# THE WISDOM OF ROBERT H. SCHULLER

# THE WISDOM OF ROBERT H. SCHULLER

## TWO COMPLETE BOOKS

## LIFE CHANGERS

## HOW TO BE AN EXTRAORDINARY PERSON IN AN ORDINARY WORLD

EDITED BY ROBERT A. SCHULLER

WINGS BOOKS

New York · Avenel, New Jersey

This 1996 edition is published by Wings Books, a division of Random House Value Publishing, Inc., 40 Engelhard Avenue, Avenel, New Jersey 07001, by arrangement with Baker Book House, Inc.

Wings Books and colophon are trademarks of Random House Value Publishing, Inc.

Random House
New York • Toronto • London • Sydney • Auckland
http://www.randomhouse.com/

Printed and bound in the United States of America

**Library of Congress Cataloging-in-Publication Data**
Schuller, Robert Harold.
   [Life changers]
   The wisdom of Robert H. Schuller: two complete books/edited by Robert A. Schuller.
     p. cm.
   Includes indexes.
   Contents: Life changers—How to be an extraordinary person in an ordinary world.
   ISBN 0-517-18065-0
   1. Meditations. 2. Christian life—Reformed (Reformed Church) authors.
3. Success—Religious aspects—Christianity.
I. Schuller, Robert A. II. Schuller, Robert Harold. How to be an extraordinary person in an ordinary world. III. Title.
BV4832.2.S33   1996
248.4'857—dc20
                                         96-14344
                                           CIP

8  7  6  5  4  3  2  1

# LIFE CHANGERS

# Introduction

It has been said that the secret of a great speaker is the ability to tell a good story. When I talk with people who listen to "Hour of Power" week after week, they often ask me: "Where does your father find all of his stories? They're so good!" I tell them that he finds his stories the same way Jesus Christ found His, in everyday situations. Everyone who is active and alive today has a story to tell. Depending upon the way it is told, it can become positive or negative, uplifting or deflating, inspiring or demeaning. My father has the ability to see the positive, the uplifting, and the inspiring side in every situation and story. This is because he understands the reality behind the promise of Romans 8:28: "All things work together for good to those who love God." He understands that God can turn "Scars Into Stars"; that a greater good can develop from tragedy, if we only believe and have faith in our benevolent and omnipotent God. This is what he calls "possibility thinking." This is what produces positive attitudes. This is what moves mountains and changes lives. With this attitude you will see the positive, the uplifting, and the inspiring side of every situation and story in your life.

This book is a compilation of my father's best stories. Some are funny, some are inspiring, others enlightening, and all of them are positive. It has many functions:

1. This book can be read simply for the enjoyment, the inspiration, and the enlightenment that its pages contain.
2. It can be read as a devotional. Simply read one story every morning, and you'll receive a little positive boost.
3. This book can be used as a spiritual pharmacy. In the back of the book is an index which can

be your guide to finding the exact story you need
to lift you out of a negative attitude.
4. This book can be used as a resource for speakers.
As one prepares his message he can use the index
to find the story he needs to illustrate his point.

No matter what your reason is for reading this book I'm
sure that you will find it positive, uplifting, inspiring, enlightening and humorous.

# Carol's Arabian Colt

Some of you may know that my daughter Carol was nearly killed in a motorcycle accident and did have to have her left leg amputated. Carol loves to ride horses, and as a gift, she was sent a magnificently beautiful, purebred Arabian colt by Doug Griffith of Imperial Farms in Baltimore, Maryland. The sire of this colt is a purebred Egyptian; the dam, or mother, is pure domestic Arabian. This beautiful animal has a fantastically impressive bloodline. When the cargo plane landed in the Los Angeles airport, and the elevator lowered this noble creature to the ground, his royal lineage showed itself in the way he arched his neck and tail, flared his nostrils, and tipped his elegant head. There is tremendous potential for greatness in this young colt, but he needs training.

Carol has been training this horse to lunge. Carol is a great inspiration to me, for when she trains the colt, she stands on her one good leg and uses a crutch in place of her other leg. With her free hand, she holds the lead rope and her other crutch. Already the colt is responding beautifully to her training. At her command, he walks slowly, then trots in a circle around Carol, as she balances on her one leg and pivots to face him. The horse knows her touch and readily obeys her command. It's a remarkable, inspiring sight to see this beautiful growing relationship between a fourteen-year-old girl and an animal of princely bloodlines.

Yesterday, while I was meditating and praying in my bedroom on the other side of the house, Carol was lunging the horse with her schoolmate. (We won't allow her to train alone, until she has her prosthesis and can use both legs again.) In a rare moment, the horse raised its head sharply, caught Carol a little off balance, and pulled the rope out of her hands. As the rope fell, it hit the horse's hoof and spooked him. He took off and ran around some trees, but as he ran, the rope only became more entangled about his front hoof, which really frightened him. So like his ancestors who ran against the wind through the great desert sand dunes of Cairo and carried their masters to safety in battle, the colt flew across the lawn. And as a bird fails to see the clear glass of a window, so the horse did not see the glass of our sliding doors and exploded through them into our living room.

I've never seen a bull in a china closet, but I've seen a gelding in a living room! I was meditating when I heard the most thunderous explosion of shattering glass that I've ever heard in my life. I leaped out of bed and ran into the hallway to see the rear end of the horse, Hofstar, disappear into the kitchen as he sauntered into Carol's bedroom! You can't imagine what it's like, living in the Schuller household—never a dull moment!

My brother, who came for my oldest daughter's wedding and stayed to enjoy the peace and quiet, cornered the Arabian colt in the closet. Fortunately the horse was not injured, though he did appear to be quite embarrassed. But the living-room floor was showered with glass.

When my wife arrived home from her Saturday-morning shopping, our twelve-year-old daughter, Gretchen, ran to greet her with the latest news. "Mom," she cried, "you'll never guess what happened!" "What happened?" my wife asked. "Wait 'til you see what the horse did in the house!" she exclaimed. "It's a mess!"

Well, that's life at our place. But you know, Carol went right back to training Hofstar. She really loves that horse; we all do. We recognize that his great ancestry gives him tremendous potential, just as God loves you and sees your tremendous potential. You can't imagine the extent of the potential and intelligence you have inherited from your ancestors. You are a descendant from God! Like you, your ancestors were made in His image. All you need is God's training and control. That's why Jesus Christ wants to be your Savior. He wants to bring out the potential that lies within you and transform you so that others can find strength and comfort in you.

# Try Giving Yourself Away

Years ago I read a story in a book entitled *Try Giving Yourself Away* by David Dunn. The author told about a woman in the lobby of the Union Depot in Cincinnati, Ohio, waiting for the train. She saw a young girl, about fifteen years of age, sitting alone in the corner of the depot. Then she saw a mother with two crying children and an armload of packages enter the train station and sit down across from the young girl. Before the woman could get settled into her seat, the teenage girl hopped up and ran over to her. "Can I take care of your two children while you go out to get something to eat?" she asked. "You look a little tired and the next train isn't due for a while, so why don't you let me help you? I'm very good with children." Startled, the mother said, "Oh, thank you! That would be wonderful." And she left the two little girls in the care of this anonymous and generous baby-sitter.

A little later the mother returned looking relaxed and refreshed. "Thank you so much," she said. And the young girl enthused, "Are you catching the next train?" "Yes," she replied, "as soon as I can get everything together." "Let me help you," the young helper said. And then she gathered all of the lady's packages and headed towards the train. After they boarded, she waved and said good-bye. Then she turned and went back into the train lobby and sat down.

She wasn't seated more than ten minutes when she spotted another mother with children. So she walked over and volunteered to baby-sit once again. And after a while that mother boarded the train, and then this drifting helper found another mother and did the same thing.

By this time the observer was puzzled, so she approached the young girl and said, "I'm curious. I've been watching you for an hour or so, and you've spent the entire time helping these young mothers and their children. Why are you doing this?"

"Oh," she said, "I was one of five children. My dad was in the army and we were always moving from one place to another. My mom got so tired carrying the packages and suitcases and caring for all of us. I remember her saying to me, 'You are so good with children.'

"My dad went to war in Europe and he never came back, so that left my mom alone. And she just recently died, so I thought that maybe I could do something for others because she said I was so good with kids. I thought there would be a lot of mothers who would be tired here so that's why I come to the depot! It makes me feel good. It really helps."

That's understanding Christianity the self-sacrificial way—and it's wonderful!

# Let It Flow

Frank Laubach, one of the great inspiring persons in my life, tells a story about the time he was in India and decided to take a tour of a new electro-generating plant. He saw an enormous dam, which was used for the production of electrical energy. He took an elevator down to see the massive turbines driven by the pressure of water against the curved vanes of the wheels. But he noticed that no electricity was being generated. "Why isn't energy being produced?" he asked the tour guide. "I mean, there's the dam, the water, and the turbines; why isn't it working?" And the guide replied, "The valve is closed. The water is not flowing through right now. And until the valve is open and the water flows through, there is no power produced."

If you come to church and absorb the message, but keep it within yourself and don't share it with your friends at the office throughout the week, or with your wife and your children, it doesn't flow through. You don't understand it. Christianity is Christ being accepted into my heart; into my mind; into my life; and then flowing through me—out of me, reaching the people who need my love.

# Gail Bartosh

I want to share with you about a person named Gail Bartosh. She and her parents have been members of this church almost from the very beginning. In the early days of our ministry, when we had only a couple hundred members, her father, Francis, was an elder of the church. Our communion set was dedicated to him when he passed away. I remember Francis used to say to me, "I wonder what will happen to Gail." Although no one ever said much about it, some thought Gail was mongoloid; others thought she was mentally retarded.

Today, Gail is one of the greatest workers we have in this church. She works in the nursery and cares for more than two hundred infants a week. During the week, Gail works in our day-care center. She beautifully and lovingly cares for these little children of all nationalities, creeds, and colors while their working mothers make a living for their families. Gail is a terrific girl, and God is using her to touch so many young lives.

Recently Gail went into the hospital for a checkup and a lump was discovered in her breast. She went into surgery for removal of the lump, but the doctors decided that her condition required a radical mastectomy. So at age thirty-seven, Gail lost her breast. I went to call on her the other day, and found her weeping into the pillows. She said, "Doctor Schuller, look at me. Now Mother has a mentally retarded cancer victim on her hands." I reached over and took her hand and said, "No, Gail, you're wrong! Wrong! *Wrong!* Your mother has a bright, brave, beautiful, inspiring gal on her hands. Now you say that." And smiling through the tears, she repeated with perfect diction, "Now Mother has a bright, brave, beautiful, inspiring gal on her hands."

"You know, Doctor Schuller," she continued, "when I was a child I was taken from one doctor to another and none could agree exactly what was wrong with me. One doctor would say, 'She's a mongoloid.' Another doctor would say, 'No, she's not a mongoloid; she's mentally retarded.' And still another would insist, 'She isn't mentally retarded; she's just slow.' So finally I stopped seeing doctors, started going to church, and decided to develop the potential God has given me the very best I could."

And that is exactly what Gail Bartosh has done. She touches the lives of children daily and inspires them to be beautiful, brave, and successful persons. She decided to make the most of what she had, and she has become a fantastic human being.

Whether you realize it or not, you have the inherited potential for greatness. All you have to do is let God hold the lead line, and He will train and control you. You will be pleasantly surprised when you see the life that can be yours, as you put yourself in the Master's hands.

# Mom Schug's Love

I conducted the funeral service for a woman that I called Mom Schug. Her real name was Bernice Schug, and she thought of me as her adopted son. She was well into her eighties when she passed away, peacefully and swiftly like a flower that had come to full bloom and was ready to drop its petals, so the new seeds could sprout. She lived the full cycle! I saw Mom Schug hours before she passed away in the hospital. We talked and prayed together. She smiled and her dimples were as bright as when she was a girl. Her eyes were as attractive and saucy as when she was sixteen. Only a week before her death, she had been working at our twenty-four-hour New Hope Telephone Counseling service.

Mom was a poor woman. She lived in a tiny mobile home that she bought thirty years ago. But every Sunday she would take 10 percent of her Social Security check and place it into the offering plate at our church.

Dear Mom Schug, what a happy woman! Oh, you may say, "She had a good life. She had such few problems." The truth is, she lost her only son, Bob, years ago in World War II. He enlisted in the navy, so he could join the fight to liberate our country from a horrible war. Bob was in the Pacific when he was struck by a shell in his leg. They quickly transported him down to the medics. Doctors were preparing to amputate his leg when a Kamikaze pilot, on a suicide dive, struck the side of the ship right where the medical center was, killing Bob, the medical team, and many others. What a crushing grief that was to Bernice Schug. But you know, God can take a crushing grief, and He can come rushing in! Mom Schug found a joy in her sorrow because she experienced the perfect love that came from God.

Several years later, Mom received the bulletin from our church and saw that a former Japanese Kamikaze pilot was going to be the guest on the following Sunday. She couldn't believe it! Days before he was to carry out his suicide plunge, the war ended. He went back to Japan and there he met a missionary and was introduced to Jesus Christ. Now, he was traveling around the world, sharing his testimony of what Jesus Christ had done in his life. Mom Schug called me and said, "Bob, I don't think I'll be in church this Sunday," and told me why. "Well, Mom," I replied, "I can understand.

You are human. If you don't want to come to church, then stay home and pray or read your Bible, or watch a church service on TV."

Saturday came and I received another call. "Bob," Mom Schug exclaimed, "are you sure you are going through with this?" "Yes," I answered, "this man is a terrific Christian. He has a personal relationship with Jesus Christ." She said good-bye, and I could hear her sobbing on the other end of the line. The next morning, the church was filling up fast, when I saw her come in through the side door and sit in the back row. She figured that she could sneak out before the service was over.

The service began with a few hymns and then the guest approached the podium. He shared a beautiful testimony and then closed with prayer. This was the time when Mom was supposed to have slipped out, but she forgot. By the time she opened her eyes to still try to make an early exit, the Japanese man was standing only a few feet away from her. She could have exited out the side door or gone down the aisle, but she didn't. Instead she walked over to the man, opened her arms, and embraced him. She whispered in his ear about her son and tears started streaming down both of their faces. When you've got love in your heart and Jesus Christ in your life, you can love the unlovely.

# True Confession

A priest, a rabbi, and a Protestant minister got together and decided to talk openly about themselves. The first religious leader was very frank, admitting some sins that he had committed. The other two men were shocked. Their mouths fell open, and they became quite flushed. The rabbi was next, so he regained his composure and walked to the front of the room. He began, "Normally I could never confess this, but since my friend was open and honest I will be, too!" And he confessed every sin that he had committed. Then came the Protestant's turn, so he stood before the group and said, "Well, I would never have dared confess my secret sin, but after hearing my colleagues openly admit their sins, I will, too. I admit that I'm an incurable gossip. I can't keep a secret and I can hardly wait to get out of here!"

# "Mount Everest, You Can't Get Any Bigger!"

When I was in London, England, a couple of weeks ago, I visited a hall where a man named Mallory was honored with a banquet years ago. In the 1920s Mallory led an expedition to try to conquer Mount Everest. The first expedition failed, as did the second. Then, with a team of the best quality and ability, Mallory made a third assault. But in spite of careful planning and extensive safety precautions, disaster struck: an avalanche hit, and Mallory and most of his party were killed.

When the few who did survive returned to England, they held a glorious banquet saluting the great people of Mallory's final expedition. As the leader of the survivors stood to acknowledge the applause, he looked around the hall at the framed pictures of Mallory and his comrades who had died. Then he turned his back to the crowds to face the huge picture of Mount Everest, which stood looming like a silent, unconquerable giant behind the banquet table.

With tears streaming down his face, he addressed the mountain on behalf of Mallory and his dead friends. "I speak to you, Mount Everest, in the name of all brave men living and those yet unborn," he began. "Mount Everest, you defeated us once; you defeated us twice; you defeated us three times. But Mount Everest, we shall someday defeat you, because you can't get any bigger and we can!"

Where are you today? Whether you find yourself at home, in a lonely hotel room, a hospital, or a prison, possibility thinking can work for you to perform healing of body, mind and soul. It will help you to see that Jesus Christ wants to come into your life and transform you. When you give your life to Jesus, you will become a beautiful new creature. Doors will open. Freedom will come your way. And when you run into problems, you will have the calm assurance that they can't get any bigger—but you can!

## Never Listen to a Negative Thought

Negative ideas multiply rapidly. If you want to attract tuna, you use one kind of bait; if you use a different kind of bait, you'll attract the sharks. A negative idea manifested in a moment of self-pity, jealousy, resentment, or anger—even a simple, seemingly innocent moment of unkind thought—harbored, nurtured, and acted upon, can be very destructive in its ultimate consequence.

Once there was a devoted pastor who counseled a woman suffering from a very rare, fatal disease. A secretary in the church saw them together and started a rumor that he was being unfaithful to his wife. The pastor could not defend himself without violating a pastoral confidence. When the woman died, the true story came out. The church board and the intimates knew that there was no foundation to that ill-fated rumor at all. But nevertheless, his reputation had been demolished in the community. When the pastor discovered the source of the rumor, he called the secretary, who was quick to come. In tears, she lamented, "I don't know how to apologize. What can I ever do to set things right again?" "Here's what I want you to do," he replied. He gave her a pillow full of goose feathers and said, "Go to the high hill outside of town. When the wind blows, just let the feathers fly, and bring back the empty pillow." "Oh, thank you," she cried. She went to the hill and scattered the feathers to the wind. When she returned, she showed the pastor the empty pillow and asked, "Now, can things be as they were? Will you forgive me?" "One last thing," the pastor said, "go back and pick up all the feathers."

If you respond to a negative thought, it will come back to you.

## Cast Your Bread on the Waters

Cast your bread on the waters and it will come back to you!

Ecclesiastes 11:1

When I first began studying this verse, I came to the conclusion that it honestly didn't make much sense. If you throw seeds on the water, they will float back to the shore, *if* the current flows in the right direction. But if you throw bread on the water, it will dissolve; it will get soggy. And if it does come back, I don't think any of us would care to eat it. The text doesn't make much sense, until you realize that the phrase was originally spoken in a culture where fish provided the basis for economic survival. If you throw bread on the water, the bread itself will not be edible, but it will attract the fish to the surface so you can net them.

Years ago, Mrs. Schuller and I bought a two-acre parcel of ground in the country. The previous owner had made several little fish ponds, so I put water in the ponds and bought a bunch of two-inch-long, little koi fish. Since that time, they have done very well and have multiplied to number more than two hundred. Koi fish are beautiful Japanese carp and come in more than forty-seven colors and varieties. They are unusually tame; they will eat out of my hand. I can caress them on the back, and they really like it. If I don't see them lurking behind the lily pads, all I have to do is throw a piece of bread down, and they surface from out of the deep to congregate near the surface of the water. That's what the writer of Ecclesiastes had in mind. If you're hungry, take your bread and throw it into the water. You'll lose your bread, but you'll come back with a meal for the whole family!

Like a crust of bread, a God-given idea can attract enormous resources that come from far corners, out of the darkness. Hold this Bible verse in your mind today: "Cast your bread on the waters and it will return to you." When you give to God, your gift will really return to you multiplied.

# There Is a Purpose to Everything

Not long ago, I sat next to a man on a plane and he asked me what I did. I told him I was a minister. "What do you do?" I asked. "I'm a gambler," he replied, tossing a silver dollar carelessly into the air. "Do you have a faith?" I inquired. "Yes," he replied, "I believe there is a purpose to everything on planet earth." "That sounds like good theology," I responded. "I really believe that," he asserted. Then, as if he were testing me, he challenged, "What's the purpose of a mouse?" Frankly, he caught me speechless. I hadn't the foggiest idea what the purpose of a mouse could be. But he had an answer on the tip of his tongue. "The purpose of a mouse," he explained, "is to generate job opportunities." "How can a mouse generate job opportunities?" I asked.

Then he told me exactly how many jobs in our economy exist to deal with the problem of mice. He rattled off the number of people that work in factories that make mouse traps and produce mouse-control poisons. And he cited the billions of dollars spent each year on cat food. As he went on and on, I was impressed. I thanked God for these lousy mice! And I've been grateful for them ever since.

Ecology has taught us there is a purpose to everything under the sun. The delicate balance between every earthly element ties the whole dynamic creation together. And if there's a purpose to the wind, the water, the plants, insects, and even mice, then you can be sure there's a purpose for human beings. It is good psychology, good theology, and good biblical interpretation to say that our purpose on planet earth is to develop our God-given creative potential that we might truly glorify our heavenly Father. When we do that, we make God's creation more beautiful, and we leave the world a better place because we lived in it.

## Look in Unlikely Places

A couple of years ago, I was invited to go up to Vancouver, Canada, to lecture to about two hundred ministers representative of the religious groups of that great province. At the opening of the conference, I recall meeting the treasurer. He was seated at the registration desk where he collected money to cover the expenses of food, lodging, and rental of the auditorium for the conference. When all the members had registered, he had a total of about six thousand dollars in cash, which he put in a little metal box. When the conference opened, he began to feel very nervous about carrying that much cash, so he put the money in the safest place he could think of—in the trunk of his car. That afternoon, after the last lecture, he went to the garage to get his car and found it was gone. It had been stolen! Downcast, he reported the theft to the police.

Five or six days later, the police found the car abandoned. It had been completely stripped. An officer called the man and informed him that they had found his car. To add insult to injury, he had to pay to have the car towed back home. But amazingly, when he opened the trunk, there was the little metal box still holding the entire six thousand dollars! The thief had never bothered to look for anything of value in the trunk.

The truth is that we oftentimes overlook the greatest potential and value, because we simply can't envision such a productive concept coming from such an unlikely source. Some of the greatest concepts come out of the most unlikely ideas. When God comes into your mind, He will give you ideas that will enable you to develop your possibilities to their fullest potential.

# Your Problem Is Not a Banyan Tree

On my first trip to Thailand, I went on an elephant hunt in the jungle. The wild elephants come thundering out of the jungle into an arena, and a massive log gate is dropped to close off the exit. Once the elephant is made captive, the men tie the end of a long chain around the elephant's foot. The other end is tied to a huge banyan tree. The great elephant will pull with all its strength, but it can't budge the banyan tree. Finally, after struggling for days and weeks the elephant will barely lift its ponderous foot, and when it feels the chain just begin to become taut, it drops its foot heavily to the ground, because it knows further struggle is useless. The elephant surrenders to the chain.

At this point, the hunters know the elephant is really trapped forever. For when they take the elephant and chain it to a little iron stake by a circus tent, the elephant never attempts to pull away, because it still thinks it is chained to a banyan tree. The elephant never realizes how easily it could achieve freedom.

God's love tells you that you are not chained to a banyan tree! Your problem is not insurmountable! Perhaps you're in the hospital, and you are fighting disease. Remember, disease is not a banyan tree. Maybe you're having problems in marriage. Remember, your problem is not a banyan tree; it is a stake.

# Love Liberates

One of my most delightful memories as a small child on our Iowa farm is of the days in the spring when we would receive our little baby chicks. I used to take the soft, fuzzy, newly hatched little things and rub what felt like silky fur against my cheek. Sometimes I would squeeze too tightly, because I loved them so much, and I didn't want them to get away. "Don't hold so tight," my father warned. "But I love it so," I protested. "If you love it so much," he said, "you have to let go."

If you really love your wife, don't be so possessive; if you love your husband, don't be so jealous. Real love is not possessive; it does not manipulate or intimidate. Real love liberates. God's love is like that. First He elevates you beyond the guilt that could give you a negative self-image, which would cause you to lose all self-confidence and render you woefully and totally ineffective. Then He sets you free to become the person you were meant to be.

# Sheila's Dream

Many years ago my daughter Sheila was at a very low point emotionally. Ever since she was in the fifth grade she wanted to be a medical doctor and serve as a missionary. Finally she graduated from Hope College with a major in chemistry and a grade point average somewhere between an *A* and a *B*. But there were fifty-four thousand graduating seniors applying for medical school and only fourteen thousand openings in all the medical schools in the United States. She was one of the forty thousand not accepted. Now she had to decide whether she would study for her master's degree, and then reapply for medical school, or make a midflight correction. She chose the latter, because she discovered the real reason she wanted to be a doctor was because she wanted to be a part of a ministry of healing. She concluded she didn't have to be an M.D. to do that. So she tried to find herself through ministry in the youth department of our church.

Somewhere along the line she had an unfortunate, heartbreaking experience with a young man. They simply were not meant for each other, and the relationship left her with a deeply negative self-image. One morning she and I were sitting around the table in the kitchen and I quietly asked, "Sheila, what do you really want out of life?" With tears streaming down her face, she poured out her heart. "Dad, I guess all I really want is a home like the one I was raised in. I want children like my brother and sisters."

She paused for a moment, and as I gently brushed the tears from her cheeks, I cried too. "You know," she continued, "I don't care if I have a husband who's rich or famous. I don't have to have a man like that. All I want is a man who will treat me like a precious gem."

As we wept together, I shared her inner anguish and lovingly assured her, "Sheila, that is a noble dream. God will give you someone like that." All persons—whether they are little or grown, young and strong, or bent-backed and old—need somebody who will treat them like precious gems. That's why we, as clergy, still challenge the groom and the bride to take each other for better or worse. Those vows signify a commitment to care forever. Every person needs someone who will treat him or her like a precious gem! God does that for us.

Casting all your care upon Him for He cares for you.
1 Peter 5:7

# Never Count Up the Might-Have-Beens

I was born and raised on an Iowa farm. I vividly remember the dust-bowl years. When I was a child, in the thirties, the drought swept in from the Dakotas. The wind was dry; the wind was dusty; the wind was violent; and the wind was fierce. The wind became our enemy, because it would peel the dry, rich, black soil, and swirl it like drifting dunes in the gullies and canyons of our fields. We prayed for the rains, but the rains did not come. I shall never forget that difficult year. We walked around our farm with white towels over our faces to keep from suffocating in the driving dust.

Then harvest season came. My father would normally harvest a hundred wagons full of corn. But I remember the harvest that year. My father harvested not the one hundred wagon loads we usually harvested—but a meager one-half wagon load. I can see the old wagon standing in the yard—only half-full. It was a total crop disaster that has never been equalled before or since!

You know what happened? I shall never forget it. Seated at the dinner table with his calloused hands holding ours, my father looked up and thanked God. He said, "I thank You, God, that I have lost nothing. I have regained the seed I planted in the springtime!" He used a half-wagon load for seed, he got a half-wagon load back. His attitude of gratitude was that he didn't lose a thing, while other farmers were saying, "We lost ninety loads," or, "We lost one hundred loads." They counted their losses by what they hoped they could have accomplished. And I'll never forget my father saying, "You can never count up the might-have-beens or you will be defeated." Never look at what you have lost; look at what you have left. Those words of wisdom from my father, who never went past the sixth grade, were immeasurable in making me the possibility thinker that I am today. The attitude of gratitude gave my father surviving power. He went right back and planted that seed the next year. When he finally retired, he was no longer a poor farmer. With this attitude he prepared and left a nice estate for his children.

# High-Flying Balloons

A man was selling balloons on the streets of New York City. He knew how to attract a crowd before he offered his wares for sale. He took a white balloon, filled it up, and let it float upward. Next he filled a red balloon, and released it. Then he added a yellow one. As the red, yellow, and white balloons were floating above his head, the little children gathered around to buy his balloons. A hesitant black boy looked up at the balloons and finally asked, "If you filled a black balloon, would it go up too?" The man looked down and said, "Why, sure! It's not the color of the balloon, it's what's inside that makes it go up!"

What's inside of you determines whether you achieve peak success experiences in your life. Climbing to the peak depends upon your mind and your attitudes.

# The Great Houdini

It's fascinating to read the stories, many of them legendary, about the late Houdini. That masterful magician was probably a better locksmith than he was a magician. He had a standing challenge that he could get out of any locked jail in sixty minutes, providing they would let him enter in his regular street clothes and not watch him work.

One of the stories is about a little town in the British Isles that decided to challenge (and perhaps embarrass) the great Houdini. This town had just completed an escape-proof jail, and so the townfolk invited Houdini to come to see if he could break out.

He accepted the challenge. He was allowed to enter the jail in his street clothes. People said they saw the locksmith turn the lock some strange way, and then with the clang of steel, everybody turned their backs and left him alone to work. Houdini had hidden a long flexible steel rod in his belt, which is what he used to try to trip the lock. He worked for thirty minutes. He kept his ear close to the lock—forty-five minutes, and then an hour passed; he was perspiring. After two hours, he was exhausted. He leaned against the door, and to his amazement, it fell open. They had never locked the door! It was their trick on the great escape artist!

The door was locked only in Houdini's mind. That's the *only* place it was locked! Some of you think that you can't overcome your problem. The only place where it is impossible is in your thinking. That's the only thing that's locked!

# The Treacherous Coral Sea

Some years ago, Mrs. Schuller and I were faculty members on the Chapman College Campus Afloat. We were on the ship for the summer, sailing to the South Seas. I shall never forget the time when the captain said that the next day the ship would go through a very narrow crevice in the Coral Sea. The following day, we were told the ship was approaching the crevice. The passengers were all on deck. We were told the ship needed thirty feet of water to avoid grounding. In the shallow coral regions that we were passing through, there was only one place where the water was deeper than thirty feet, and this passageway was so narrow that I had the impression that it was hardly wide enough for our ship. To maneuver such a huge ship through such a narrow crevice was indeed precarious.

As we came closer, the captain cut the forward speed, and then off in the distance we saw a little motorboat coming toward us, leaving its wide white wake. In that motorboat was a special captain in uniform from Australia. He stepped out onto our ship through a little hole down below. You could see him come in. He came up the elevator, and the captain of our ship saluted him and stepped aside. And this special captain from Australia took the helm, because he specialized in taking ships through this narrow passage. That was teamwork.

You know who that special pilot must be for you, don't you? His name is Jesus Christ. Make sure that Jesus Christ is at the helm and, as you go through some narrow waters, you'll reach port safely.

# "What's Green Bay Without the Packers?"

One day I sat next to a man on a plane in Los Angeles. "Where are you from?" he asked me. "Garden Grove, California," I enthused. And then—he insulted me. "Garden Grove? I never heard of it." "Where are you from?" I inquired, hoping it would be a town I had never heard of. "Green Bay, Wisconsin," he replied, which, unfortunately, I had heard of, being a Packer fan.

Then I thought, *How can I insult him back without violating my Christian ethics or self-respect and self-esteem?* That was challenging. I came up with what I considered to be an ethical, subtle, clever, Christian insult. "Green Bay?" I questioned, looking him straight in the eye, "What does Green Bay have outside the Packers?" "I don't have the faintest idea," he exclaimed, "I'm the coach!" "How are you going to do next season?" I asked. "Terrific!" he enthused. "Well, how can you say that?" I countered. "Because," he said, "we've got talent." "Talent? Is that right? What's talent?" I questioned.

Since he was a coach, I thought he'd say "speed" or "coordination," or maybe "intelligence"; but he didn't reply with any of those answers. "Talent? Why, it's character!" he exclaimed. "What do you mean by 'character'?" I queried. "I mean loyalty to the team, that's what I mean," he answered.

Success isn't a matter of having *things,* it's a matter of having the right thoughts, character, integrity, enthusiasm, and determination. God wants you to be a success, because God wants you to enjoy self-esteem. You are His child, not just a glorified monkey. If He gave you a thing, it wouldn't feed your self-esteem; but when He gives you an idea, it leads you to success. You gain wholesome self-respect in the process of achieving. So, you can be sure it is God who is feeding you with those success-generating ideas and opportunities.

# The Ray Kroc Story

Have you ever gone by a store that had lousy management and then, one day you passed by and saw a banner that read UNDER NEW MANAGEMENT? It's amazing what can happen when management changes.

Some years ago, there were a couple of brothers named McDonald who owned a hamburger shop in San Bernardino. Then along came a fifty-nine-year-old man with a thousand dollars to invest—and a better idea about how the shop should be managed. He bought the brothers out. His name is Ray Kroc. He brought to the business fresh new ideas, and that's what made the difference. Today *McDonald's* is a world-wide, multimillion dollar enterprise.

Maybe you think you're doing a pretty good job managing your life, but you haven't seen anything—until you let your life come under the management of Jesus Christ. Fly a new banner across your mind that declares UNDER NEW MANAGEMENT. Receive Him as your Savior—as your Lord—and say, "From this time on, I'm going to talk to You; I'm going to walk with You; I'm going to love You; and I'm going to let You call the shots in my life."

# The Influence of the Insignificant

Once there was a dear lady named Hazel who loved to sing simple, common gospel songs. She decided to try out for the church choir. She told the choir director that she couldn't read music, so he said, "We'll let you sing, but just stay on tune." But she couldn't stay on tune, so she had to drop out of the choir. Nothing really seemed to have any meaning in Hazel's life. Her mother had recently died. When Hazel was young, she had spent most of her time caring for her mother, instead of dating and enjoying her adolescence. Consequently, she had never married.

At the age of sixty, she felt as though she had failed in her attempt to find happiness in life. Alone, with no spouse or children, she couldn't even fulfill her life goal of singing. Distressed and worried, as you can well imagine, she lived in a tiny one-bedroom apartment three or four flights above the street level in a big city. With her mother gone, she lived alone in an old, run-down, apartment building where only old people on Social Security usually live.

One day, as Hazel was on her way out, she saw a young hippie-looking guy moving into one of the small tenements. He had a full beard and long hair. When she returned, all of her friends were talking about the new tenant. "We're in real trouble now," said one lady. "Once these tough-looking characters move in, they always take over!" And all the old folks living in the apartment building started taking extra precautions, just in case the stranger was a thief. Many even put extra locks on their windows and doors. Nobody trusted him.

This went on for several weeks. Then one night Hazel came in later than usual. She entered the lobby very quietly, so she wouldn't disturb any of the other tenants. After climbing two flights of stairs, she saw a suspicious-looking man in the hallway. Instead of screaming or running back down the stairs, she began to sing! In her own off-key way she sang the first words that came to her. "When you walk through a storm hold your head up high and don't be afraid of the dark." That's the only song she could remember and she wasn't even sure if the words were right. She sang on:

". . . Hold your head up high and you'll never walk alone. Walk on, walk on, with hope in your heart and you'll never walk alone." By this time she had reached her apartment. So she quickly opened the door and locked it securely, listening at the door for some kind of sound. She heard nothing, so she went to bed, grateful that she had made it safely to her place.

The next morning she saw a torn, crumpled piece of paper under her door. It was from the rough-looking young man that everyone feared. This is what it said: "I don't know who you are, but thank you for singing to me last night. I was ready to cash in—to commit suicide—but then you started to sing: 'When you walk through a storm hold your head up high and you'll never walk alone.' I want you to know that you saved my life. I'm going to another city where I know I can find the job I need. Thank you. Good-bye."

The power of a smile or the words of encouragement! Only God can say how valuable it is! Any impossibility thinker can count the seeds in an apple. Only God can count the apples in a seed! Only God knows how powerful your gift is.

# Do the Dogs Like It?

A sales manager developed a new dog food. All the proteins, minerals, fats, and carbohydrates were included in the product. The company came out with a brand-new package and a national advertising program that included full-page ads and ingenious commercials. But after six months, the sales (which had started slowly) had finally dwindled to nothing. So the chairman of the board called all the district sales managers together in a major convention in Chicago. "What's wrong?" he asked. "Look at the beautiful full-page ads we have in national magazines. Look at the expensive commercials on television." Then he held up a box of the dog food and pointed to the back of the box. He read the contents and admired the beautiful packaging. "The cost is even lower than our competitors," he added. "Now tell me why you people aren't selling this dog food!" You could hear a pin drop. Then someone in the back of the room slowly came to his feet and said, "Sir, the dogs don't like it!"

The secret of success is not to sit in an expensive leather chair in a plush office and dream up your dreams. The secret of success is to find the need and fill it, to find a hurt and heal it, to find somebody with a problem and offer to help solve the problem.

# The End Becomes a Bend

I remember when Mrs. Schuller, the children, and I came from the Midwest to California. We came across a mountain ridge and stopped to view the great valley beyond. The road stretched as straight as an arrow, for as far as we could see. But as we came closer and closer to the mountain ridge, it looked like the road stopped dead. But we didn't stop and turn around—we kept on going. And sure enough, twenty miles down that straight road, we saw that the road gradually curved. And as we followed the curve, it became a pass through the mountains.

That's the way God deals with us! You get started, even though you see a huge mountain range that makes it impossible to see beyond. You just keep on going, and at the right moment, the end becomes a bend!

# Kyle, I Love You

An elder of our church named John Joseph shared this story with us at devotions the other night. John began by explaining that his wife and three daughters were back East. "I love my children and my wife. I miss them when we're separated—even for a little while. So we talk on the phone every night. One night my wife called me, and while we were talking, she told me Kyle, my nine-year-old daughter, wanted to talk to me.

"Kyle got on the line and said, 'Oh, Dad, I'm having such a wonderful time.' 'Kyle,' I said, 'it's so good to hear your voice. I . . .' I started to say, 'I love you.' But before I could say the words, she interrupted. 'I had such a wonderful time at the fair today, Daddy. It was so beautiful!' Again, as she paused, I tried to tell her, 'Kyle, I love you.' But again she interrupted, 'I'm so excited! I won the trophy, Dad.' And she proceeded to tell me all about the trophy. Once more I tried to tell her how important she is to me, how much I love her. But Kyle never gave me the chance. She interrupted once more and then said cheerily, 'Mom wants to talk to you again,' and handed the phone back to my wife.

"I was so depressed after that phone call I nearly cried. I wanted to say so desperately, 'Kyle, I love you. Kyle, I'm praying for you today.' I wanted to tell her, but she couldn't hear a word I said because, you see, Kyle is stone-deaf.

"It made me feel terrible to think my little Kyle couldn't hear what I wanted to say to her, until I realized that God has this problem with His children all the time. We're always in a hurry. And by nature, we're often stone-deaf to God's voice. When we pray, we do all the talking. God doesn't have a chance to say anything."

But God has a word for you. He has a plan for your life that will reflect His awesome, limitless love for you. All we have to do is listen.

# A Report From "The International Psychological Convention"

Several years ago at the International Psychological Convention in Paris, France, I was involved in a fascinating seminar. A report was made of a study that was first begun approximately thirty years ago by graduate students at Johns Hopkins University. These students were told by their professor to go to the most emotionally, economically, and culturally deprived inner-city ghetto to analyze and document the lives of two hundred selected young men between the ages of twelve and sixteen. When they had completed their analysis of the subjects' economic, social, and cultural environment, they were to make a prediction based upon this data as to where these boys would be twenty-five years down the road.

When this portion of the study was completed, the graduate students predicted that of the 200 boys, 196 would spend at least some time in jail. I found that to be an incredibly gloomy prediction.

Twenty-five years later, another group of graduate students were assigned to find the 200 boys and check on the predictions. Eventually they found 180 of the 200. Of those they were able to locate, they discovered that only 6 of the 180 had ever spent any time at all in jail. The predictions of the previous behavioral scientists were totally wrong!

The students were then challenged to discover why, given the negative social environment which surrounded these young men during their formative years, they had not behaved as predicted. The students interviewed the men and asked them what was the most positive influence in their lives. Seventy-five percent of those questioned said the most positive influence in their lives was a teacher. Again and again one name emerged—the name of a woman teacher.

The students sought out the woman and found her in a retirement home. Whey they told her the results of the study she replied, "Is that right?"—not at all surprised. "How did you communicate with these young men, and what values did you impart in them? Did you have a specific strategy?" the students asked. "No, no," the old lady said shaking her head. Then slowly she smiled. "I just loved those boys," she replied. "I just loved those boys. That's all."

There's no force in the world as strong as the life-changing influence of a person who truly loves you. I've experienced that from Jesus Christ.

# Dream Risky Dreams

She was a beautiful young girl, not more than twenty-one years old. She came to me this past week for counseling and guidance. She told me about a marvelous new friendship she has with this great guy. "You know, our relationship is so wonderful," she said. "We have such fun together. We can talk about anything and feel comfortable. And we both share the same love for God.

"But you know," she continued, "I'm afraid that this relationship we share is leading somewhere serious. I look around and see the unhappy marriages and the divorces, and I don't know if I should dare to believe I could be married in our kind of world."

"As I see you and listen to you, do you know what I think about?" I asked her. "No," she replied.

"First of all, let me tell you that I've been a pastor for twenty-nine years. In those twenty-nine years I have married and baptized a lot of people, and conducted a lot of funerals. When I look at you and listen to you, I can see funerals."

"Funerals!" she exclaimed in astonishment. "Yes," I replied. "I don't know how many dozens of times I have conducted a funeral for a man in his seventies or eighties. And as I walked the widow from the cemetery back to her car, she would look at me and say, 'You know, Reverend, I first met him when I was a teenager. Oh, we used to have so much fun. But secretly I wondered, *Can it last?* Then he asked me to marry him. I was so unsure of myself at first, but I said yes. And still I wondered, *Can it last?*

" 'Oh, we had our share of troubled times, but we grew together and learned to love each other even more. And before I knew it, we were celebrating our twenty-fifth wedding anniversary. We were so very happy that, in the midst of celebrating, I thought to myself, *Can it last?* And then, not long ago, we celebrated our forty-sixth year together. The children were all there, and we had such a wonderful time. And I thought to myself, *I'm so in love; how long can it last?* We were married forty-six years, and they were forty-six of the most beautiful, fulfilling years any person could ever hope for. He was such a good man. And we loved each other more with each passing year.' "

As I studied the face of the young girl sitting across from me, I said, "When you describe your young man, I can suddenly see you when you're eighty years old, and you're saying to your pastor, 'You know, we had such a great relationship when we were teenagers. We shared so many wonderful things together and had so much fun. Then we got married, and we were so happy that we wondered, *How long can it last?* Yes, we had our share of tears and of growing times, but we've shared over forty years of joy. He was such a good man, and we loved each other all our lives together.' "

It takes courage to dream risky dreams. It can be seen in a young bride going to the altar, or in the groom who makes a commitment. They're people who dare to commit themselves to a dream, regardless of the risk they take, and it's beautiful.

# Be Supportive

Yesterday I called on a lady in the hospital. "They say I'm terminal. They're not even giving me chemotherapy anymore. Everything has failed," she said. "Mary Lou," I soothed, "if what they mean by that is correct, the word is not terminal, it's *transitional*. You're not going to die; you're going through a transition." "But everything seems so hopeless," she persisted. Taking her hands in mine, I assured her, "When everything else fails, get ready to meet God, because that's when God steps in. He's always there. He never fails. This isn't an end for you; it's a beginning." And then she smiled at me and squeezed my hand and said, "Thank you. That helps."

For a brief moment I had the most wonderful feeling. I had been her supportive beam.

It's important that you take the time to get involved and become that supportive beam, that lift, that so many people need. When you become that kind of person, life becomes more exciting than you can imagine!

# You Are Brilliant!

The head of a well-known company decided to test the creativity of average people, so he selected ten men from one of his factories. They were noneducated people at the bottom of the corporate ladder. The president led them into the executive headquarters and told them to sit in the big leather chairs around the huge board table. After they all sat down, he stood before them and explained why they had been chosen. "I have observed you people for some time now, and it has come to my attention that you all have remarkable gifts of creativity. This is why I have called you together today. Our company is facing a problem, and I believe that you ten men can come up with a solution." He explained all of the details and then left the room for a few hours, a little cynical of the whole idea. When he returned, he discovered they had found a solution.

It was in that meeting that a great breakthrough was made. They had found an answer to the problem that his top corporate research and development personnel had overlooked! The average "bottom-of-the-ladder person" is potentially as creatively brilliant as the top executive who is sitting in the big office. The only drawback is that the person on the bottom doesn't *realize* he's brilliant and doesn't believe in his own ideas.

The executive appealed to the employees' pride! He appealed to their self-worth! This is how he explains it: "Every person is creative! They only have to believe it. When I told the men they were smart, they believed it! They came up with a solution, because they were not informed enough to know that the suggestion they made couldn't be done. So, they came up with an idea that the rest of us never seriously considered because in our minds it was technologically impossible. And when they came up with the idea, we established it as a goal and solved the problem!"

Every human being has virtually equal creative possibilities. But why isn't the average person more creative? One simple reason: They don't *think* they are creative. Nobody's ever told them they're creative, so they have never tried to be. There are incredible ideas that come to their minds once in a while, but they don't do anything about them. And then, years later, they read that somebody else did something with the idea. And they say to themselves, "I thought about that; why didn't I do something about it?"

I don't suppose there is one fact that I can try to communicate to you that is more important than this next sentence: "All of you are brilliant!" That's a *fact*. All of us have incredibly creative potential, because all creative ideas come from God.

# Believe in Yourself

The glass elevator in our Tower of Hope was inspired by the El Cortez Hotel in San Diego. The owners of the elegant hotel decided they needed additional elevators, so they hired a group of architects and engineers to figure out the best location, both in terms of appearance and cost. If they put the elevators inside the hotel, they would have to cut a hole in all the floors. What a mess! Plaster dust would be everywhere.

As the planners stood in the lobby deliberating over the placement of these elevators, a janitor overheard the conversation. All he could think of was the mess the hotel was going to be in while all this reconstruction was going on inside. And the more he thought about it, the braver he got, until finally he went up to the group of men and said, "Why don't you put the elevators outside the building?" Nobody had thought of that! The professionals listened and the idea clicked in their imagination. "Why not?" they said. "It's never been done before, but let's try and see how we could do it." So the elevators were built outside the El Cortez Hotel and since then, many well-known buildings have done the same!

Common people are brilliant if they'll only believe in their own ideas! I don't care who you are. I don't care how poor you are. I don't care how illiterate you are. I don't care how educated you are. I don't care what your race is. I don't care where you are on the economic ladder. You have the same basic brain as any other human being! Believe in yourself.

# No Idea Is Perfect!

Remember John Steinbeck's famous story "The Pearl"? A man found a beautiful pearl, but it had one tiny flaw. He thought if he could just remove that little imperfection, the pearl would be the biggest and the most priceless one in the world. So he peeled off the first layer, but the flaw was still there. Then he took off the next layer, thinking it would disappear, but the flaw remained. He continued to take off each layer, until finally he had no pearl. The flaw was gone now, but so was the beautiful prize.

No idea is perfect! No idea is without its problems. God sets it up that way in order for us to be humble enough to seek His help all along the way.

## The Faith of Stanley Reimer

Every Sunday morning I see a very special person sitting about ten rows back on the right side of the auditorium. His name is Stanley Reimer, and he's an elder on our church board. I'll never forget the day when I received the tragic news that Stanley had a heart attack. Stan was a chemist with a large company, and the news was that he had a twenty-two-minute cardiac arrest. Twenty-two minutes! You know what that means. There was a considerable amount of time when oxygen did not reach the brain. And if Stan survived, he would probably be a vegetable all of his life. They managed to get him breathing again, but he was in a death coma. He was placed in the intensive care unit immediately, and his body was breathing on its own, but he was still in a coma. There was no sign of life other than the breathing that was going on. The neurosurgeon told Stan's wife that there was no hope. "If he keeps breathing, he'll be a vegetable all his life. He'll never close his eyes. They'll be open in a death stare as you see now. Totally, a vegetable."

I rushed to the hospital as soon as I could, praying the whole time. "God," I prayed, "what will I say?" What will I say to his wife? And then I remembered what I was taught in theological seminary: *Someday, as a pastor, you may be talking to someone in a death coma. When that happens, only think life! Only talk life! If you're ever at the bedside of a presumably dying patient, and he's in a coma so deep that no response is indicated, talk life! He may lack the power to move his lips or manifest a physical indication that he is hearing, but his subconscious may hear! And you must not place a negative thought in that mind!*

So I went into the intensive-care unit where he was lying, and there was Billie, his wife, standing at the bedside, tears streaming down her face. My once outgoing friend looked like a statue. He couldn't move—dead for all practical appearances—but he was breathing. His eyes were wide open. I put my arm around Billie and prayed with her. Then I took hold of his hand and softly said, "Stanley, I know you cannot talk. I know you cannot respond, but I know that deep down within you, you can hear me. I'm Bob Schuller. I've just come from church where everyone is praying for you. And Stanley, I've got news for you. You had a bad heart attack, but you are going to recover. You are going to live, and it's going to be a long battle. It's going to be hard, but you're going to make it!"

And at that point I had one of the most moving experiences of my life. A tear rolled out of my friend's eye. He understood! No smile, no quiver of a lip, but a tear rolled out of his eye. The doctors couldn't believe it! That was over a year ago and today Stanley is able to speak full sentences, he can hear, and his faculties are becoming normalized.

A miracle? Remember:

"If you have faith as a grain of mustard seed you can say to your mountain, 'Move' and nothing will be impossible."

In the darkest time, tell yourself that faith will move the mountain! Faith will help and faith will heal, but you must not give up believing.

# Run, Patty, Run!

Patty Wilson was thirteen years old when she discovered she was an epileptic. Her dad did everything he could to convince her that she shouldn't have a negative self-image because of this condition. He knew that she would encounter discrimination, and he didn't want to see her get hurt. One day Patty's dad was driving to work, when he saw a man running along the sidewalk in runner's shoes and clothes, but there was something strange about his feet. They looked like the hoofs of a horse! Mr. Wilson did a double take and threw his car into reverse. He later found out that the man was born with no feet, and his custom-made running shoes looked like the hoofs of a horse. That one incident inspired Patty's dad to run! Mr. Wilson thought, "If he can run, so can I!" And it was at this point that he vowed to teach Patty that she was normal. And he was going to make her believe it!

As Patty watched her dad run each morning, she became interested and was soon running alongside of him. Day after day, week after week, month after month, you could see the father-daughter team running through the neighborhood. Then Patty was inspired with a dream. *How can I encourage the world to treat epileptics like normal people?* she wondered. She asked her dad what the women's record for long-distance running was and set a goal to break it. She decided she'd run from Orange County to San Diego, 100 miles; to Las Vegas, 300 miles; and then to San Francisco, 500 miles. These were her major goals.

She trained for a year to make it. And she said, "At the end of my sophomore year, I'll run from Orange County to Portland, Oregon [1,000 miles]." She didn't stop there! "At the end of my junior year," she determined, "I will run from Orange County to Saint Louis, Missouri [2,000 miles]. And at the end of my senior year, when I graduate from high school, I'll celebrate by running from Orange County across the United States of America to Washington, D.C. I want to shake hands with the President at the White House."

How's that for big thinking by a teen-age epileptic girl? Talk about possibility thinking! Well, she tried and last year she made it! She ran 500 miles from Orange County to San Francisco, California. And this year, at the end of her sophomore year, she was ready to try for Portland, Oregon—1,000 miles. And when the event was to occur, her high-school classmates had a big paper banner stretched across the street, and they wrote in red, sloppy ink—RUN, PATTY, RUN! There were some ceremonies, and I said a prayer. I even placed my medallion around her neck!

What an exciting moment when Patty ran through and ripped the paper banner! She went running down the road, on the way towards the coast, on the way to Portland, Oregon, 1,000 miles. Driving behind at a safe distance was her mother, a licensed vocational nurse, with medication in case she had a seizure. And tacked on the back of the van were the words: PATTY WILSON, WORLD'S WOMEN'S LONG-DISTANCE RUNNER RECORD-HOLDER—RUNNING FROM CALIFORNIA TO OREGON. We followed her every day with our prayers. She did great until 28 miles later, when she cracked a bone in her foot. Her parents took her to the emergency room of the hospital, praying that it wasn't serious. Doctors X-rayed her foot and concluded that it was fractured. The doctor said, "Patty, you'd better not run, because if you do, you may have permanent injury." Patty knew that there were thousands of people that were expecting her to run and complete the adventure. "Doctor," she said, "if you wrapped it tight, don't you think I could keep running?" "Yes, you might do it," he explained, "but you'll get terrible blisters." "That's just water under the skin," Patty enthused. "My mother's a nurse. Couldn't she take the liquid out with a syringe?" "Yes," the doctor replied. "Just be careful." So Patty tightly wrapped her foot up and went back onto the road. It hurt! But she kept on running—*500* miles, *600, 700, 800, 900, 1,000!*

They decided to take the coastal route, not stopping to think that it was 300 miles farther. One thousand, 1,100, 1,200, 1,300—and when they were about a mile outside of Portland, Oregon, the governor got his running suit on and ran with her the last mile. The entire city was out to greet her, and what a welcome she got! She endured the pain! There was no permanent injury to her foot, so she's in great shape. And Patty's already talking about running across the U.S.A. And when she makes it, you'll hear about her!

Stop and think. *How?* Have you been as faithful to your dream as Patty Wilson has been to hers?

Faith will never fail you—unless you give up! Patty didn't give up! And she's still climbing! Today's impossibilities are tomorrow's possibilities! Keep on keeping on! Believe in yourself!

# We Need You

If you've taken a cruise on an ocean liner, you've had the thrill of first catching sight of the shore. When you come into a new port, you see a huge mass of floating hotels with their precious cargo of hundreds and hundreds of persons and their property. A tugboat brings the ship in slowly and carefully, until it's right against the pier. Now the ship has to be tied firmly to the dock, or the gangplank will tip and topple with the slightest swell of the water. The ship has to be tied tightly! And if you've been past the dock or pier, you've seen these huge ropes thicker than your arm that hold the ship tight against the dock. The crew doesn't throw the big rope onto the shore, for it's too heavy. A sailor at the bow with another at the stern holds in his hand a little ball. He throws the ball onto the dock, and trailing behind it is a thin line, like a kite string. Somebody on the dock picks up that ball and pulls in the kite string. And tied to the thin string is a little rope, the size of a clothesline. When he gets hold of it, he and his crewmen can pull the boat to the dock.

So the great liner unloads its cargo and is ready to set sail again. Who made it possible? The captain? Yes. But it was also that thin little line that was the key for all of the maneuvering. The captain, the tugboats, and those who work on the pier would fail if it weren't for that thin string tied to a rope. The crew can keep the ship running, but when it gets to the bottom line, it takes a thin thread to make a journey a success.

# You Are Important

Many of you think you're not important; you don't see life in its whole perspective. We have a furnace in our home that has a little pilot light. That small flame has to be faithful in order for the big furnace to work. The pilot ignites the bigger furnace, which heats the entire house. Friends visiting my home on a cold day might comment on the comfortable temperature inside the house, but nobody ever compliments the pilot light. Nobody thinks about the poor little flame. I have news for you. In every successful institution and enterprise, there is at least one person who is the pilot light. He or she throws on the big furnace to make things happen.

I went to Hope College, in Holland, Michigan, a great institution with very high academic standards. When I was there, the president of the college was Dr. Irwin Lubbers. Every so often I would see him cut across campus on his way to a meeting. He would rarely talk to the students, for he seemed to have so many things on his mind. In fact, there was only one person that I ever saw him stop and talk to, and that was the gardener. Now I knew that young man. He had suffered from a childhood illness and was limited in his mental capacity. Sometimes I'd be sitting on the lawn reading, when Dr. Lubbers would walk by and stop to talk with the man. They would laugh and shake hands, as if they were good friends. The college president always seemed to have a new spring in his step as he walked on. He was the furnace, and the gardener was the pilot light. Every institution has to have that kind of pilot light! You can be an inspiration to somebody!

# The Inspiration for Mary Crowley

Mary Crowley, president of Home Interiors, a very prosperous business, was in Nassau, in the Bahamas, with her husband some years ago. It was a Sunday morning, so they decided to go to church. They found a local church filled with nearby citizens. There were all black people in the congregation. She tells the story of how the huge, silver-haired preacher, with a thundering voice and a rusty, gravelly tone, kept pounding home one theme to his people all morning. Talking to his people he bellowed out, "Be somebody! God never takes time to build a nobody. Everybody God creates is created to be *somebody!*"

That black preacher probably never knew what an inspiration he was to Mary Crowley. Little did he realize that he would be the one to inspire a woman to go back to the United States with that positive message: *"Be* somebody! God never takes time to create a nobody!" And she has been sharing that theme now until her organization reaches into every state in the country! Be somebody! God never takes time to create a nobody!

# The Inspiration of George Truitt

When I was a theology student, I was assigned to write a term paper on a minister named George Truitt. At that time, I had never heard of him. I discovered that he had come to a tiny congregation in Dallas, Texas, and decided to spend his life in that church. He labored in his congregation for forty years, until it became one of the largest and the finest Baptist churches in the world. I was so inspired by this story that I prayed then and there: "God, I'm a young man; lead me to some place where I can spend forty years and start a church from scratch." George Truitt was the pilot for this church. Now we, in turn, are inspiring others. You can be an inspiration to somebody if you have the right source—if you're set on the right course, and if you have the force behind you. Jesus Christ is the source of my inspiration. He said:

> "For the Scriptures declare that rivers of living water shall flow from the inmost being of anyone who believes in me."
>
> John 7:38 LB

# The Saudi Problem

> It is the glory of God to conceal a thing. And it is the glory of kings to reveal it.
>
> Proverbs 25:2

Dr. Paul Harrison, one of the great surgeons of the twentieth century spent most of his life in Saudi Arabia as a missionary for our church. I remember he used to tell of one tremendous problem the Arabs (who lived in bleak, sandy deserts) constantly had to deal with—the problem of keeping their sheep alive. It seemed that the sheep were constantly being poisoned by a black substance which oozed from the ground and swirled through the animals' watering holes. At that time, the Arabs didn't know that that black substance was of far greater value to them than their flocks of sheep. Unknowingly, they had discovered oil. *It is the glory of God to conceal a thing. And it is the glory of kings to reveal it.*

## An American Success Story

Not long ago I had dinner with a remarkable man at his home in Miami, Florida. This man was born in a very tough neighborhood in Flint, Michigan. When I met with him, he said, "Doctor Schuller, you asked me what kind of neighborhood I lived in, how tough my gang was. Let me explain. Of my friends, eleven are dead. Five were murdered. And four are serving life sentences for murder." That man is, today, forty-three years of age. He showed me his hands. They had been scarred from innumerable street battles. Even today the carriage of his body still reflects the attitude of the street.

At eighteen he dropped out of high school with a *D* average. He met a young girl and soon married when she became pregnant. Their first child had barely been born when the young man's wife became pregnant once again. He had no idea how to support his new family and little hope for his marriage. Desperation drove him to seek help from a black marriage counselor.

After talking to him for a while and giving him some aptitude tests, the counselor said, "You should either be a mechanic or a salesman." So the young man enrolled in mechanic's trade school sponsored by General Motors. Two weeks after he began working he looked at his grease-covered body and thought with despair, "I just can't do this for the rest of my life!" While walking home, he passed a used-car lot. He wished he could have money for a car and wondered, "Could I be a salesman?"

The manager of the lot asked, "You, looking for a car. You got any money?" "Maybe," the man replied. "Maybe I'm looking for a job." The man gave him a job working on the lot for forty dollars a week. His first week on the lot, the young man astounded everyone, including himself, by selling fifteen cars.

He'd not been at the lot very long when one of his customers offered him a job selling furniture for a small base salary plus commission. At the end of his first year on the job he had a pregnant wife, two children, and a gross income of twenty-eight thousand dollars. He was not yet nineteen years old. His second year he earned forty-two thousand dollars.

At twenty-two, he borrowed ten thousand dollars from his father (who had mortgaged his house) and set up his own furniture store. During his first thirty days in business he sold two hundred thousand dollars in gross sales, fifty thousand of which was his net profit. By the end of that year, he netted $1 million. He retired at the age of twenty-eight with a personal fortune of $15 million.

Today he spends his time working on the boards of directors of various Catholic institutions and charitable organizations. In addition to being a father to nine children and a grandfather, he's using his energies to inspire people who are looked upon as hopeless punks to "believe you can do something and be somebody." My friend, you have the possibilities within you you haven't dared to believe.

# "Follow More Closely"

Recently I was scheduled to speak to a group of bishops and leaders in the Roman Catholic Church as well as leaders of the Protestant churches in New Orleans. Because I had so much work to do, I booked the 12:30 flight to New Orleans, which would arrive at 6:00 P.M.—one hour before the dinner was to begin. I figured that if the plane arrived at 6:00, that would give me a half hour to be briefed. I thought I had it timed perfectly.

The problem was that the plane ran into a problem in Los Angeles and didn't leave on time. Fifteen, then thirty minutes passed. Finally, forty-five minutes later, the plane took off, and I landed in New Orleans about twelve minutes to 7:00. The two principal officials of the event were waiting for me when I stepped off the plane, along with a police officer. We left the airport, and I climbed into the waiting car. The police officer led the way in his car. All of a sudden, the light on the police car started turning and the siren blew. I was soon aware that we were having a police escort.

You know, that's really kind of an ego trip. Having a police escort really made me feel important. And I must confess, it's a lot better feeling having the siren ahead of you than behind you!

The policeman was leading the way down the expressway and everybody was pulling to the side to let us pass. Then suddenly the police car pulled over to the curb. Our driver didn't know what that meant, and we were still some minutes from our destination, so we kept on driving. Soon, however, he pulled beside us. Through his megaphone I could hear him say, "You've got to follow me more closely." Boy, we had to hang right in there behind him, as he led the way.

In the same way, God moves ahead of us. He thinks bigger than either you or I can think. He knows you have far more potential than you give yourself credit for. He has more, far more, faith in you than you have in yourself. And your job is to "follow more closely."

# Look for the Rainbow

I suppose the most successful publishing venture in American outside of the Bible is the *Old Farmer's Almanac.* It's a super success and has been for almost a hundred years. In July, 1883, the editor was finishing the final draft for the year's almanac. He had worked all the way into the following year, estimating what the weather would be every day from January through July 12, 1884. But as the accomplished writer neared completion, he grew tired. So he thought he'd pick up the next day with July 13, 1884.

Just as he was about to go home, a boy came running in and exclaimed, "You can't go! The printer is demanding the remaining pages tonight—all the way through July thirteenth. You must stay and finish!" "I've had it," the editor said. "Just write in some kind of temperature and weather for July thirteenth. Frankly, your guess is as good as mine." And he forgot all about it.

So the young boy wrote in his weather forecast: "Wind, hail, and snow." When the almanac finally came out and was being distributed, the editor looked through it and saw what the boy had written. He was furious! He called the boy in and said, "This is outrageous! We're barely making it, and now this is going to ruin us. There's no way there can be wind, hail, and snow on July thirteenth!" Well, on July 13, 1884, there was wind, hail, and snow, like never before and never since. And when the United States read that the *Old Farmer's Almanac* had predicted it ten months before, their reputation soared overnight to make them a national success!

Sometimes we think that everything that happens to us is

bad news. Remember this: Good news will always follow bad news! There is a rainbow that rises out of the storm. You may have to wait a while, but good news always follows bad news. That's why you need a connection with God through Jesus Christ, and if you have that, you may have problems, but you can make it!

# Take a Look at Your Good Times

Look at what you have left. Don't look at what you've lost. Look at your good times—don't look at your bad times.

I had lunch with a very good friend last week to check up on his health, because he's been very ill. I asked him how he was. "Oh, I'm terrific now," he answered. Six months ago he was in very bad shape. We prayed together often on the telephone. "You know, Bob," he shared, "there was a time when I was so sick that I thought every day was a bad day and every hour was a totally bad hour. Then one day I said to my wife, 'Honey, I haven't had five good minutes today.' 'That's not true,' she enthused, 'you just don't remember the good minutes.' And I thought to myself, 'She may be right!'

"The next day I went to the store and purchased a loose-leaf notebook, so I could start my own personal diary. My plan was that any time in the course of the day when I felt good I would write it down. For instance, right after breakfast I said, 'The bacon tasted good.' That was a good experience so I wrote it down. At the end of the day, I looked at the good things that had happened. It really wasn't all bad after all! The next day I did the same thing. Now I have a very thick diary!" In the worst time a lot of good things can happen!

# Inflate Your Possibilities

The other day I read about a man who was marooned on an island a year ago. According to the anecdote, he was not rescued until the year 2000. The first thing he did when he returned to civilization was to go to a pay phone, where he dropped in a coin and called his broker.

"Hey, I'm back," he said. "You know, of course, I've been gone for twenty years. Tell me, how did my General Motors stock do?"

"Oh," the broker said, "It's done incredibly well. It's now worth nine million dollars."

"How about my house?" exclaimed the man breathlessly, "What is it worth?"

"Oh, your house is worth about two and a half million," the broker replied.

The man was rejoicing over his good fortune, when the operator broke in. "I'm sorry," she said, "your three minutes are up. Please deposit one million dollars."

None of us knows what the future will bring. We know we're caught up in economic inflation—but will your possibilities also inflate? Will your personal development also inflate? It can—if you practice right thinking, believe, pray, and live the kind of life God has planned for you. You, too, can say, "I can do all things through Christ which strengtheneth me" (Philippians 4:13 KJV).

# Listen: Your Key to Harmony

When I was in high school, I sang in a male quartet. Later, when I entered college, I made it a point of joining another quartet. We made many concert tours throughout the United States. In fact, I made my first trip to California when I was in the Hope College traveling, touring quartet. I'll never forget my high-school music teacher saying, "Boys, the key to a good male quartet is equal balanced harmony. All voices *must* be equally balanced!" Then she went on to explain how to obtain harmony.

"Listen to yourself sing, but also listen to the other voices on each side of you," she explained. "If the voices on either side of you are a little louder than you, you know that you have to sing a little louder. If you hear yourself louder than you hear those on each side of you, then you are singing too loud; tone down a little. All you have to do is use your ears! Make sure that you don't sing louder or softer than the voices around you. *Listen!*"

I have discovered that that is also an important principle for interpersonal relationships. The tragedy is most people listen to their own will. They listen to their own wishes—to their own desires. They hear the inner voice of their own selfish desires so strongly, that when somebody else comes along with a suggestion or an idea, a request or an appeal, they really don't hear it. They only hear what satisfies their own desires. Then they wonder why they fail, or why things fall apart, or why disharmony moves in. They wonder why they are not happy, and why they are not enthusiastic, why they are not sparkling and twinkling. Disharmony produces gloom. Harmony produces sparkle. The key is listening to what others are trying to say to you. And most important— this listening must be with regularity.

# The Place for Negativity

A very negative-thinking minister was given a promotion. He was to leave his pastorate and become a bishop. He was replaced by a young, positive, enthusiastic fellow who had just graduated from theological seminary. This young minister entered the stiff, stodgy, and stuffy old church with great ideas. He initiated some recreational programs and led a more liberal service on Sunday mornings. When his predecessor heard what was happening to his old pastorate he became distressed. The bishop couldn't see his previous church led down the road to destruction, so he pulled his rank of authority and demanded an opportunity to return to his old pulpit.

The bishop came with determination to straighten out the congregation—to correct this impetuous, impulsive, ridiculously progressive and ultraliberal successor. He stood before the congregation and berated the young pastor. It was a very embarrassing and sordid scene. When he was finished, with flushed face, the humiliated minister came up to the pulpit to conclude the service. With his head hung in remorse he addressed the people. "I'm sorry; I can make mistakes." Then pointing to his beloved congregation, he said, "You can make mistakes." And turning to the bishop he said, "And the bishop can make mistakes." There was complete silence as he continued. "I can sin. You can sin. And the bishop can sin. I could go to hell, you could go to hell, and the bishop can go to hell." There is a lot of negativity in religion!

A lot of religion can go to hell because that is exactly where it is! That is the truth! What is hell? Hell is a state of being separated from God. Hell is a state when we are not consumed by His love and by the awareness of His Presence. Whatever hell is, wherever hell is, this we know: There can be no hell if you stand in the heart of the presence of the love of God.

# "He Was Leaning Against the Wind"

I was in Bóston recently and the wind was blowing fiercely. It reminded me of the experience of Bill Stidger, a student at the Boston University. Bill always walked to school early in the morning. One morning he noticed a large group of people gathered at the base of a skyscraper being built, so he moved into the crowd. "What's happening?" he asked a man with a hard hat who looked like a foreman. "One of the workers just got killed," the workman replied. And Bill Stidger, a student for the ministry, asked, "How did it happen?" "The fool," the foreman angrily answered, "he was leaning against the wind!" And then with tears in his eyes, he added, "When I hired him last week I distinctly said, 'Don't lean against the wind!' "

"What does he mean?" Bill asked another hardhat standing nearby. "What does he mean, *leaning against the wind?*" "Oh," the other steelworker said, "here in Boston there is always a steady breeze in the morning. A firm, pressurized wind comes off the ocean and leans against the skeleton of this building. So when we work up there, it's so easy to lean against the wind. But about nine o'clock in the morning, the wind always cuts off. And always without any warning! This new guy had just come from Indianapolis. He was used to working on a highrise, but he's not used to working in Boston. He was leaning against the wind, and when the wind cut off, he fell."

If you are down on living, you are leaning against the wind. Don't lean against the wind; lean upon a solid rock. Lean against Jesus Christ.

> "Every one then who hears these words of mine and does them will be like a wise man who built his house upon the rock; and the rain fell, and the floods came,

and the winds blew and beat upon that house, but it
did not fall, because it had been founded on the
rock."

Matthew 7:24, 25 RSV

# How to Succeed in Tough Times

I want to share with you the story of a very dear friend of
mine who, incidentally, prefers to remain anonymous. He
was a salesman during the Great Depression in the early
1930s—a time when salesmen as a whole weren't doing well
at all. One night at a sales meeting a fellow salesman told
him the story of a man who had made a lot of money with
the Coca-Cola Company. "Did you her about the guy who
went to Coca-Cola with an idea which would vastly expand
the sales of their product?" he asked. "No," someone in the
group answered. "What do you mean?"

"Well," the man continued, "this guy wrote to Coca-Cola
and told them he had an idea that could be enormously
profitable to their company. All he asked was a fraction of
one percent of the gross sales realized as a result of his idea.
At first he was ignored, but he kept badgering everyone so
consistently that finally management agreed to see him and
hear him out.

"Do you know what the idea was?" the man asked. "He
told those smart executives that they would multiply sales if
they would sell only bottled Coca-Cola."

Up until that time Coca-Cola had been sold only in large
containers to drugstores. Nobody had ever thought of putting it in bottles and selling it to grocery stores and other retail outlets. Coca-Cola agreed to his terms, tried the idea,
and it was so successful that the man made multiple millions.

My friend went home that night and thought about what

he had heard. The next day he took his car to a service station to get oil put into it. The only way to get oil was for the service-station attendant to pump it out of huge drums, and then pour it into the car. *I wonder if I could bottle automobile oil? my friend mused. No, he thought. If the bottles broke, that would really be a mess. I wonder if I could put oil in cans and sell it that way?*

He went to a friend in Pennsylvania who owned an oil refinery that was refining more oil than could be marketed. His friend agreed to allow him to have the excess oil for a reasonable percentage of the profits. Then my friend went to a can company and made arrangements with them to purchase some cans. Finally he went to the A&P and said to the marketing manager, "How would you like to expand your retail sales enormously by selling car oil in cans?" All he asked as payment was seventy-five dollars for each freight carload of canned oil that was sold. In the middle of the Great Depression, this man made millions of dollars. He used that money as the basis for establishing what is today an incredible financial empire. And he's given millions of dollars to numerous great causes. In the worst of times, somebody is going to get a bright idea!

## "A/440"

When Jesus becomes Lord of our lives, He becomes our solid, single integrating force—our "A/440."

Let me explain: Suppose that a concert was planned featuring the three greatest pianists in the world, perhaps Van Cliburn, Liberace, and Rubinstein. Each will play in a different city—one in New York, one in Tokyo, and one in Paris—and the three will be simultaneously broadcast via international satellite. In America, and around the world, viewers could see and hear these three great artists playing the same composition at the same moment on a triple screen. Such an event is technically possible.

However, we encounter one problem: How do you make sure all pianos are tuned exactly alike? You can't, very practically, get all three pianos on a plane, tune them and then ship them to three different concert halls. Could you tune them using a taped recording of one piano as the basis for tuning the remaining two? The variable for error is still too great. How could it be done? By tuning the three pianos by *A*/440 above middle *C*. The *A* above middle *C* is tuned to produce 440 vibrations per second when it is struck. This measure will be the same in Tokyo, Paris, and New York City—*A*/440 is an absolute, international measure in relation to music.

When the angels appeared at Christmastime, what they were really announcing was the arrival of God's greatest gift to the world—an international standard by which we could tune our lives. Whatever your race, culture, religious belief (or lack of it)—you, without exception—need an internationally valid moral, spiritual, and emotional standard that can determine your human values. Who do you tune your life by? The moral standards and human values of others? If so, that's perfectly normal. But it is probably a basic reason why you're not happy.

Can you imagine how an orchestra would sound if each musician was pursuing his own ego trip and said, "My pitch is perfect. I'll tune my instrument by my own ear." The result would be a maddening cacophony. Instead the oboe is tuned to *A*/440. (The oboe is chosen for the purity of its notes. More than any other instrument, its sound is free from overtones.) And the remaining instruments take their pitch from the oboe.

Until Jesus was born, the world was like an orchestra without an *A*/440. Jesus became the integrating force upon whom we can form our basic value system. Before Him, there was no standard for all human beings. No other religious leader in history ever said, "I am the Way, the Truth and the Life." No other human being claimed to be humanity's guiding North Star—the moral, emotional, and spiritual *A/440* above middle *C.* Jesus is God's standard for every person for all time to come.

# My Most Memorable Christmas

The other day someone asked, "Doctor Schuller, what is your most memorable Christmas?" "I think I can answer that," I replied, "and I don't think it will change during my lifetime. I can't imagine any Christmas more memorable than the Christmas of 1978." That was the year—and I shall never forget it—when our young daughter Carol, age thirteen, was thrown from a motorcycle on which she was a passenger. She sailed eighty-nine feet through the air and landed in a ditch where she almost died. My wife and I were on a mission in Korea when we got the news that the doctors were in the process of amputating her left leg.

Our plane flight home took twenty-two hours. I suppose I did more crying on that flight than I ever have in my entire life. When my wife and I arrived at my daughter's side, unable to think of adequate words of comfort, surprisingly enough, Carol began the conversation. "Dad," she said, "I think God has a special ministry for my life to help people who have been hurt as I have." She saw possibilities— positive ones—in tragedy! What a lift those words gave me. But we were just beginning what would prove to be a long, exhaustive battle. Carol's femur broke in four places and plunged through the thigh bone and into the ditch of an Iowa farm, next to a slaughterhouse. There it picked up a form of bacteria, which had previously been resistant to any known antibiotics.

The accident happened in July. In November, Carol went back into the hospital for surgery which would, hopefully, release muscles in her knee that might make her leg more usable. The doctor was so delighted when he opened her thigh and knee and discovered no pus pockets. But the hidden bacteria which, until that time had remained dormant, erupted like a prairie fire when exposed to the open air. Three days after surgery she was the sickest little girl I've ever seen.

Each passing day, the bacteria multiplied with increasing impatience. Carol's fever soared to 104 degrees and lingered there day after day, night after night. Her leg continued to swell and the infection raged out of control.

About that time we were blessed with a minor miracle. With no knowledge of my daughter's need, the Federal Drug Administration released, for the first time, an antibiotic that was declared significantly effective against that specific strain of bacteria Carol contracted while lying in that Iowa ditch. She was the first human being in Children's Hospital, Orange Country, California, to receive it. In a matter of hours after the first dosage, her temperature went down. Each successive culture reading showed fewer and fewer bacteria until, about three weeks before Christmas, a culture came back that showed no bacteria growth.

Lying in her hospital bed with the intravenous tubes still in her hands, Carol asked the visiting doctor, who was standing in for her own surgeon, when she would be released. "Will I be home for Christmas, doctor?" she asked. "I don't know," he replied cautiously. "Will I be able to get my new prosthesis? All I want for Christmas is my new fake foot," she chimed. "Well," the doctor cautioned, "I don't believe you can get it yet."

But when her doctor returned from his lecture trip to Spain, he checked her over. That same day Carol called me at my office. "Daddy, I have good news," she announced. "What is it?" I asked. "Doctor Masters is an angel," she exclaimed. "He said I can come home for Christmas!"

On December 16, a Saturday night, Carol was released from the hospital. I was told to stay home and await a surprise. My wife went to pick her up. I saw the lights of the car, as it rolled up the driveway. Then I saw the taillights go on as the brake pedal was pressed, and I ran to the front door. My wife opened the door and said, "Bob, you have to go back in and wait. Carol wants you to wait by the Christmas tree."

So I waited nervously by the Christmas tree, counting the seemingly interminable seconds. Then I heard the front door open and the squeak of rubber on the wooden floor. I knew the sound came from the rubber tips of Carol's crutches. Then she stepped into the open door, ten feet away from my seat by the Christmas tree. She had gone straight from the hospital to the beauty parlor (typical girl) where she had had the most beautiful permanent. Then she stood with the most lovely curls framing her face. And I looked down and saw two shoes, two ankles, two legs—a beautiful girl. Carol got her new foot for Christmas. In my mind, *that* Christmas will always be the most memorable!

# The White House Experience

Not long ago I was in the White House on a Wednesday and a Thursday. On Wednesday, I was invited by Mrs. Carter to attend a press conference which announced the launching of a national campaign, one which would announce and promote television programs for the deaf. A new technology has been developed which allows a deaf person to attach a small adaptor to the television set. When this is accomplished, this person can see the words spoken and sung by television personalities move across the bottom of the screen. Only on a television set fitted with this adaptor will the words appear. So if a person has impaired hearing or is totally deaf, he can read every word, just as a hearing person would read the subtitles of a foreign film. However, in order for the adaptor to be effective, the program must be specially produced. And that can be very expensive.

When we heard about the breakthrough some time ago, we immediately decided to implement the technique into our production of the "Hour of Power." In order to do this, we authorized the spending of an additional two thousand dollars per week to cover the expenses of this special facet of television production for the deaf. At the time we didn't realize it, but we were the first secular or sacred syndicated television program in the United States to use this special technique! So I was quite surprised when I got a letter from Mrs. Carter, inviting me to be with her at the White House for the press conference held in the East Room.

The next day I was invited to return to the East Room of the White House at the invitation of the President. There a group of national leaders met to talk about the problems of inflation and energy. First of all, Economic Adviser Charles Schultze spoke for about forty minutes on the problems of inflation. He urged the American people to be thrifty and pay off their credit cards.

I wanted to raise my hand and say, "I'm all for thrift. But may I suggest, sir, instead of taking a negative approach and saying, 'Don't use your charge card,' try a positive approach. Tell the people to put away as much as they can into savings accounts. Then declare that all of the interest paid to those savings accounts will be nontaxable income and eliminate the practice of allowing the interest on credit cards to be an income-tax deduction. Our tax feeds debt and fuels inflation." If the United States did that, then people would start saving and rise out of their poverty. That's what they do in Singapore and their inflation rate is only 4 percent and has been for the past 5 years. Place the emphasis on thrift and really reward the people who are saving positively by giving them incentives. Don't try to repress or restrict them.

However I didn't get a chance to voice my idea, and perhaps it's just as well. After Mr. Schultze finished speaking, Secretary Francis Duncan took his place at the podium and spoke about the energy crisis. He's right. We waste an incredible amount of energy. The President later told us that we spend 10 billion dollars every sixty minutes on imported oil. That statement really hit a responsive cord in me. We must conserve energy.

For years I've been urging my children to put the lights out, turn off the television or radio if they're not enjoying them. Even on business trips, I always remember to turn the lights out in my hotel room. Of course I'm not paying the bill, but that doesn't matter. The hotel management is getting this energy from the same ultimate source that everyone else is in America. We have to start conserving fuel and energy. Don't make unnecessary trips. Car pool whenever possible.

Then the President, too, urged Americans to be more thrifty and energy conscious. He suggested that we use solar energy. That statement immediately caught my attention, because we were sitting in the East Room on a bright sunny day with all the drapes drawn. Lights were blazing unnecessarily throughout the room! "Look," I wanted to say, "all the drapes are drawn. Why not let the natural sunlight illuminate the room?"

So when Mr. Schultze asked if there were any questions, I raised my hand. But he saw somebody else. I never got a chance to speak. Then Mr. Duncan finished his address and I raised my hand again. Although I was right in front of him, he didn't see me either. Then the President finished his speech with the words, "Everybody has to do their little part to save energy. Are there any questions?" I raised my hand and saw him look in my direction. But a congressman next to me popped up. He asked a question in the way typical with congressman—he made a speech for five minutes! When his speech was finished, President Carter said, "I'm sorry, I have to leave."

The President walked out and Mr. Schultze and Mr. Duncan followed. Since I was right there in the center aisle, the very front seat, I followed the Secretary. Tapping him on the shoulder, I asked, "Hey, we've all got to conserve, right?" "Right," he answered emphatically. "Then I've got a question," I began. "I sat in the East Room for an hour and a half yesterday and for two and a half hours today. That's a total of four hours. Both days it was bright and sunny outside. And both days all the drapes were shut, darkening the room so all the lights had to be burning for four hours. Why didn't you use solar energy to light the place?"

He blushed and stammered. Finally he said, "Well, they need the room dark for television." Shaking my head I volunteered, "You know it's possible to get beautiful television production without any drapes drawn on the windows." Quite flustered he said, "I don't know," and pushed his way ahead and left in a hurry.

Friday night of that same week, I returned home and watched the President give his public address to the nation with regard to the United States's boycott of the Olympics in Moscow. Once again he was in the East Room. But do you know what? This time all the drapes were wide open! Now I'm not saying, of course, that I'm the reason for this change in White House procedure. But maybe they did decide to listen just a little bit. The point is that everybody can do their little bit to conserve energy.

# Sealing the Windows of the Cathedral

Successful leaders must learn to manage time, money, energy, talent, and people. They also must learn to handle problems. The Crystal Cathedral, which was just constructed, is completely glazed. One of the final steps that had to be performed on the exterior was for each seam to be sealed where the windows come together. Everyone who was asked to bid on the job said it was impossible. Nobody could walk up and down on the steep sides of a slippery glass roof a football field in size. It would be impossible not to slide down.

Then one day a young man from Cupple's Company came to me and asked, "Doctor Schuller, did you see the little go-cart I invented?" It was a little device that would allow a man to sit in it and go back and forth along the roof and work the seams of the windows. "Anytime somebody says they can't do something," the young man said, "it simply means that they don't want to do it. You can do anything you want to. You just have to invent something new, that's all." He's a true possibility thinker!

# Why You Need a Positive Church

Last week I was talking at length on the telephone with Dr. Lacy Hall, who is involved in the Stone-Brandel Center in Chicago, Illinois. He was telling me about an experiment they did at the center about three years ago. First, they recruited a large number of persons. Then they asked every person to keep a diary of their daily life—to record everything that came as an input into their mind or into their lives. He believed that we are the product of what comes into our lives, our minds, our hearts, and our emotional experiences. Dr. Hall wanted to find out what percentage of input into a human brain in the course of a day was positive and what percentage was negative.

Everyone was told to record everything that came into their brains in the course of a day for a year and a half. Their diaries began with the opening of the day. If they turned on the television set, they had to write down exactly what they watched—whether it was a newscast or a talk show, they had to log it into their diaries. Was the input positive or negative? If they worked, every encounter had to be recorded, whether positive or negative. If they listened to a radio station, read a certain newspaper or book, visited with family or friends, participated in any kind of entertainment or went to church—everything had to be documented.

After a year and a half, Dr. Hall said the data was collected, calculated, and computerized under controlled research at the Stone-Brandel Center in Chicago. The people who kept these diaries came up feeling discouraged or depressed all the time. Do you wonder why? Most people experienced 90 percent negative input. Ony 10 percent of the thoughts that were fed to them, or the concepts that came into their life during the year and a half were positive! There were a few people who had a high percentage of positive input, but they were rare. These were the people who had unique relationships in marriage, in the office, and at home. And they also had connections with outstanding positive-thinking churches. But on an overall average, Dr. Hall said this group had 75 percent negative input.

Dr. Hall's closing comment was, "You see, Doctor Schuller, we are fighting against tremendous odds. The average human being (who is trying to be positive) is fighting a losing battle, unless he's tied into something unusual that constantly feeds him positive emotions."

Do you wonder why you don't have the *up* feeling all the

time? Do you wonder why you want to quit and give up? Do you wonder why you lack enthusiasm and inner spiritual power? It's quite simple. The majority of thoughts and inputs that come into that brain of yours—that soul of yours—is negative! That's right! That's why you need to attend a church where every service is positive. You need it! That's why we print books and try desperately to get you to do at least one positive thing every day. You need it! I need it! Everyone needs it!

# How to Receive Satisfaction in Life

Recently I read about Doctor William Havender, a prominent ophthalmologist. He was addressing a group of young medical students about to graduate. He said: "Students, when I was your age I could only conclude that no one knew about God. And therefore atheism was the only tenable position. Now, I know whether or not there is a God; the patients that know they have a God are much better off than those who do not believe in God. There is no question about it. There is an enormous difference! So what do we physicians do about that fact? Let me illustrate by comparing physicians to stoneworkers.

"Three stoneworkers might, depending upon their viewpoint or their perspective or their mental attitude, look upon their job in different ways. One stoneworker sees his job as carrying stone; another stoneworker sees it as building a wall; and another sees his job as creating a cathedral to the glory of God. As doctors, you have the same attitude. If you see your job as carrying stones, you will then see your patients as complaining crocks, indigent invalids, sick scoundrels, and poor protoplasm. And with that view you will soon start seeking the solace of alcohol or drugs.

"A second attitude is you can see your work as the construction of an endless wall, the futile patching up of worn-out bodies. The whole endeavor becomes senseless because you know, ultimately, that the body cannot be patched up anymore. Now with that attitude, you welcome the ultimate escape from your profession, because you'll think that at the end you're a loser and you'll welcome death.

"But if you are as fortunate as I am to come to believe that there is a God and every human being is one of His unique and special creatures, however frail and faulted they might be, then you will look upon each patient as a little cathedral—as an individual that you can build to the glory of God. I am now able to see each patient as a very special person—a child of God—deserving my best skill and attention as I rebuild that cathedral!

"What I am doing is very important, and of course, my patients sense my new attitude. They are so grateful. And any doctor is going to be happy when he is dealing with appreciative patients.

"Finally, the most important thing that I can ever say to you is: 'Live your life, doctors, as if there was a God, even if you don't believe in Him! Live your life and your practice as if there was a God of love that cares for you, too, even as He cares for every patient that comes in! And you know what? With that attitude you'll someday be an old silver-haired and wrinkle-faced doctor, but you will still have a twinkle in your eye and love in your life!' "

# The Cost of Perfect Love

You have all walked past a jewelry store and looked into the window, staring at all the beautiful jewels. You may see a little ring with a price tag of fourteen dollars or a silver neck chain that is twenty dollars, or perhaps an attractive gold bracelet that is only ten dollars. Then you see a stunning piece of jewelry that catches your eye, but the price tag is turned over. You think it's probably not too expensive, so you go in and ask the clerk what it costs. He turns the price tag over and you're shocked at the cost!

The most priceless pieces of jewelry—the kind that become lasting family heirlooms—are always made out of authentic metals and jewels. They are never cheap. So perfect love has a high price tag! It's like expensive jewelry—it's not cheap. Perfect love always calls for costly commitments to care—always.

# The Result of Fear

Once I attended a rather prestigious affair in Hong Kong. (Actually it was a banquet.) I was sitting next to a very important gentleman—a leading citizen of the city. The table was beautifully spread when we were seated. The fruit cup, which was the starter, was already set before us. Also, in front of us were the rolls, the butter, and the dessert (which was cake, as I remember). As soon as we sat down, we began to eat.

The gentleman to my right started by pushing aside the fruit cup and reaching for the dessert. He ate the piece of cake before the fruit cocktail! That struck me as rather peculiar so I said, "That's interesting—you ate the dessert first!" "Yes," he replied, laughing. "It's one of my eccentricities." An executive in a major international firm, this distinguished English gentleman explained, "I developed the habit as a child." "Oh?" I responded. "My folks always said, 'You can't eat dessert until you've finished your vegetables.'" "I'll tell you what happened with me," he went on. "My father always ate the dessert first. I can still remember him saying, 'There might be a fire so eat your dessert first!'"

These little fears do some funny things to people, don't they? I mean, if you let them get into your mind and under your skin, fears can make your decisions; fears can set your goals; fears can determine how you approach a problem, or run away from it. Before you realize it, you have surrendered leadership to your fears. And fears can kill you!

# To Handle Your Foes: Keep on Shining!

I'm reminded of the judge who was campaigning for re-election. He had a reputation for integrity. He was a distinguished and honorable gentleman of no small charity. And his opponent was conducting a vicious, mud-smearing, unfair campaign against him.

Somebody approached the judge and said, "Do you know what your opponent is saying about you? Do you know he is criticizing you? How are you going to handle it? What are you going to do about it?" The judge looked at his counselors and his campaign committee and calmly replied: "Well, when I was a boy I had a dog. And every time the moon was full, that hound dog would howl and bark at the bright face of the moon. We never did sleep very well those nights. He would bark and howl at the moon all night." With that, the judge concluded his remarks.

"That's beside the point," his campaign manager impatiently said. "You've told us a nice story about your dog, but what are you going to do about your critic?" The judge explained. "I just answered you! When the dog barked at the moon, the moon kept right on shining! I don't intend to do anything but keep right on shining. And I'll ignore the criticism, like the moon ignored the dog. I'll just keep right on shining! Quietly, calmly, beautifully!"

Remember that! It might give you courage to shine—to strive for the top and not worry about what people will say if you succeed or if you fail.

## You May Be a Late Bloomer

A student from a wealthy family barely made it through Harrow, a very famous English undergraduate school. His family wanted him to attend a very prestigious university upon his graduation from Harrow, but the young boy had to be tutored three times by a private tutor before he could even get into the upper-level-school. "I don't believe this child went through Harrow," the learned tutor exclaimed. "I think he went under Harrow. He's just not very bright!" That student's name was Winston Churchill!

There are lots of late bloomers, and if you've got courage, and you won't be discouraged if you come in second again and again and again. Someday you may well end up being Number One! But if you don't have courage, you will quit, and then you'll never succeed!

## The Courage to Face Failure

Over fifty years ago, a little lady named Lillian married a graduate of the Princeton Theological Seminary. As a minister's wife, her name changed to Lillian Dickson. She and her young husband prayed earnestly together. "God, You have a plan for our lives. Where should we spend it? What shall we do with it?" Now, they had courage. They dared to believe that they could have the number-one slot. They were willing to take a number-two spot if that's what God wanted for them, because the Reverend Dickson said, "Remember this, Lillian, let's spend our lives where the need is greatest!" That judgment led them to an island called Formosa.

So, over fifty years ago, they sailed across the ocean to help the impoverished, the lost, the illiterate, the sick, and dying in Formosa.

When they arrived, they talked to a government official in Social Services. He look at this young naive couple and laughed. "Look, go back to America. You can't possibly succeed here. There is no way. No way!" He stood up and walked over to the window and pointed outside. "Look out that window. You can see the ocean. You want to help people? Helping people here in Formosa is like getting one bucket of water out of that vast ocean." But young Lillian Dickson got out of her chair and said, "Well, then I am going to fill my bucket!" she exclaimed.

That was over fifty years ago. It was just four years ago, I recall, that I was with Lillian Dickson at a banquet. At that time, her husband had died. Today she is still alive. Today she is still on that island. Fifty plus years later she is nearly eighty years of age, and she has a new ten-year plan! And what has her bucket amounted to?

Well, Lillian Dickson has established over one thousand churches, schools, and hospitals! It all happened because she was willing to fail! To face possible futility! If she and her husband hadn't had the courage to fail, they would have turned right around and gone home. They would have accomplished nothing. You see, when you think you've failed, you don't know what your bucket of water may have accomplished. God uses ordinary people who think they are failures, and they make the world go round! They really do!

# The Truth About Babe Ruth

Everybody knows the name of a man who, until a few years ago, held the world's record for the most home-run hits in the major leagues. He hit 714 home runs, holding the world record, until 1976 when Hank Aaron passed him. His name was Babe Ruth. But how many people remember the name of the man who held the record for the greatest number of strikeouts? As I recall, the record book shows that this fellow had 1,330 strikeouts. That's the record. And I think it still holds. But how many people know his name? You just remember Babe Ruth who won the home-run record.

It was in 1927. The Yankees were playing in Philadelphia. That's when Babe Ruth got one of his home runs. You may have read the story. He came up to the plate for the first time. Babe missed the first pitch, strike. The second pitch, another strike. Swish, strike three! The second time he came up to bat he struck at the first one, strike one; struck at the second one, strike two; and the third one, strike three! Now it was the eighth inning and the Yankees were behind, three to one. The bases were loaded. Thirty-five thousand fans were on their feet as Babe Ruth came up to bat for the third time. Everyone knew that Lefty Grove could strike him out again.

First pitch, strike; second pitch, he swung so hard that when he missed, he stumbled and fell on the ground. He picked up his pudgy body, dusted himself off, put his cap back on, and waited for the third pitch. It was so fast, nobody even saw it. All they heard was a crack, and that ball went out of the stadium, over the roofs of the houses, across the street from the park for one of the longest hits in the major leagues. All the fellows on the bases came running in, and when Babe Ruth came across home plate, the Home-Run King took his hat off to the fans and smiled. You remember him—Babe Ruth, the Home-Run King! But how many of you remember the name of the guy who still today, holds the record for the number of strikeouts—1,330—his name, too, is Babe Ruth! Yes, Babe Ruth would never have become the Home-Run King if he had feared the failures of strikeouts!

# The Malibu Rock

Here is a true story that will amaze you—a story that happened recently. It's about California and Australia. In a way, it's a story that concerns you and me.

Not far from our church is a town called Malibu, situated below high hills which overlook the waves of the Pacific Ocean, as they roll over the sandy shoreline. On one particular hill stood a massive rock—a rock that had been there for thousands upon thousands of years. Californians drove by it for decades without thinking much of it. But one day a homeowner in Malibu looked up and thought to himself, *If that rock falls, my property will be destroyed.* So he organized a citizens group, and together they prepared a class-action suit against the California Highway Department, charging it with liability in the event the rock should fall. Members of the citizens group had actually climbed up to the rock and inspected it. They were sure they had seen signs of movement.

Under the threat of a class-action suit, the highway department was forced to assume the impending liability, and so accepted the responsibility for removing what was to become known throughout the country as the "Malibu Rock." They employed two of their most powerful bulldozers to dislodge the massive rock, but even together their strength was not enough to move it. Next they used a helicopter with cables an inch thick attached to the rock in combinations with the two bulldozers. Together they strained to move the rock, but it would not budge.

Finally they employed a force so powerful that by it, through time, enormous mountains and hills have been leveled—a force that nothing could resist for long—the force of rushing water. For four days and nights water under high pressure was pumped against the rock. Then the bulldozers and helicopter once again thrust their might against the huge rock and managed to dislodge it. To everyone's surprise it was discovered that the bulk of the rock was not above ground but so far beneath the surface that chances are it would never have rolled down that hill in a million years!

Nevertheless, the job was done. The rock fell and rolled into the middle of the highway. By the time the entire operation was completed it cost California taxpayers $1 million. And, ironically, the fears of the homeowners who sought the removal of the threatening rock were realized. The rock had been holding up the whole hill. When the rock was removed, mud slid down the hill and their properties were, in fact, damaged. Although they never realized it until it was too late, that rock had been their best friend.

Meanwhile, watching the media coverage of the removal of the Malibu Rock from his hotel room in Los Angeles was a young man from Australia. This young man was a possibility thinker. He saw the rock—not as a menace—but as a masterpiece. His name is Brett Livingston Strong. When he was fifteen years old, he painted a beautiful picture of a naked aborigine gazing up at the Sydney Opera House. The work was so widely acclaimed that the Queen of England accepted it on behalf of her country. At twenty-three he came to America with hopes of furthering his career as an artist.

When he heard the rock was coming down, he rushed to the site in Malibu and saw it roll into the middle of the highway. At once, he approached members of the highway department and said, "I want to buy the rock." The highway officials poked each other and snickered. They sold the rock for one hundred dollars. The young Australian felt he had just bought the best bargain of his life, as he traded his check for the receipt.

"Oh, by the way," the highway officials said, "There's just one more thing you need to know. You've got to get that rock out of the middle of the road in the next forty-eight hours." But his enthusiasm was not dampened. He set about planning how he would remove his twenty-ton rock from the center of a California highway.

He went to Century Plaza in Los Angeles and convinced the merchants there that the rock would make a beautiful addition to their landscaping scheme. The merchants agreed. So he collected an investment of twenty thousand dollars, with which to have the rock hauled to Century City. He covered the rock with a tarpaulin and, working ten hours a day with pneumatic hammers, from February 1979 to May 1979, he chiseled out of the Malibu Rock the figure of a man who, for him, the rock epitomized. "The rock reminds me of John Wayne," Brett Livingston Strong said. "Tough to bring down."

Not far from the site in Century City where Brett was working on sculpturing the rock into the image of John Wayne is a hospital called UCLA Medical Center. At that time a dear friend and neighbor of ours, named John Wayne, was a patient there. When Brett finished his sculpture of the "Big Duke," John Wayne left his hospital room before he died to look at the majestic work. "I like it," he said. "I really like it."

In Scottsdale, Arizona, a wealthy philanthropist named Tom Murphy was impressed by the sculpture and came to the young artist and offered to buy it. And the story that is circulating is that the sculpture was purchased by Mr. Murphy for $1 million. And guess what? The latest gossip is the rock is going back up the hill to be placed in the J. Paul

Getty Museum—only a couple of miles down the road from where it originally stood! So some saw the rock as a risk—but a young possibility thinker saw it as an opportunity!

There are two kinds of people in this world today—possibility thinkers and impossibility thinkers. Impossibility thinkers are constantly looking for ways of avoiding possible risks. They want insurance that covers every eventuality of life. Impossibility thinkers are seeking a risk-free society. On the other hand possibility thinkers realize there is no way to achieve success without being a sanctified risk taker.

## Viktor Frankl's Stars

Viktor Frankl, an eminent Jewish psychiatrist, was standing naked and stripped before the Gestapo. They had taken his watch, then had seen his gold wedding band, and demanded it as well. As Frankl took the wedding band off his finger to hand it to the Gestapo officer, a thought went though his brain. *There is one thing you can never take from me and that is my freedom to choose how I will react to whatever you do to me!* That we all retain to the end.

If you choose to react positively, not negatively, to the hurts of life, you can turn your scars into stars.

## Nobody Has a Money Problem, Only Idea Problems

The greatest compliment I think I've ever received came from a black cabdriver in New York City. I came out of my hotel and walked up to the first of several cabs lined against the curb. The driver was a black man with a gold ring in his nose. Immediately I experienced some cross-cultural conflict—he scared me! But before I could say hello, the man jumped out of the cab, pointed a finger at me and shouted, " 'Hour of Power'! You're Doctor Robert Schuller, aren't you?" Then he shook my hand, embraced me, and opened the door. I slid in, and he told me how our ministry has changed his life.

He was born in Harlem, and the man never knew his father. All his life he lived on welfare. He tuned into the "Hour of Power" one day and became a regular viewer.

"Doctor Schuller, me and my wife watched you," he said. "We liked to see the flowers, oranges, and palm trees—especially in the winter. It was just nice to look at. When you started talking about possibility thinking, I thought, *Yeah, you can talk that way. You're white. You live in California. Anybody who lives by Disneyland can believe in possibility thinking!*

"But then you told a story that changed my life. It was about some negative-thinking women who lived on the bayou in Louisiana, who were constantly complaining about their homes and lives. Finally one positive-thinking woman got tired of their complaining and said to them, 'Look, you live on the bayou. The bayou flows into the river. The river flows into the Gulf. The Gulf flows into the ocean. You have a boat. You can go anywhere from where you are!' "

So the man began to wonder if possibility thinking could work for him. "Why don't you get a job?" his wife suggested. "What can I do?" he demanded defensively. "You can drive," she retorted. "Why don't you become a cabdriver?" "If they knew I was black, they would never hire me," he countered. "That's impossibility thinking—just what Doctor Schuller preaches against," she persisted. So finally the man was persuaded. He went to the telephone and called the cab company. When he told them he wanted a job, they asked him, "Are you black?" "Yes, I am," he responded defensively, his heart sinking. "Great!" they said, "We need black cabdrivers. The whites don't dare drive in Harlem. You come in and you've got a job!"

As he told the story, his eyes filled with tears. He had such pride in himself and his work. "I earn more now as a cab-driver than I ever did on welfare!" he enthused. He has the pride of being a wage earner.

It's very easy to be negative. It's very easy to say, "Poor me. See what I don't have?" We all need more. But do you know what we need more of? Not a handout—but dynamic ideas to turn us into productive persons.

# How to Face Your Future

The other day I came home and saw my youngest daughter, Gretchen, sitting on the floor in her room. Scattered all over the carpet in front of her were envelopes and sheets of clean, unwrinkled stationery. With pen in hand it looked like she was getting ready to write some letters. Now, I know that Gretchen never writes letters, so my curiosity was instantly stirred.

"Gretchen," I exclaimed, "what are you doing?" Caught by surprise, she turned and looked up at me. "Oh, hi, Dad. I'm going to write my thank-you notes." "You're what?" I asked. "What do you mean?" "I'm starting to write my thank-you notes for my Christmas gifts," she explained. A little confused at this point, I went on. "Gretchen, how in the world can you write thank-you notes for gifts that you haven't received yet? How do you know who to address them to? And how do you know that you'll be receiving any?" "Oh," she enthused, "I've got that figured out. I'm going to say, 'Dear Friend, Thank you for your wonderful gift. I'm enjoying it very much. Love, Gretchen.' " I laughed and said, "But, Gretchen, how do you know you are going to enjoy all the gifts?" "Oh, Daddy, I just know I'm going to enjoy every one of them!" That's what you call advance planning! She was in such good spirits, because she was expecting something beautiful to happen. She was already living in her imagination in the arena of goodness.

Some people spend most of their lives living in the past arena of bad news. Something that happened to you yesterday is past! Expect good things to happen to you today and live high! Live in the realm of good news! Don't live in the realm of bad news!

# There's Something Good in Every Situation

A young man named Woolworth decided he was going to open a new store—a brand-new business of his own. When he was ready for the grand opening, a merchant down the street got a little nervous about this young man taking some of his business away, so he ran an ad in the local paper. It read: DO YOUR LOCAL SHOPPING HERE. WE HAVE BEEN IN BUSINESS FOR FIFTY YEARS! Young Woolworth couldn't believe it! How could he handle this competition? What should he do? The next week he countered with an ad of his own. And it read: WE'VE BEEN IN BUSINESS ONLY ONE WEEK—ALL OF OUR MERCHANDISE IS BRAND-NEW! And he was off to a great success!

Take all the good news you can. If you're faced with bad news, remember, oftentimes there is good news hidden in a bad-news scene. You have to become positively oriented before you see it.

# Take All the Good News You Can Get

On my way into church early last Sunday morning somebody called out my name. "Doctor Schuller!" I stopped and turned around. A young man was trying to get my attention. "I wanted to catch you before you went into your office," the man said. "Do you remember a little boy named Nelson— you prayed for him two years ago?" I couldn't recall, until he gave me some of the background on the child, and then I remembered. A car had suddenly gone out of control and through a backyard fence, pinning this five-year-old boy under the car. He was rushed to the hospital with a badly crushed neck. Doctors gave him little chance to live. The father of the boy saw the huge cross on the top of the Tower of Hope and came to our church for help. He knelt by the Good Shepherd statue, crying and praying that his son would live. One of the ministers found him and counseled him, trying to comfort him during this time.

After talking with the minister, the father realized that this was the church that was on television each Sunday morning. He then requested that I go see his boy. I'll never forget that child—tiny, naked, and barely breathing—lying in the crib. An iron skull, like a cross of thorns, made out of steel, penetrated into his tiny skull, pulling his head out. Iron clamps were on his tiny feet stretching his tiny, frail body. He lay there motionless, pale, and quiet, on the edge of eternity.

I prayed and prayed for little Nelson, but I never knew what happened to the little boy after that day. And then this young man came up to me with some great news. He said, "Doctor Schuller, that little boy is the child of some very good friends of mine. My wife and I were in their home this week, and that little boy has completely recovered!" Taken back by the good news, I said, "But he had a broken neck. You mean he isn't paralyzed?" "No," the young man said. "The bones were so crushed that there wasn't a bone of substantial size to sever a nerve. The nerves were never cut! He's perfectly normal in every way!"

What good news to greet me at the beginning of a new day! Take all the good news you can! Look for it; you can spot it! And try to develop a callousness for the bad news. If there's bad news, turn it into good news through possibility thinking. Take all the good news that you can!

# Break All the Good News You Can

Never will I forget the time that I was invited to make a call on Hubert Humphrey . This was after he told me that he had an inoperable cancer and that he would not return to Washington ever again. I called on him in his Minneapolis apartment. His close friends approached me before I knocked on the door. "Doctor Schuller, if you could just inspire him to return to Washington, we would be forever grateful. We think his last days would be more meaningful there. We don't know how long those days, months, or years will be."

As I stepped into his apartment, I saw a gaunt and lean man who after having an ileostomy, colostomy, chemotherapy, and radiation treatment, had changed drastically. But there was still a sparkle in his eye, as he greeted me and welcomed me to Minneapolis, Minnesota.

I was a little nervous about what to talk about, but once we got started it was easy. We talked about his prognosis. Then we began to thank God for all He'd done—for the successful surgeries that my friend had gone through; for his beautiful wife, Muriel; for his lovely daughter and her little mongoloid child, who has brought so much joy into Hubert's and Muriel's lives; for the many years of service to his country; for the excellent medical care; that there is always hope even though everything may seem hopeless; that when it seems nothing can happen for good, suddenly there can be a total turnabout and we see the light; for Jesus Christ who came to the world to give us courage in tough times and hope in dark times and an awareness that what seems like the end of the road is only a bend in the road of life. Instead of dwelling on the negative, we concentrated on the positive. And we had a beautiful time together, sharing good news!

## "God Loves You, and I'm Trying"

It was Christmas Eve, and I was running late, so my wife and two girls jumped into the car and we took off for church, trying to make the service on time. As we neared the campus of the church, I suddenly realized that I had to make a left turn. I was in the right lane, so I hurriedly looked into my rearview mirror, saw that nobody was behind me, and swerved over into the left lane. Well, what I didn't see was a guy in my blind spot! I cut him off and almost clipped his front bumper. I don't normally drive that way; I try to be very careful, but I just didn't see him behind me. I made the lane, just as the light turned red.

Well, the next thing I knew, a large man was standing outside my car, motioning me to roll down my window. He was furious! I could see the blood vessels swelling in his neck! And his mouth was expelling some words I can't repeat. Hesitating a moment, I rolled down my window and tried to say I was sorry. But he wouldn't let me utter a word! I have never heard so many obscenities in my life. I tried to interrupt him, but he would just go off on another tangent. I tried to smile but that even made him madder. Finally, he had to take a breath and I moved in.

"Hey! Wait a minute! You know what? It's Christmastime . . . ." But he had taken a deep breath and started in again. I wanted to break some good news, but he wouldn't give me the chance. Fortunately, he had to take another breath, so I jumped in again. (Now I know why God made the lungs with a limited capacity—it's the only way negative people can be turned off for a second.) I looked him in the eye and I said, "God loves you, and I'm trying!" And I saw a look come across his face that I've seen many times when people recognize me in a restaurant or an airport. He got a little pink in the face and went back to his car without saying another word.

Break all the good news you can! You can do this by sharing your faith! Good news doesn't just happen. *You* make it happen!

# "What a Pitcher!"

I am reminded of the story of the little boy overheard talking to himself, as he strutted through the backyard, baseball cap in place, toting ball and bat. "I'm the greatest baseball player in the world," he said proudly. Then he tossed the ball into the air, swung at it—and missed. Undaunted, he picked up the ball, threw it into the air and, as he said to himself, "I'm the greatest ball player ever!" he swung at the ball again. And again he missed. He paused a moment to carefully examine his bat and ball. Then once again he threw the ball into the air. "I'm the greatest baseball player who ever lived!" he said. He swung the bat hard and again, he missed the ball.

"Wow!" he exclaimed. "What a pitcher!"

There's nothing in the world like a positive mental attitude. It can transform situations and experiences in life into great possibilities.

# The Sky Is Falling

Not too long ago America warned the world that Sky Lab was going to fall to earth. I have a friend who was in Australia during that time. He made some very interesting observations. "Everywhere I went in Australia people were talking about the probability of Sky Lab falling into their country. Inevitably they reacted in two totally different ways. Some people reacted fearfully. 'Oh,' they exclaimed, 'what if it hits our property?' They saw Sky Lab's imminent descent to earth as a potential menace. Others reacted not with a negative, but with a positive mental attitude. 'What if it lands on our place?' they said. 'Won't it be a valuable souvenir? We could even take it to San Francisco and collect the ten thousand dollars cash reward offered by the San Francisco newspaper.' "

When Sky Lab did fall to earth, it did, in fact, fall in Australia. Some of the people on whose property it fell never touched it for fear of contracting radioactive poisoning. But one young man believed what he had been told about the pieces of Sky Lab being absolutely safe to touch. He flew to San Francisco with his piece of Sky Lab and collected the ten thousand dollars in cash. Because he held onto a positive attitude, Sky Lab was no menace to him; it was a masterpiece!

A natural law states that whenever a person begins to practice a positive mental attitude, there is a power released—a very natural, human power. God designed human beings so that we produce constructive energy when we think positively and begin to sense the unlimited possibilities in little ideas.

# Knott's Berry Farm

I have a dear friend named Walter Knott. Some of you may have visited Knott's Berry Farm in Southern California. It is one of the first comprehensive recreational parks to be founded in America—a favorite place visited by tourists from all over the world.

Walter Knott and his wife, Cornelia, started their now-famous enterprise only a few miles from our church. They began many years ago by raising boysenberries. Today it's hard to believe how much mileage they've gotten out of a boysenberry!

A few years ago Walter Knott stood in the pulpit of this church. "What gives you your greatest fulfillment, Walter?" I asked him. "My greatest fulfillment comes from the knowledge that I am creating job opportunities for hundreds of people," he answered. "It takes me only five thousand dollars of capital investment to create one new job," he calculated. Of course that was a few years ago. But as a successful capitalist, Walter Knott saw his situation as an opportunity to create job opportunities for people. Isn't that beautiful! One small idea has such tremendous reproductive capacity!

# Melrose Suspension Bridge

In California we are very proud of the beautiful San Francisco Golden Gate Bridge. As a suspension bridge, it is an architectural marvel, still unsurpassed in beauty and grace. However such a feat of engineering followed a history of suspension bridges, and one cannot ignore the influence of the Melrose Suspension Bridge, which spans the Niagara River.

In 1848 an engineer by the name of Theodore Elliot solved

a problem that had hindered commerce for decades. For years farmers and businessmen alike had thought how wonderful it would be to have a railroad that could cross from New York to Canada. But in order to build such a railroad, a bridge was needed to span the Niagara River. Traditional bridge-building schemes simply would not work. But Theodore Elliot conceived of a brilliant solution. He proposed the first suspension bridge. He envisioned supportive towers twenty-four and eighty feet high on either side of the roaring, raging waters of the Niagara River. From the towers he would suspend a cable which in turn would support the bridge.

But he had one problem. How could he get started? There was no way to work from a boat at that point on the river. There was no shoreline to work from, only sheer, rocky cliffs. And yet he knew that beginning was half-done.

So he decided to start by stringing a cable from one side of the river to the other. "A cable made from thirty-six strands of number ten wire will be thick and sturdy enough to suspend two buckets capable of holding two workers. These workers could go from side to side and begin construction of the bridge," he said. "But how can you get a steel cable that thick across the gorge?" someone asked. "You can't throw it across. It's too heavy." Elliot was puzzled for a moment. Then he got an idea: Why not have a contest for the kids in the neighborhood—a kite-flying contest?

Elliot announced the kite-flying contest and offered a prize of ten dollars to the first boy who could fly a kite across the gorge and tie the rope down on the other side. There were many contestants—ten dollars was a lot of money for a little lad in those days. But none succeeded, until one day an eleven-year-old boy named Homer Walsh took advantage of a good south wind. His kite took off and, instead of falling short as all the others had, it landed on the other side. His friend, who was waiting across the river, tied the string down on the other side. Homer won the ten dollars!

The next day Elliot tied the kite string to a slightly heavier rope. He pulled the rope across the gorge, so that it spanned the gap. Then he tied that rope to still-thicker rope and pulled it across. This rope he attached to the steel cable and, by repeating the process, he strung the cable from one side of the gorge to the other, thus enabling the two workers to move back and forth and begin the construction of the suspension bridge.

You may be faced with what seems to be a risky but insignificant decision. It may be only a kite string, but like Homer's kite string, it can pave the way for something as monumental as the first suspension bridge. Just like Theodore Elliot and Homer Walsh, you may be the inspiration for great future accomplishments—as great as the Golden Gate Bridge! Next time you pass over the Golden Gate, say a word of thanks to a little boy named Homer Walsh.

# What Makes a Large Fish?

Some of you know that as a hobby I raise Japanese carp known as koi fish. These fish are really amazing creatures. Some of the larger ones will actually suck my fingers (they have no teeth), and let me stroke them on the back.

The carp are used to taking a whole slice of bread and passing it around to one another, taking a bite as they do. One day I was leaning over the pool and my wallet fell into the water. I watched as one fish passed it to another, hoping they would soon tire of the game. (I called it carp-to-carp walleting.)

Some people have asked, "Why are there some big fish and some little ones? How big can they get?" That's a fascinating question. The size of the fish depends on the size of the pond. A koi fish can live in a small tank, but it will never grow longer than two or three inches. In a larger pond they can grow from six to ten inches. In ponds the size of mine, they will grow up to a foot and a half in length. But if they live in a huge lake where they can swim and stretch, they will grow up to three feet long. It's the stretching that lends itself to greater growth. The size of the fish is in direct relation to the size of the pond.

This observation leads to an interesting principle: Little ideas which fall into little-thinking minds produce little achievements. But when those same little ideas drop into big-thinking minds, they become enormous achievements! The size of your thinking determines the growth of your idea in its ultimate development!

# Fence Out

Not long ago I read a story about a salesman who, in 1800, came from the East to a small frontier town in Texas. He came to sell his goods to the merchant at the local general store. Just as the salesman was about to show the storekeeper his merchandise, a local rancher came in to make a purchase.

"Excuse me," the merchant said, "but I have to wait on my customer." Turning to the rancher he said, "What can I do for you, Josh?" Josh pointed to several items around the store, and then asked the storekeeper to put the things on his account.

"Oh," the storekeeper said knowingly, "so you want credit. Let me ask you something, Josh. Are you doing any fencing this spring?" "Yes, I am, sir," Josh replied. "Well, are you fencing in or are you fencing out?" the merchant queried. "I'm fencing out," Josh answered. "Going to add three hundred and sixty new acres." "Well, then," the shop owner said, "if you're fencing out, go ahead and see Harry at the back of the store. He'll help you get what you need."

Having listened to this exchange, the salesman was somewhat puzzled. "You know," he said, "I've heard of all kinds of systems of credit, but I've never heard of your system. What kind of credit is that?"

"Well," the merchant explained, "we've got two kinds of ranchers and farmers here—those who fence in and those who fence out. Those who fence in are people who are afraid they might not make it quite as well next year. They are afraid of what the weather might bring, or of wasting too much seed, so they pull their fences in. Then there are others who have confidence in themselves and their work. Slowly, gradually, they fence out, adding a little more land to their farms and ranches. People who fence out have hope. And I give credit to anyone who has hope!"

## Life's Greatest Prizes

After several months in our first drive-in church, we were finally able to afford our first professional minister of music. Her name was Lea Ora Mead, and she took charge of our first choir (composed of an odd number of volunteer singers who met for rehearsals in our home). When we first hired Lea Ora, I took her aside and said, "Lea Ora we don't want to build just an average church. We want to do something that's really outstanding, and so we want our music to be outstanding. With God's help, I know you can lay the musical foundations, so that this church will have the finest quality music heard anywhere. If the foundations are laid correctly, we know the rest will fall into place."

Lea Ora did that. For six years we conducted this church in the drive-in theater. Every Sunday morning I climbed up on the sticky tar-paper roof of the snack bar and delivered my messages in the rain, the chilly wind, or the blazing sun. And standing right behind me, leading the choir, was Lea

Ora Mead. When we finally moved into a building of our own, she continued to direct the choir and bring beautiful music into the lives of countless people.

Lea Ora is still a young woman, but today she is dying of cancer. She has been fighting it courageously for a long time; and we don't know how many more days she has left to go on fighting.

Recently, someone who prefers to remain anonymous sent the first gift for the Pillars of Steel in the Crystal Cathedral in Lea Ora's honor. So Lea Ora became our first "Iron-Pillared Friend."

I went to call on Lea Ora one night. She had received the medallion and a letter informing her of the gift given in her name. When we greeted one another, she was crying. "Bob, who gave that gift for me?" she asked. "Lea Ora," I explained gently, "the giver of the gift asked to remain anonymous." "Yes," she continued, "But who would do something like that? I moved away from here years ago. Who could possibly remember me?" Taking her hand in mine, I looked at her and replied, "Lea Ora, stop and think of every person who ever heard music while you were choir director of our church. Think of all the people who might have been inspired and lifted because of your ministry. You brought a lot of joy into a lot of people's lives."

There's no way she could ever guess who it was who chose to commemorate her contribution to the church. As I turned to leave, she said, "You know, maybe I really did something worthwhile in my life after all." "Lea Ora," I assured her, "there's no way you can ever know how much good you did for people in your lifetime, for music has a way of reaching into the hidden corners of the mind and heart and stirring a soul."

As I've said before, any fool can count the seeds in an apple, but only God can count the apples in a seed. When you draw near to the end of your life and you feel that you've done something wonderful for God—that you've been an inspiration to a fellow human being—then you have received one of life's greatest prizes.

# Jim Poppen

Jim Poppen was a student at Hope Academy, a high-school division of my alma mater, Hope College. But Jim was not exactly an exemplary student. There were people at that institution who questioned his intellectual capacity. Many of his teachers remarked, "I don't think he is ever going to amount to much. Jim Poppen just isn't very bright."

But to prejudge the intellect of another is one of the most audacious presumptions anyone can be guilty of. We know that child prodigies are not born; they are developed. That scientifically proven statement was first introduced to me in Paris at the International Psychological Conference. If a child prodigy is developed and not born, then the average person has the potential for becoming a genius.

Jim Poppen graduated from Hope Academy and astounded his former teachers by going on to study at Northwestern University.

One Christmas, Jim's father awoke suddenly when he heard a noise in the night. Convinced that there was a burglar in the house, Mr. Poppen stole downstairs and tiptoed into the dark kitchen. There he found Jim tying knots around chair legs as fast as he could. Sure that his son had flipped, Mr. Poppen exclaimed, "Jim, what in the world are you doing?" "It's okay, Dad," Jim explained. "I've decided I'm going to be a brain surgeon. I've got to teach my fingers to tie knots very fast and accurately where I cannot see anything—just like a surgeon operating on a human skull."

His father laughed that night, but Jim did become a brain

surgeon—one of the best in the world. When Bobby Kennedy was shot at the Biltmore Hotel in Los Angeles, Dr. Jim Poppen was chosen by the President of the United States to fly to Bobby Kennedy's side and attempt to save his life.

William Loeb, from New Hampshire, a listener to "Hour of Power," recently sent me an editorial from his newspaper the *Manchester Union Leader,* about Jim Poppen. The letter says, "Doctor Schuller, you mentioned Jim Poppen as a friend of yours. He was my friend too. Did you know he died just a few months ago? I think you should know a little more about him.

"You have spoken of Dr. Poppen's connection with Bobby Kennedy and the attempt on his life. Did you know that just a few months before that tragic incident Aristotle Onassis' only son was involved in an airplane crash? Jim Poppen, accompanied by Aristotle and his wife, Jackie Kennedy Onassis, sped across the Atlantic in a Lear jet to Greece to be by the young man's side. International leaders, ministers of finance, presidents, and kings knew Jim Poppen as the greatest brain surgeon in the world.

"Just a year ago," the letter continued, "I wanted to reach Doctor Poppen. By telephone, I finally tracked him down in a remote village 12,000 feet high in the Andes, in Bogota, Colombia. 'What in the world are you doing in Bogota, Jim?' I asked incredulously. 'Oh,' he replied very quietly and matter-of-factly, 'There are some people here who have some problems. They can't afford the high cost of medical care in Boston, so I decided to come here and take care of them.'

"When Jim Poppen died a few months ago, the services held for him in the New England Baptist Memorial Chapel were jammed with great people, whose famous faces many would know. But there were also many unknowns present— red, yellow, black, white, rich and poor. Many nurses came to the chapel directly from the operating rooms. They stood quietly in the back of the chapel, still dressed in their green surgical robes and caps. Hundreds came to pay tribute to a man who proved that, by giving life all you've got, you can leave a mark behind and do something beautiful."

God has a prize for you. If you will trust Him with your life, you will have the incomparably beautiful assurance that you have done something great for God.

## There Is Hope for All of Us

Here's another story about this very remarkable human being, Jim Poppen. This amazing man used to hunt ferocious jaguars in the jungles of Brazil, using a .22 short bullet. Once, when he told a fellow hunter what kind of ammunition he preferred, the hunter asked derisively, "Why don't you just use a slingshot?" "But a twenty-two short is plenty good for hunting a jaguar," he argued. "After all, I aim at the eye." When asked how he expected to hit the eye of a jaguar he replied, "Simple. I just close in to thirty or forty feet."

Of course, anyone who hunts knows that a Brazilian jaguar can jump forty to sixty feet easily. "They're not going to jump," he explained, "because I stand at the end of the branch the jaguar is standing on and swing it back and forth to keep it off balance. It can't possibly jump!" He was an incredible man!

## God's Unconditional Love

We have some very dear friends who live on a farm in Minnesota. God blessed them with two sons, but their first son died in a tragic drowning accident when he was a teenager. The couple was heartbroken, but they comforted themselves with this thought: *We still have a beautiful son.*

*We still have a wonderful marriage. We'll look at what we have left, not at what we've lost.* But two years later their remaining son was killed in a farm accident, when his tractor rolled over on him and crushed him.

Not long after that second sad event, the couple came to visit us here at Garden Grove Community Church. "How did you pick up the pieces of your life and keep on going?" I asked them. "We received letters from across the country," the woman relied. "One letter, which was from someone we had never met, was especially comforting. It simply said, 'After what's happened, we just want to tell you that God still loves you. Nothing can stop that.' "

One of the most beautiful rewards of salvation is the awareness of God's unconditional, undying, imperishable love. No matter what happens, He has a plan of infinite beauty for your life.

# He Loves Me

Yesterday our youngest daughter, Gretchen, and I were out in the garden cutting fresh flowers. Rather mischievously, I clipped one and said to her, "Gretchen, this one is for you." Then as I pulled off the petals one by one, I recited a rhyme from my youth: "She loves me. She loves me not. She loves me. . . ." Gretchen got a quizzical kind of expression on her face and said, "I know Daddy. I'm going to pick one for God." And as she plucked the petals of the flower, she gave me a lesson I'll not soon forget. As she pulled the first petal, she said, "He loves me." Then she pulled the next, "He loves me." And the next, "He loves me." Until she had but one petal left and, smiling brightly, she finished the rhyme: "He loves me."

# Does God Care?

The other day I heard a story about a salesman who came home from the office to find his house in complete disarray. His wife was usually a wonderful housekeeper, so he simply couldn't understand why everything was in such a mess. "What happened?" he asked in amazement. "Remember how you always ask, 'What could you possibly be doing all day?' " his wife replied. "Well, today I didn't do it!"

If we experience troubled times because God is trying to preach to us, that is fantastic! We can always stand a good word from our ultimate Source of wisdom, can't we?

# The Way in Which God Uses Troubled Times

There was once was a company that required 100 percent cooperation and agreement by all the employees before they could sign up for a new pension-insurance plan. Everyone in the entire company was anxious to enter into the new plan, except for one stubborn, selfish, ego-involved man, who refused to see the benefits of the new plan. He found all kinds of reasons for not joining with the others and refused to sign the consent form. Every one of his fellow employees tried to induce him to sign, but he stubbornly refused.

Finally, his boss called him into the office. He handed the man a pen and said, "Look. Here's the paper. Here's the pen. Sign it or you're fired." Smiling cheerfully, the man picked up the pen and signed his name to the consent form. In exasperation, the man's boss demanded, "Why haven't you signed it before?" "Well," the man replied, "no one ever explained it to me so clearly before."

Often troubled times are God's way of giving us the shove we need. Sometimes we postpone a decision until He really presses us.

# How to Handle Boredom

The great Christian industrialist, Foster McGaw, who is the founder of American Hospital Supply Corporation, once told me an interesting story about his father. Foster's father served as a Presbyterian pastor and missionary in Warsaw, Poland, for the greater part of his life. At the age of eighty-one he retired and returned to the United States. But Mr. McGaw found retirement dull and soon became bored. He began thinking of things he had dreamed of, but never had a chance to do.

*You know,* he thought to himself, *one thing I've always wanted to do since I was a young man was to become a missionary to Africa. Well, why not?*

So Mr. McGaw called his son, Foster, who was age forty-two, the founding chairman of a multimillion dollar corporation. "Foster, this is Dad," Mr. McGaw began. "I'm going to Africa to be a missionary. I'm going to fly to New York and make a reservation on a ship to Africa. I know God will provide the money for my ticket. All I'm saying is, I want you to come and see me off."

Foster recalls the day when his father set sail. "Of course I was the way God provided for my father's ticket. I still remember my last sight of him as he stood ramrod straight, chin out, waving at me from the upper deck. 'See ya, Foster,' he cried out. He sailed to Africa and worked as a missionary from the age of eighty-two to eighty-six. He died and was buried there." Your troubled times may come when you're old, bored, and feel nobody needs you. Let God prod you! Let Him show you how to be productive at any age.

# God Wants to Promote You

Maybe God is trying to promote you through your troubled times. I remember counseling a member of this church who was feeling hurt and betrayed. He was a high-ranking executive in a major corporation. Suddenly, for no apparent reason, he received his dismissal notice—he was fired after seventeen years with the company! He was unemployed for several months. Each time he applied for a new position, the interviewer would say, "Sorry, you're overqualified." But finally he did get a job. It is the best job he's ever had. He started at 33 percent more money per year than what he was paid in his former position; and he faces more challenge and opportunity than ever before! His dismissal was God's way of promoting him!

# God Will Give You What You Need

This week I served communion to Corrie ten Boom. As some of you may know, Corrie is now over eighty years of age. By some miracle, she survived a concentration camp in Germany during World War II. She lost both her father and her sister while a prisoner. She told me a story from her childhood in Holland. One day she said to her father, "Papa, I don't think I have the faith to handle real trouble. I don't know what I'd do if you should die. I don't think I have the faith that some people have to face trouble."

Corrie's father looked at her tenderly and said, "Corrie, dear, when your father says he will send you to the store tomorrow, does he give the money to you today? No. He gives it to you when you are ready to go to the store. And if you are going on a train trip and you need money for a ticket, does your father give you the money when we decide you may take the trip? No. He gives it to you when you are at the depot, ready to buy your ticket. Corrie, God treats us the same way. He doesn't give you the faith until you need it. But when you do need it, He will certainly give it to you." Corrie's life is a testimony to the truth of that statement.

## The Key to Economic Security

Today, everybody seems to have their own ideas on how to make the dollar stretch. I heard a story recently about a woman who had a very unique answer to the problem of economic security. At her funeral, the mourners were told that during her lifetime she had four husbands, and apparently she had planned all four. First, she married a millionaire. Then she married a Hollywood producer. Third, she married a life-insurance salesman. And, finally, her last husband was a mortician. Her plan worked well—*one for the money; two for the show; three to get ready; and four to go!*

If you want to achieve financial security, you don't have to marry a millionaire. I've got a better idea for you. The idea is simply this: Pray that God will give you the health, strength, and opportunity to earn some money. Then, once you've earned this money—however small that first check is—take 10 percent of it and drop it into the offering plate of your church.

## Praise the Lord

I like to tell my old story of the minister with the unusual horse. This horse didn't respond to the usual commands of *whoa* and *giddy-up*. Instead, when the preacher wanted the horse to go, he would yell, "Praise the Lord!" The horse would hear this command and gallop full speed. When the preacher wanted the horse to stop, he yelled, "Amen!" When the horse heard this word, he would dig his hoofs into the dirt, sending the sand flying in a spray behind him as he came to a screeching halt.

When the preacher sold his horse to a man who was not well acquainted with religion, he told the man about the special commands he must use with the horse. "If you want the horse to go, say, 'Praise the Lord!' If you want the horse to stop, say, 'Amen.'"

The man bought the horse and set out on rocky terrain. As he approached a steep cliff, he wondered what the word for stopping was. "Praise the Lord!" He shouted. And the horse took off at a gallop. Then, just as he was about to plunge over the edge of the cliff, he remembered to shout "Amen!" And the horse dug his hoofs into the dust inches before reaching the edge of the cliff. Shaken, and very grateful, the man looked toward heaven and said, "Praise the Lord."

Praising the Lord really gives us go-power. Thank God for ideas that give you go-head, climb-up-the-ladder power. Then thank God that you have life.

## You Are the Energy

A while back I bought an interesting flashlight. Before I decided to buy it, I asked, "How long will the battery last?" "As long as you do," the saleslady replied. "What do you mean?" I queried. "*You* are the battery," she explained. "There is no battery inside. You have to pump to make it light." I tried it, and sure enough, when I pumped the handle at the bottom of the flashlight, I generated the electricity to make the light! As soon as I stopped pumping, the light went out.

There is a beautiful principle illustrated in this little anecdote. If you make the right commitments to an idea that is
beautiful, but seems impossible, all you have to do is pray
and possibilitize—keep pumping! Bright ideas will come
your way—ideas that come from God.

## The Importance of Beauty

The importance of beauty in our lives was first impressed
upon me when we hired the architect years ago to build the
Tower of Hope and our sanctuary. At the time we decided to
build the new structures, Richard Neutra's face had just appeared on the cover of *Time* magazine. He was recognized as
one of the great architects of the twentieth century. We retained him to design the sanctuary and Tower of Hope.

When we began to explore the possible styles of architecture which would suit the purposes of our church, I said to
him, "Richard, I'd like a church which incorporates the
mood of the Twenty-third Psalm. 'Cool waters and green
pastures' are universal tranquilizing elements." He loved the
idea. "We'll do it!" he enthused. And so the structures were
erected.

When we originally conceived of the plans of our present
buildings, one person saw the plans and urged me to replace
the grass, flowers, and pools of water with concrete.
"Schuller," he exclaimed, "look at the waste of money you
propose! You certainly can't eat it!" "You're wrong," I cor-
rected, "we will eat it. We will feed emotionally on the
beauty of the trees, flowers, grass, water, and sunshine. And
as we sense the beauty of it all, something beautiful will
happen in our lives. *Beauty isn't a luxury; it's a necessity.*"

# A Letter of Sanity

Leslie Hale, an evangelist from Belfast, Ireland, told an interesting story. He was speaking in a large public meeting, when a man shouted above the heads of those gathered, "Leslie, I have to talk to you after the meeting." Leslie spoke soothing words to calm the man and assured him he would see him at the close of the meeting. When the meeting ended, again the man shouted, "Leslie Hale, I'd like to see you before this meeting is over." "The meeting is over," Leslie answered, "come see me."

The man urgently pushed his way through the crowds and reached into his pocket to withdraw a letter, which he handed to Leslie. Leslie was aware of the need for caution. In war-torn Ireland, trusting is a difficult thing. Anything, including a plastic explosive, could have been in the envelope. He didn't know what he was in for.

But when he opened the letter, he recognized the letterhead of a mental hospital. The letter was signed by the superintendent of the hospital. It read: "To whom it may concern: This is to certify that [the name of the man who delivered the letter] has been a patient at the mental hospital in Belfast, North Ireland. It is the judgment of those in authority here that he is now deemed capable of living life normally on the outside. In our judgment he is considered sane and sensible."

"Did you read it?" the man demanded. "I read it, every word," Leslie assured him. "That proves I'm sane, doesn't it?" the man implored with true desperation. "That proves I'm not crazy!" "That's right," Leslie agreed. "They should know. They're experts." "They're experts. They should know," the man repeated, smiling.

That was the only boost he needed. He returned the letter and envelope to his pocket. "I watched him go out of the door and climb on his bicycle," Leslie said. "Just before he pedaled away, he turned, smiled and said, 'Hey, let me see *your* letter.' "

Do you have a letter? I don't. Every human being, at some point in his or her life goes through an experience that involves such emotional turmoil that he or she asks, *Am I going crazy? Am I losing my mind?* It can be a horrible, frightening experience, but if you have encountered it, join the human race. It's normal. We all need the affirmation of our basic sanity once in a while.

# The Comedian Without a Voice Box

Good clean comedians are ministers of God. I remember my boss from the only other job I ever had as a young man in Chicago, Illinois. His name was Bill Bruin. Bill had had cancer of the throat which necessitated the removal of his larynx. The only way he was able to communicate was with the aid of a little instrument, three inches long, which looked like a flashlight. He would put the instrument up to his throat, and when he talked, his voice sounded like that of a robot.

But Bill turned his problem into an opportunity through possibility thinking. He developed a marvelous comedy routine. Every time there was a party, Bill became the center of attention. Just as the gathering would get kind of loud, he would make a sirenlike sound. Everybody would drop what they were doing and look around for the cops; Bill would have a laugh. He was a beautiful person—the comedian without a voice box. A beautiful person is an *amusing* person.

# Take Time to Listen

Take the time to listen to people who need advice and comfort. Everybody needs a counselor at some time in their lives. I know a minister who decided to become a bartender. After years away at college and seminary, he went to school to learn how to mix drinks. He decided that most people who have problems don't talk to ministers, psychiatrists, or professional counselors. He discovered that many of the people with hurts often try to escape through alcohol at the neighborhood bar. He decided he'd have to get close to them, so for three years he worked as a bartender. He became a beautiful influence upon the lives of many people. He uplifted, guided, and taught the people who came to him for advice. And he led many to Christ and the Church.

# Father of the Bride

I'll never forget when, for the first time in my life, I was the father of the bride. What a joyous event!

I must tell you I was a little worried because, at times, I can get very sentimental. I have been officiating in marriages for thirty-one years—since my ordination in 1950. At many of the weddings I've performed I have been so moved that I nearly choked up. So when I enjoyed the privilege of joining the first of my beloved daughters in marriage to a very special young man, I was afraid I would puddle up and weep with joy and happiness.

Several months before my doctor had given me some mild medication that would help keep my emotions under control. Frankly, I just threw the pills away and decided I would try possibility thinking instead. Through possibility thinking I have discovered a cure to that tearful ailment that has blighted the fathers of brides for centuries! If you're going to

be the father of the bride and you're nearly overpowered by
the joy and delight of the occasion, all you need to control
the joy that would cause you to weep with happiness is this
reminder: "Remember, Daddy, you're paying the bill." That
should balance your joy for a moment.

Sheila's wedding was just naturally the kind of family
event that could fill me to overflowing with happiness and
love. Our three younger daughters were Sheila's brides-
maids. I was so very proud of my fourteen-year-old daughter, Carol, who so beautifully achieved the goal she had set
for herself after the accident (which necessitated the amputation of her left leg). Just as she said she would, she walked
down the aisle at her sister's wedding, her bouquet firmly
taped to the top of her crutch.

After I had escorted my lovely daughter down the aisle
and given her away. I then stepped forward to perform the
ceremony. (I must say I delivered my lines quite well!) As
they took their vows to love and honor each other, I main-
tained marvelous control—I didn't puddle up once! Later at
the reception, many people came up to me and marveled,
"Doctor Schuller, you were so relaxed! You seem to be enjoying all this." "Absolutely," I replied, "I decided I would
enjoy it, after all I was paying the bill!" So I had a wonderful
time.

I think the reason why it was such a super event for me is
because it underscored the fact that I am a success in the
most important area of my life. Some people might question
my success as a clergyman, or a pastor, or an author. But nobody can debate the fact that I am a success as a husband
and a father!

# The Tassel Is Worth the Hassle

My son, who was a student at Fuller Theological Seminary, graduated from my alma mater, Hope College in Holland, Michigan, seven years ago. The moment he received his B.A. degree was one of the proudest moments of my life. I watched as he received his diploma and moved the tassel on his mortarboard from the left side to the right.

After the ceremony we met outside. Beaming with delight, we hugged each other and slapped one another on the back. "You made it!" I exclaimed. "Yes," he said, grinning broadly. "I made it. But it was tough." "But it was worth it, though, wasn't it?" I asked. "It was worth it," he repeated. "But at times I wondered. It was quite a hassle." As he spoke those words, my eyes were drawn to the tassel flowing from his cap. Touching it lightly, I said, "The tassel is worth the hassle." "You bet!" my son affirmed enthusiastically.

If you make your decisions based upon how comfortable, easy, convenient, or painless your choices are, then don't ever expect great rewards. Hassle-free living is tassel-free living. You can be sure that the tassel is in proportion to the hassle. Pay a big price and you can expect a good return!

# Hassles Can Help You Grow

Do you remember the story of the little boy who stormed angrily home from his first day at kindergarten? "How did you like school?" his mother asked gently. "I didn't like it," he replied sulkily. "In fact," he continued, "I not only didn't like it, I'm quitting!" "You're quitting!" his mother exclaimed incredulously. "Why, you can't do that!" "I don't care if I can or I can't," the little boy said. "I'm quitting." "Why do you want to quit school?" she questioned. "Look,

Mom," the child replied, "school is an awful place. I can't write. I don't know how to read. And they wouldn't let me talk. There's nothing to it, so I quit!"

Personal growth comes when we learn through our hassles what our potential capabilities and capacities for learning really are. Hassles show us how we can grow.

# A Glorious Impossibility

Not long ago I heard on television an interview with one of the runners in the Boston Marathon. "Why did you run the race?" the young woman asked. "I know you weren't paid for it. Was the race a physically pleasurable experience?" "No," the runner answered. "As a matter of fact, it was pretty painful—especially the last few hills."

Running can be painful, but it can also be sheer joy. This morning I rose before dawn and went out on the road to run a few miles. I experienced a wonderful feeling. As I ran through the silent neighborhood, I felt that I was alive and the rest of the world was dead and hadn't resurrected yet. I had eyes that could see the drifting clouds and the sun as it struggled to break over the horizon, while the sleepers were blind as they huddled under their warm sheets in their darkened bedrooms. I could hear the sound of the birds singing and the light breeze softly ruffling the leaves of the trees, while they were deaf to the music of an awakening world. I could feel strength building through my veins, I could feel strength building and energy flowing through my limbs. I was alive!

But I must admit, not every morning is like that. Some days it's difficult to drag myself from bed and run those miles in the early morning. And, like the marathon runner, I often find that pushing myself to the limits of my endurance can be a less than pleasurable experience. So I listened with anticipation when the reporter pressed the marathoner to tell why he had subjected himself to that grueling twenty-six-mile race. The runner said, "I ran the race because of the glorious impossibility of it." Until we are faced with a glorious impossibility, we don't know what we are, who we are, or what we can do.

## Hidden Treasure

As I recall my visits to the shimmering emerald waters which surround the Greek peninsula, I remember a tour into the hinterlands of that country. My guide took me through some of the glorious temples built in the age of Pericles some 2,360 years ago. As he gestured toward the empty marble pedestals in and around the temple grounds, he explained, "On these pedestals once stood some of the most beautiful pieces of marble sculpture ever created in the Ancient World. Most of them were lost when the Romans invaded Greece. These works of art were carted down to Roman ships—many of which were lost at sea."

Greece's most magnificent treasures now lie hidden under the waters of the Mediterranean. Like the talents and treasures that lie within you, they are just waiting to be discovered.

## Gold of Glacier Bay

If you've ever had the opportunity to journey up into the far north near Glacier Bay, you know it's a spectacular experience. Glacier Bay is located in a region so far from civilization that it is as primitive, virginal, and unspoiled as the dawn of creation. There are no cars, houses, or neon lights for as far as the eye can see. I took a tour of the bay by ship. As we approached the three-hundred-foot high, sheer cliff of diamond-blue ice, we heard it creak and groan. Then suddenly the cliff splintered from top to bottom and, with a screeching crack and deafening snap, a huge chunk of this millenniums-old glacier slid thunderously into the ocean and exploded in white foam. The echo of the explosion reverberated through the hills of the desolate countryside.

Many geologists feel certain that, as this river of frozen ice scoured the bottom and sides of the valleys through the centuries, it carried with it vast, unknown amounts of precious metals. Within that glacier may be the largest, purest gold nugget that has ever been created! It simply hasn't been uncovered yet!

Could there be a gold nugget within you that you haven't yet discovered?

## Bear Quarterback Finds Religion

Once someone sent me an article from the *Chicago Tribune*. The headline read BEAR QUARTERBACK FINDS RELIGION— EVANS' LIFE CHANGES OFF THE FIELD TOO." The story told of how Vince Evans, quarterback for the Chicago Bears, had suddenly developed a tremendous sense of self-confidence and was showing remarkable potential. In the previous few weeks, he had thrown more than his share of touchdown passes. He had suddenly begun to develop his potential for greatness. In short, he was worshiping God in the beauty of holiness which, for him, was playing great football.

What made the difference? He was suddenly inspired by a new idea. Anytime you act upon a great new idea, you are going to become a different person. What new idea inspired Vince Evans? According to Evans, something happened the previous Easter that made him more confident. "I was looking at Reverend Robert Schuller of Garden Grove, California, on television," said Evans. "I've watched him before because he talks about positive thinking. He was talking about the Resurrection. It was cloudy at that particular time. Just as he said Jesus had risen, the sun came out.

"My television is on a loft under a skylight. The sun shone in and beamed on my face. I knew Jesus Christ had come into my life and I overflowed with tears. I was always religiously inclined, but I never had a personal relationship with God until then." The rest of the story told how Vince Evans now lets his faith make a difference in his attitude toward daily life.

Worship the Lord in the beauty of holiness. Be daring and courageous enough to open up to beautiful new ideas. When you do, a lot of things are going to open up to you.

## Cut the Motor

One morning I took a motorboat ride across the Sea of Galilee. Suddenly, in the middle of the lake, the operator of the boat cut the motor, and I wondered for a moment if we were out of gas. When I inquired, he said, "No. I thought it would be nice, Doctor Schuller, if you could just listen to the quietness out here." Soon the boat stopped rocking and the only sounds we heard were the sounds of the water lapping gently against the stern and the majestic silence of the centuries, as we sat in the very same sea Jesus fished nearly two thousand years ago.

There must come a time in each of our lives when we cut the motor, stop the boat, and just pause to be still and recognize the mighty presence of God. Most of us allow ourselves to get into a rut. We think we know the answers to all the important questions in our lives. We think we have our philosophies, ideologies, theology, and psychology all neatly packaged and labeled. When we feel safe and secure in our knowledge, when we think we have all the answers, then it's time to stop the motor and ask ourselves, "Am I ready for a new idea?"

# Boiled Peanuts

I tried something this week I want to share with you. I was in Georgia to give a lecture. While being driven to the lecture hall, I saw little roadside stands all along the way which read BOILED PEANUTS FOR SALE. I had never heard of boiled peanuts before, so I asked my driver about them.

"You've never had boiled peanuts?" my driver asked incredulously. "No," I replied, "do they actually boil them?" "Sure," he said. "Be adventuresome. Try them." So he pulled over to the side of the road, and I followed him to one of the stands where there was a big pot of boiling water. Floating on the surface like sea kelp were peanuts still in their shells. The man took a dipper and scooped the soggy peanuts up into a paper bag.

When I returned to the car, I went to crack the nut and water squirted me in the nose. When I finally got it out of the shell and into my mouth, I discovered it really was very good. I feel I must commend Georgia and President Carter for giving us boiled peanuts.

But when I went to hand the bag of peanuts to my friend in the front seat, the bottom dropped out and all the peanuts landed in my lap.

It's fun to try something new. But what is really fun is when the new thing you try really puts beauty into your life. What we all need are beautiful ideas. And Jesus Christ is my idea of a beautiful idea.

# The Glorious Buffet

This summer I was traveling with my wife and our two youngest daughters. We were the guests of a company up north where I spoke, and they provided accommodations for us at a lovely hotel. The first morning I was there, I arose early and went out on my usual morning run. On the way back to my room, I saw the buffet table. It was glorious—piled high with everything imaginable: fruit, all kinds of meats, eggs, fish, blueberry and bran muffins, pancakes, waffles, and French toast. Although I usually shy away from big breakfasts, I decided to indulge that morning.

When I returned to our room, I found our daughter Gretchen cuddled up in our bed dozing peacefully. "Gretchen," I said, "come on out! Let's go to breakfast!" "Nope," she answered, "I'm ordering room service." "Gretchen, do you know what you get here for room service?" I asked. "Yes," she said, "Breakfast in bed. I've never had breakfast in bed, and today I'm going to." "But Gretchen," I argued, "all you get from room service is cold cereal and milk." "I like cold cereal and milk," she answered. "I want breakfast in bed."

"Gretchen," I exclaimed, "you should see the buffet table! They have scrambled eggs [her favorite], bacon, French toast. . . ." And she pulled the covers over her head. She didn't want to hear. "Gretchen," I continued, "they also have blueberry muffins." And she pulled a pillow over her head. "They have bran muffins and pancakes, too," I shouted, as she buried her head deeper into the pillows and pulled a second blanket over her head. She didn't want to hear, because hearing meant changing her way of thinking. Hearing meant getting out of a comfortable bed, getting dressed, and going down into the dining room—something she wasn't prepared to do.

You may be missing a super banquet—the banquet of love, joy, and peace of mind you could be enjoying through a relationship with Jesus Christ. Make the necessary changes, get ready to wake up and embrace Jesus Christ. Accept the banquet He offers you. Dare to try something you never have tried before.

# A Hole in the Boat

We had a staff meeting some months ago, and during that meeting I drew a sketch of an oceanliner with about seven different stories. At the top level was the captain, looking at the splendid view. The next level was the lounge, where people were having intimate conversation. At the next level were people enjoying the excellent cuisine. The next level was the sundeck, where people were sunning themselves. And finally you came to the cabin area. Way at the bottom in one end was the theater, and at the other end was the engine room. And next to the engine room, just slightly above the mechanical room, was a little room called the washroom. In it were automatic washers and automatic dryers. This room happened to be run by one simple fellow who was getting sick and tired of all the rich tourists who used the washroom and ran off with the towels. And nobody paid attention to him. He was forgotten, isolated, and abandoned. Even the people who came to use this little room didn't listen to his rules.

Finally he decided that he was not going to stand for it anymore, so he got a hammer and some nails and hammered the towels to the wall. "Now they won't run off with my towels!" he said. The captain, who couldn't have cared less, didn't know about it. The people up in the bar and in the restaurant and the people sunning themselves really didn't care. Nobody cared what the little fellow did with his towels. If he wanted to hammer them to the wall, then he could just go ahead.

But what the man who hammered the towels to the wall didn't know was that it was an outside wall. He had never seen the ship blueprints. But suddenly the water was leaking in. He jammed it with a bar of soap, and that just dissolved. He stuck his fingers in the hole, but that didn't seem to be the most fruitful solution to the problem. And finally, in desperation and hysteria, he pulled his fingers out and the water was up to his ankles. It would only be a matter of time before the captain was going to be concerned about some little fellow who hammered the towels to the wall of the ship.

The real point is, *a hole in a boat is a hole in a boat.* All human beings who live on planet earth are on the same ship, spinning at an incredible speed through space. We can take an I-don't-care attitude like the captain at the top toward the little man in the washroom. We can take that kind of an attitude towards other people in other states, other professions, other races and nationalities. But you can be sure a hole in a boat is a hole in a boat is a hole in a boat.

# The Americans and Their Houseboy

Four servicemen, who were assigned to the East Coast, were given living quarters and a private houseboy who would take care of their laundry, make up their beds, and clean their room. Well, these young American soldiers loved pranks, so they decided to pull a joke on the fellow.

The first night on the base they waited until he was asleep and then one of the GI's slipped out of bed and went into his room. Then he carefully proceeded to nail his shoes to the wooden floor. The next morning they were awakened with a knock at the door. When they opened the door, there was the houseboy. "Good morning," the aide said. They looked down and saw that he was wearing his shoes. He was carrying a tray and on it were four cups of black, thick, hot, steaming coffee. "Here's your coffee," he enthused without saying another word. And so, the four servicemen drank their coffee.

The next night the Americans decided to pull another prank and put sand in the houseboy's bed. The following morning there was a knock on the door. One of the men opened it, and there was the aide once again. They expected him to be very angry, but he was smiling again, "Good morning," he said, holding the tray with hot, thick, black steaming coffee. He didn't even hint that he had a bad night of sleep.

Well, the young men couldn't take it. They couldn't stand pulling pranks on such a nice fellow. They felt so bad, so repentant, and so remorseful that they called him in and told him to sit down. "Look, we're very sorry," they explained. "We have been very mean and rude to you. We're very sorry that we nailed your shoes to the floor, and we're sorry we put sand in your bed last night. We are not going to play any more pranks on you ever again, you are just too nice." He smiled. "You no more nail my shoes to the floor?" "No," they answered in unison. "You no more put sand in my bed?" "No," they answered again, "Okay. Then me no more put mud in your coffee."

Everything we do provokes an action or reaction from someone. You and I are either part of the problem or part of the solution.

# The Sanctified Hypocrite

Henry Fawcett was one of the great distinguished members of Parliament in England. William Gladstone appointed him Postmaster General, and he made one of the greatest contributions to England in the whole area of the postal services and telegraphy. The story behind it is this: Henry Fawcett was blind! He had every reason to be bitter. It happened when he was twenty years old. He and his dad had a super relationship. One day they were out hunting, and the father accidentally discharged the gun and shot his son in the face. This bright, healthy, mentally alert young boy of twenty dropped, covered with blood. The father rushed over to his son's side and took him home. The boy lived, but he was sightless the rest of his life. The father wanted to kill himself. And young Henry wanted to die, too. He had no hope, for he would not be able to read again. He would not be able to study or go back to school. All of these negative thoughts went through his mind over and over again.

Then one day he overhead his father crying. He was swearing out loud and condemning himself for ruining his son's life. This was when Henry decided to build his father's hopes. He would pretend! "It's okay, Dad," Henry said. "Don't worry, I'll soon learn to read. Others can read to me." But in his heart it was a lie. So only to keep his father from self-destruction, young Henry Fawcett lived a lie of laughter, and optimism, and enthusiasm. He lived the life of joy. But he didn't have joy; he didn't have enthusiasm. He was, you might say, a sanctified hypocrite.

But then something happened. There came a moment when the lie became a reality! The act became the real thing! The play became the truth! He had hope! And his hope produced results! And results produced progress! He began, you see, to listen to his own positive statements, even when he didn't mean them.

# Bright Faces

Edward Rosenow was one of the great doctors at the Mayo Clinic for many years. His career as a doctor really started for him when he was a little boy, living in Minnesota. His brother was critically ill, so his parents called for the doctor. He said, "I'll never forget when the doctor came to the house. My father's and my mother's faces were strained with fear and worry. The doctor told them to wait with me around the table in the dining room while he went into the bedroom and closed the door. He seemed to be gone a very long time. I looked at my dad and his face was dark. I looked at my mother and her face was dark. When the doctor came out of the bedroom and closed the door, he looked at each of us for a moment and his face broke into a smile. "You can relax, folks, he's going to be all right!" Young Ed said, "at that time I saw a light come into my dad's face, and a light come into my mother's face. And I decided then and there I was going to be a doctor when I grew up, because I wanted to put light in people's faces."

There's a calling for you! There's a plan and a dream for you! Every life is to be a light.

## The Bridge of Moses

I'm reminded of a story about a little boy who came home from Sunday school, bragging about how good the class was, so his mother said, "What did you learn today?" And the boy replied, "I learned how Moses got the Israelites out of Egypt." "How did he do it?" the mother prodded. "Very simply," he continued, "Moses hired some bridge experts and they built a suspension bridge ten times as long as the Golden Gate Bridge. It went clear across the Red Sea!" "That's hard to believe," his mother laughed. "Look," the persistent child said, "if I told you what they really taught me, you'd *never* believe me!"

## Motivate Me

Be motivated! Like the story of the little boy whose mother was a psychologist, and he came to the breakfast table one morning, refusing to eat his cereal. She tried all of the manipulative tactics, but nothing worked. She tried all of the tricks of behavioral modification, but none of it worked. Finally she lost her cool and yelled at him. He looked coolly across the table and said, "Motivate me!" How do you motivate people? God uses impossible situations to motivate persons. God deliberately throws mountains in front of us, so we'll fall on our knees and ask for help!

# A Brand-New Car

A funny thing happened to me this morning on the way to church. I was driving the old car that I bought seven years ago. It's been such a faithful old car. A few miles from church, I looked down at the speedometer and watched the little blocks change: 99,999.5 ... 99,999.6 ... 99,999.7 ... 99,999.8 ... 99,999.9 ...—then the odometer read 00,000.0, and I had a brand-new car!

Now we all know that you cannot tell the newness of a car by the odometer, and you can't tell a book by its cover. That's not a new car just because the odometer reads 00,000.0! That car can't be recreated into a brand-new car, but *you* can be *re*created into a brand-new person! You can become a totally new creature, if you will let Jesus Christ come into your life.

# A Courageous Woman

In 1921, Lewis Lawes became the warden at Sing Sing Prison. No prison was tougher than Sing Sing during that time. But when Warden Lawes retired twenty some years later, that prison had become a humanitarian institution. It was a model for other prisons to follow. Those who studied the system said credit for the change belonged to Lewis Lawes. But when Warden Lawes was asked about the transformation, this is what he said: "I owe it all to my wonderful wife, Catherine, who is buried outside the prison walls."

Catherine Lawes was a young mother with three small children when her husband became the warden at Sing Sing prison. Everybody warned her from the beginning that she should never step foot inside the prison walls or in any other facility that the prisoners would be using, but that didn't stop Catherine! When the first prison basketball game was held, she insisted on going. She walked into the auditorium with her three beautiful children and sat in the stands with the hard-core criminals. Other guests came up to her afterwards and asked, "How do you dare sit with these men? Why do you take your little children in there?" And her reply was, "My husband and I are going to take care of these men, and I believe they will take care of me! I don't have to worry!"

She even insisted on getting acquainted with the records of the men. She discovered that one of the men convicted of murder was blind, so she paid him a visit. She stepped into the cold cell and sat down next to this man. Holding his hand in hers she warmly said, "Do you read Braille?" "What's Braille?" he asked. "Don't you know? It is a way that you can read with your fingers," she explained. "Well, I've never heard of it," he replied. "I'll teach you then!" she enthused. And she taught that blind killer how to read Braille. Years later he would weep in love for her.

Later Catherine found that there was a deaf-mute in the prison, so she went to school to learn sign language. Soon she was communicating with him through the use of her hands. Many said that Catherine Lawes was the body of Jesus Christ that came alive again at Sing Sing prison from 1921 to 1937.

Then one evening the car in which she was riding went out of control, and she was killed. The next morning her husband did not come to work, so the acting warden came in his place. In an instant, the whole prison knew something was wrong. When they heard the news that their beloved lady had died, everyone wept.

The following day her body was resting in a casket in her home, three-quarters of a mile from the prison. As the acting warden took his early-morning walk, he was shocked to see a large crowd of the toughest, hardest-looking criminals, gathering like a herd of animals at the main gate. It looked as if they were ready to launch a riot. He walked over to the group and, instead of seeing hostility in their eyes, he saw tears of grief and sadness. He knew how much they loved and admired Catherine. He turned and faced the men. "All right, men, you can go. Just be sure and check in tonight!" Then he opened the gate without another word and a parade of more than one hundred criminals walked, without a guard, three-quarters of a mile to stand in line to pay their respects to Catherine Lawes. And every one of them checked in that night. *Every one! It's amazing what one life can do when it has the Spirit of Christ within.* Catherine Lawes believed there were no hopeless cases, only hopeless thinkers!

The warden's wife had the courage to take her little children and sit among murderers and rapists. Do you have courage? How much nerve do you have? Do you have enough courage to trust God as He comes to you and says: "I believe in you! I have a dream for your life!"

# The Hands of Christ

In a small French country village during World War II, there was a beautiful marble statue of Jesus with His hands outstretched before him, standing in the courtyard of a quaint little church. One day a bomb struck too close, and the statue was dismembered. After the battle was over and the enemy had passed through, the citizens of the village decided to find the pieces of their beloved statue and reconstruct it. It was no work of art by Michelangelo or Bernini, but it was a part of their lives, and they loved it just the same. And so they gathered the broken pieces and reassembled it. Even the scars on the body added to its beauty. But there was one problem. They were unable to find the hands of the statue. "A Christ without hands is no Christ at all," someone lamented. "Hands with scars—yes. But what's a Lord without hands? We need a new statue." Then someone else came along with another idea, and it prevailed. A brass plaque was attached at the base of the statue which reads I HAVE NO HANDS BUT YOUR HANDS.

# The Three Pennies of Sister Theresa

Sister Theresa had a dream one day. She told her superiors, "I have three pennies and a dream from God to build an orphanage." "Sister Theresa," her superiors chided gently, "you cannot build an orphanage with three pennies. With three pennies, you can't do anything." "I know," she said, smiling, "but with God and three pennies, I *can* do anything!"

# Don't Miss the Positives

There was once a professor who took a piece of paper and pinned it on the board in his classroom. Then with a felt-tip pen he made a circle and colored it in with black. When he finished, he asked his psychology class, "What do you see?" One person said, "A black dot." Another person said, "I see a round circle and it's dark." Another one said, "I see a round circle colored solid black." And so he went through the class, until finally the professor said, "Doesn't anybody see a piece of white paper?" They all picked out the black dot. Nobody pointed to the white sheet of paper.

Most of the people you work with and live with are negative people. They look at the faults; they pick out the shortcomings; they point out the defects; they show the imperfections; they spot the flaws; they focus on the wrinkles; they check the stains; they look for the negatives. They miss everything that's positive and great.

## Life Can Be Great at Ninety-Eight

This past week I talked to a beautiful gentleman. This man was one of the most inspiring men I have ever met. He was not exactly young when I met him last year. Six months earlier he had celebrated his ninety-eighth birthday. But what a chipper old fellow he is! He works six days a week in his factory, operating America's last hand-hewn-copper-kettle factory. What a bright and alert man!

I know people who, when they get older, don't like birthdays. They are always complaining about getting old. I love birthdays! You know why? Because if I didn't have a birthday every year, I wouldn't be here! That's what you call a positive attitude. I asked my friend, "How long are you going to live?" Smiling, he said, "Oh, I'm planning to live to one hundred!" "Wow!" I exclaimed. "How can I live to be one hundred?" "Very simple," he enthused, "anybody can live to be one hundred. All you do is live to be ninety-nine— and then be *very* careful!"

When I saw my friend this time, it happened to be a very unpleasant day for me, and I made some negative comment about it. He looked me in the eye and said, "Doctor Schuller, every day is a good day! Every day is better than no day at all!" Think of that. *Every day is better than no day at all!*

Ninety-eight years old and a great believer in God and possibility thinking! Some people look upon the years as burdens. My ninety-eight-year-old friend looks upon every added year as another blessing. It's all a matter of your mental attitude. And you have the freedom to choose how you will think!

# The Courage of Hubert Humphrey

I first met Hubert Humphrey in 1971. I received a letter from him saying that he and his wife, Muriel, watched the "Hour of Power" and that it was a great help to them on a very deep and personal level. He told me to stop in and see him the next time I was in Washington, so I did! When I found his office, I told his secretary who I was and she smiled and said, "Oh, Doctor Schuller, he really wants to see you!" Then she had a member of his staff take me to the Senate Chamber where Senator Humphrey was speaking.

He was finishing, just as I entered the room. When he rushed over and warmly embraced me, I didn't know exactly what to say, so I handed him one of the little gold cards with the possibility-thinkers' creed printed on it. "What's this?" Hubert asked. And I told him to read it. In his strong and sturdy voice, he began reading:

> When faced with a mountain I will not quit, I will keep on striving until I climb over, find a pass through, tunnel underneath or simply stay and turn the mountain into a gold mine, with God's help.

Tears filled his eyes before he could finish. This was only the beginning of what would become a deep, personal relationship.

People have said it through the years and I affirm it today—Hubert Humphrey had great courage! People who fight a terminal illness, and keep on fighting bravely, have courage! I have always admired their perseverance. I have always admired their faith. But I used to say, "Why do you call it courage? What's so brave about it? Perseverance? Yes. Toughness? Of course. But courageousness? But why do you say it's *courageous,* when somebody's fighting a battle of cancer?"

It's courageous because a person who fights a brave battle with a terminal illness, is making a commitment! There can be no courage unless there is a choice between alternatives. And the person who is fighting a terminal illness is making a choice between two alternatives. One is to overdose and slip away quickly. The other is to hang in there as bravely and optimistically as possible, until God stops the heartbeat. When you're faced with alternatives, you choose the one where the personal price is high but the rewards in terms of inspiration to those around you is high. That's *courage!*

# Dear Abby, "What's Wrong With Suicide?"

In my latest book, *Peace of Mind Through Possibility Thinking,* I tell about a conversation I had with a good friend—Abby. She writes her own syndicated newspaper column called "Dear Abby." We were at dinner together in Beverly Hills, and I was telling her about our ministry and the suicides that we prevent through our twenty-four-hour life-line telephone Christian counseling program. She was surprised when I told her that we operate the longest-standing, continually operating New Hope Telephone Counseling Center right here on the campus of the Garden Grove Community

Church. I told her how proud we were of the fact that no ministry saves more lives than we do!

Abby's reply was a question: "Dr. Schuller, what's so wrong about suicide?" "What's wrong with suicide," I replied, "is that your friends and relatives are left behind to live with the terrible hurt! They are the ones who must carry the scars for the rest of their lives!"

Your life and mine will be judged before Almighty God on this question: "When I was faced with alternatives, did I choose the brave way?" And if I did, I uplifted the collective level of social self-esteem in the process.

## Charlotte Valente

I have never met Charlotte Valente but I surely want to some day. I became acquainted with her story through some literature I received from the Children's Hospital in Los Angeles. Mary Ames Anderson, now the retired editor, said if she were to pick one child in the Children's Hospital who inspired her more than anybody else, it would have to be Charlotte Valente. And here's Mary Anderson's beautiful story.

"I was walking through the corridor of the Children's Hospital in 1953, when I heard a young voice say, 'Here I am!' I stopped and turned to see where the voice was coming from. And that's when I saw a little girl, barely two years old, lying in bed hugging her teddy bear. She seemed so young to be speaking so clearly. Both of her tiny legs were hanging in the air, in traction. 'Well, hello!' I enthused. Smiling, she asked, 'How are you today?' But before I could answer, she interrupted, 'I have brittle bones. This one is broken. Last time it was that one,' she said, as she pointed to her right leg. 'But this time it is this one. I have had eleven fractures!'

"By the age of six Charlotte had been in and out of the

hospital eighty-five times. She has a rare disease, which makes her bones break very easily. She had over two hundred fractures by the time she was ten, but she was a delightful little girl, always smiling and very positive.

"I only saw her cry twice," Mrs. Anderson wrote. "Once when she fractured her arm the day before her sister's wedding, and she had to stay in the hospital. The other time was when she made a community appeal to urge people to give so crippled children could walk. 'I will never walk,' Charlotte said in her plea, 'but hundreds of others can walk if only you'll help!' Charlotte couldn't walk because by the time she reached puberty, the disease had arrested itself. Her normal development had been permanently distorted. She would probably never weigh more than fifty pounds in her entire lifetime. But this brave young girl didn't cry until she was recognized by community leaders. And do you know why? Because they gave her a typewriter—the one material thing that she'd wanted ever since she was a child. She didn't want a bike, because she could never ride one. She wanted a typewriter! And when she was presented this gift, she cried and cried. 'I'm the luckiest girl in the whole world!' she exclaimed."

Charlotte went on to high school and graduated. Then she picked a university that had ramps equipped for the handicapped. She was accepted and graduated four years later cum laude! But Charlotte did not stop there! She went on to law school and passed the state bar exam. All fifty pounds of her!

# The Ideal One

The late Ozzie Nelson used to tell this story about a friend of his son Ricky.

He said, "Ricky was just a young boy when he begged me to let his friend Walter come over and spend the weekend with him. And after much persistence, I gave in. On the day that Walter was to come over, I got off work a little early, so I could play with the boys. We went into the backyard and started throwing a football around. I was getting really good, when Ricky said, 'Hey, Dad, you're great!' And Walter piped in and exclaimed, 'Gee, Mr. Nelson, you've got a pretty good arm, but not as good as my dad.' When it came to dinner time I carved the roast so beautifully with thin and even slices. 'Look at those nice slices, Walter,' I bragged. 'You carve the roast pretty good, Mr. Nelson,' Walter enthused, 'but you should see my dad do it!' I couldn't believe it! I couldn't do anything as well as this kid's father.

"Well, when their bedtime came I decided to tell one of my best stories. Their eyes were popping out of their heads! 'That's a great story, Mr. Nelson, but my dad is one of the best storytellers there is!' And the next day the same thing happened—no matter what we did together. I was starting to dislike a man I'd never even met. I couldn't wait for Walter's mother to pick him up, so I could find out about this superdad! When she came to the door, I said, 'Hi! I'm delighted to meet you.' 'How was Walter?' she asked. 'Oh, just great,' I exclaimed. 'I'd sure like to meet your husband. He must be something else!' 'Oh, no!' she said, 'has Walter been talking about his dad again? You see, Walter was only three years old when his dad was killed at Corregidor.' " That little boy had an Ideal One who lived within him.

My Ideal One died before I was born—at Calvary! His name is Jesus! That's where I get my courage. That's where I get my nerve. He lives in me and He wants to live in you!

# Dr. Henry Poppen

A visit to Hong Kong brought back some beautiful memories of a good friend, Dr. Henry Poppen. He was on my staff for many years, until he went to be with the Lord at the age of eighty-three. Dr. Poppen was one of the first missionaries to go to China. After spending over forty years there, he was called into public trial in the main city square. Over ten thousand people jammed the square as accusation after accusation was read against him. Finally, he was declared guilty on all counts and told he must leave the country.

Dr. Poppen and his wife boarded a bus and headed to Swatow, hoping to board a steamer and leave for freedom in Hong Kong, and then back to America. But in Swatow, Henry was pulled off the bus, brought to solitary confinement and confined to a little cell, six feet by eight feet. The ceiling was so low, he couldn't stand up straight. He didn't know what was going to happen to him, but he did know that most missionaries who were prisoners of Mao Tse-tung never lived to tell about it.

Mrs. Poppen was put on a train, then a boat, and finally found herself in Hong Kong. She waited anxiously in a hotel, not knowing where her beloved husband was.

Dr. Poppen spent hour after hour, and day by day in his small, dark cell. After four and a half days, he could stand the blackness and the mental torture no more. At midnight he got on his hands and knees by his small wooden cot and prayed, "Oh, God, you know I am not Saint Paul, or the Apostle John or Saint Peter. I am only Henry Poppen, and Henry Poppen can take no more! Lord, open the door!"

He fell asleep on his hands and knees, only to be awakened about an hour later by the creaking of the hinges on his cell door. The guards came in and tied a rope around his neck with a slipknot, ran it down his backbone and bound his arms behind him so tightly that if he struggled at all, he would strangle himself. Then they led him down a dark, winding cobblestone street, until he saw the reflection of light in rippling water. He heard the hum and chunking of an engine. Then he saw the dark outline of an ocean steamer, waiting, with its gangplank down. The guards shoved him onto the deck and said, "Now get out of our country!"

The gangplank was raised, and the steamer blew the whistle. The captain took the rope off his neck and cut it loose from his hands. Dr. Poppen raised his proud head, a free man under God! The gift of an open door—what greater gift can God give you than that? God heard Dr. Poppen's prayer, and He opened the door and delivered him! The power of positive prayer.

# Three Little Whacks

I'm reminded of a story Mary Goforth's father told in one of his books. There was a young woodpecker who was given training on how to properly go about drilling holes in trees. He was taught the correct method to throw his head back to achieve maximum thrust. He learned how to sharpen his beak to a perfect point on the bark of a tree. And, being the determined woodpecker that he was, he graduated in the top 10 percent of his class.

As a new graduate, he was given his first assignment and his instructors pointed him to an appropriate tree. With extreme confidence, this cocky young woodpecker stretched his wings and flew to the assigned tree. Grabbing hold of the bark with his sturdy feet, he inspected the wood and, as he had been taught to do, threw back his head and took his first whack. A chip of bark flew from the trunk of the tree and the eyes of the woodpecker sparkled with pride—finally he was doing what he was meant to do. Again he threw back his head and took another whack. This time an even larger piece of wood flew from the tree. He was doing great. Then, just as he threw his head back and took his third whack at the tree, lightning struck, splintering the trunk into fragments, and sending the woodpecker tumbling to the ground.

Dazed, but not seriously hurt, the young woodpecker flew with feeble wings to a tree adjoining the one he had been working on so industriously. He looked at the splintered tree trunk and said incredulously, "Wow! To think I did it with only three little whacks!"

Most likely our difficult situations will not be solved with "three little whacks" of our own. We as human beings simply aren't that smart. But if we're really in tune with God and His will, He intervenes in our lives. Only He can know what great things we can accomplish with Him.

# The Skeptic

Here's a funny story that illustrates lack of faith.

The Japanese are famous for their skill with computers. Recently they installed a fully computerized scale which, instead of giving you a ticker-tape readout of your height and weight, gives you personal data via a mechanical voice.

A skeptical American dropped in a coin and out of the speaker of this inventive Japanese device came the following announcement: YOU ARE AN AMERICAN. YOU ARE 5'10" TALL. YOU WEIGH 185 LBS. AND YOU ARE BOOKED ON FLIGHT 408 TO LOS ANGELES, CALIFORNIA. The man was totally incredulous. He was sure someone was playing some kind of practical joke on him. So he sneaked back into the club lounge, changed his clothes, put on a different coat, and pulled his hat over his ears, so that it hid his face. Hobbling like a shrunken old man, the American stepped onto the machine, dropped in his dime, and waited for the announcement. YOU ARE AN AMERICAN, the voice announced from the speaker. YOU ARE 5'10" TALL. YOU WEIGH 185 LBS. AND WHILE YOU WERE CHANGING YOUR CLOTHES, YOUR PLANE LEFT FOR LOS ANGELES.

Any counselor will tell you that it is very difficult for people who naturally employ manipulative avoidance reaction response or intentional inattention to believe.

# The Child With an Exceptional Future

Yesterday I met with a young couple who came to visit our church campus from a city far away. They were a beautiful couple—a happy husband and wife, and in her arms, the young woman held a beautiful little baby boy. As we stood together outside the Tower of Hope, they said to me, "Doctor Schuller, this ministry has given us real faith—faith that can turn our scars into stars. It's made us strong for our little boy." And I looked at the darling little three-month-old baby boy, sleeping in the blanket. "May I hold him?" I asked. As I held the warm, sleeping bundle, I wondered what they could have meant—what scars could this small child have put upon their lives?

But without my asking, they explained, "You see, Doctor Schuller, we just got word that both of our child's little legs must be amputated below the knee. He was born without bones between the knee and ankle. God really used your daughter Carol's accident to help us see a bright future for him. You gave us faith. We know he's going to be an exceptional child with an exceptional future." And we held hands and prayed together and claimed God's promise in Jeremiah 29:11: "I have a plan for your life. It is a plan for good and not evil. It is a plan to give you a future with hope."

# George W. Campbell

George W. Campbell was born blind. When he was a child, there was no cure for the disease known as congenital bilateral cataracts. The doctor said to the father, "At this time, there is absolutely no cure. He will be destined to be sightless all of his life." The child grew and learned to walk, laugh, sing, and play. At six years of age something happened. He was playing with a friend who had forgotten for a moment that he was sightless. The friend threw the ball at him and saw that it was headed straight for his little face. The friend shouted, "George, look out! It's going to hit you!" The ball hit him in the face. He went to his mother and said, "How did Roy know something was going to happen to me before it happened?"

His mother sat down and took his little hands in hers. She counted his fingers and began, "George, I want to tell you something: People have five senses. The thumb stands for hearing; you can hear me talk to you. This little finger stands for touching; you can feel me touch you. This little finger stands for the tongue; you can taste food. And this little finger stands for smelling; you can smell when I bake bread. And this little finger stands for seeing." Then she took that little finger and with a rope she tied it into the palm of his hand. She said, "George, you're different from other people. With you this little finger doesn't work. You cannot see. But now you have four fingers and I've got the other one tied down. I want you to put both of our hands out and I'm going to throw a ball to you. Catch it; here it comes!" He caught it and she explained, "See, George! I want you to know that as you grow up, you can catch a ball, even though you're missing one finger. You can catch hold of life and live a full and wonderful life, even though you cannot see." And that beautiful, positive possibility placed in his little life made him a positive, creative, and fruitful person.

At age eighteen he was sick in the hospital with a minor ailment, when the news came out that a treatment had been discovered that might be helpful to congenital bilateral cataracts. It was risky, but the father determined after discussing it with George that it was worth the risk. So they performed two surgeries on each eye over a six-month period of time.

During this long period of surgeries, they were prayerful and hopeful. When the last surgery was complete and the bandages were removed, the doctor asked, "George, do you see anything?" He could only see what seemed like a dull blur, so he was still considered legally blind. And then something happened. He heard a voice over his face saying, "George, this is your mother. Can you see?" The blur turned into a color, the color took shape, and suddenly he, for the first time in his life, saw a human face. It was the face of a sixty-two-year-old woman, wrinkled, with white hair. When he was old, he said, "It was the first face I ever saw—and was it ever beautiful." He didn't see her wrinkles. He didn't see the old lines that had begun to form. He didn't notice that her hands were gnarled and old. They were the hands that had held his little hands. This was the voice that had spoken to him all those years. This was his mother. He lived a normal and beautiful life and he said, "The most beautiful moment of my life was when my eyes were opened, and I saw the face of my mother."

There are many of you who know what I'm talking about. Do you remember when your eyes were first opened to the possibilities that God had locked up for you? The most beautiful moment in life is when your eyes are opened and you see the face of Jesus. When you became a possibility thinker and stopped being a negative thinker, you discovered the potential of power within yourself. I believe God is going to do something in your life, and you'll see what you have not seen before and will never forget it.

# Mine Your Mind

One Saturday morning I was on a plane flight to Los Angeles and I had to work on my Sunday-morning message. I was not in the mood to communicate with the person who sat next to me—not because I'm unfriendly, but because I have only limited hours left, and nobody else is going to prepare my brain for Sunday morning. My suitcase was open; one of my books was there; and my picture was on the back of the jacket. The man who sat next to me saw it, looked at me, and interrupted my solitude, saying, "Are you an author?" I said, "Yes." He said, "So am I." Then he asked, "What do you write about?" I said, "Possibility thinking. What do you write about?" He answered, "Applied mathematics." I hoped he wouldn't pursue the conversation. Then I had a revelation: "You know, I write about impossibility and possibility thinkers. Obviously possibility thinking doesn't apply in mathematics. I mean, two plus two equals four, and four plus four equals eight."

And he said, "Doctor Schuller, let me tell you a true story: I was a graduate at Berkeley thirty years ago. I came to class late and copied what I believed to be the homework: two problems that were written on the blackboard. Later I said to my professor, 'I haven't been able to solve the homework problems yet, can I have a little more time?' He said, 'Sure, George. When you do, put it on my desk.

"In due time I did solve them and turned the homework in. Several weeks later, one Sunday morning, there was a great pounding at my door; it was my professor. He was all excited, for it turned out what I mistook for homework were two famous unsolved problems of mathematical statistics.

"Now, Dr. Schuller, do you suppose I would have solved these two problems if I knew that they were two well-known unsolved problems?"

What keeps the average person from mining his mind and

discovering this power God put in it? I can tell you, it is pre-conceived, prejudicial, negative information that's put into us. We think it's impossible. The most dangerous person on planet earth is the negative-thinking expert. Because he's an expert in his field, nobody challenges him. Therefore you accept it as fact. You spend your life believing the lowest, instead of beginning to believe the possible.

## Test Your Possibility Thinking

Let me ask you a question: Are you a possibility thinker or an impossibility thinker? Here's a test: Tonight the sun will set at approximately 7:30. Suppose it's a beautiful sunset—red, green, purple, blue, orange, and yellow—until twilight and darkness comes and the lights twinkle. Somebody says, "Did you see the sunset?" And you say, "No, I missed it." Is it possible to have a replay? Is it possible to catch the sunset once you've missed it? The answer is no. *Agree?* Wait a minute!

When we left Paris, Mrs. Schuller and I had to get to Honolulu, where I had to deliver the major address to an eight-thousand-member convention. People told me it was impossible to leave Paris and still get to Honolulu on time. There just aren't planes to get you there that fast. Suddenly somebody said, "You can make it if you fly the *Concorde*." So, Mrs. Schuller and I booked ourselves on the *Concorde*. It was 8:00 P.M when we were to take off. I was excited because the sun was setting at 9:05 P.M., and I expected it would be glorious to catch the sunset at sixty thousand feet in the air. I was told you could see the curvature of the earth at that altitude.

During the takeoff I made this exciting discovery: I can understand Greek, Hebrew, English, and Dutch, but I didn't know I could understand French. As we were powering down the runway, suddenly there was a screech of brakes, smell of rubber, and a Frenchman rattled something off that I understood. He said, *"Le problem,"* and I knew we had a problem. We went back to the gate and we waited. The sun was dropping lower and lower. Finally at 8:45 the sun was horizontal in its beams. We waited until 10:00 P.M. By now it was very dark. We went back with the lights on in the plane, we took off down the runway, and suddenly we were up in the air. It was an exciting, steep, vertical ascent, like a missile. The flight attendant told us that the screen in the front of the fuselage was not a television screen, but we would see a digital dial and the numbers would register our speed. Suddenly, it was 45, 50, 90, 98, 100—meaning Mach 1—then 1, 2, 3, 4, 5, 6, 7 . . . 198, 199, Mach 2. We were now going over 1,400 miles per hour. Then, out of the blackened window, I could see from the west the horizon. Where moments before it was black, it had now turned gold, then orange, and then streaks of pink, purple, red, and blue. And then it happened—sunrise in the west! The sun began to climb. We literally were catching up with the sunset that we had missed! The whole sun was up in the sky sending its late afternoon sunlight into the fuselage. The flight attendant came to me and said, "Doctor Schuller, the pilot would like to invite you to the cockpit." As I went into the cockpit, we were going Mach 2.4. And the cockpit was bathed in golden sunlight.

Today I can tell you it's possible to have a replay of the sunset if you've missed it, given the right circumstances and conditions. A year ago, I would have told you it's impossible. What is my point? My point is: What may be impossible today, may be possible tomorrow.

# R. G. LeTourneau

Robert G. LeTourneau was probably one of the great geniuses of our time and a great Christian. He had the subcontractor's job for the Hoover Dam. He had underestimated, because he ran into deep, solid rock and the cost for fulfilling his commitment bankrupted him. In deep despair he turned to God and became a believer. Napoleon Hill traveled with him for one and a half years and tells this story: "One night when LeTourneau finished his lecture, he and I went into his private plane. The pilot took off, and LeTourneau sat on one side and I sat on the other. It wasn't long before LeTourneau was praying silently, and in his prayers he fell asleep. He was a huge bulk of a man and he was sleeping deeply." Napoleon Hill said, "I've seen people walk in their sleep before, but I've never seen anything like this.

"In his sleep, LeTourneau reached in his pocket, pulled out a notebook and a pencil, wrote something in the notebook, and put it back in his pocket without opening his eyes. When we landed and he awoke, I said, 'Mr. LeTourneau, do you remember writing in the notebook?' He said no. He quickly reached into his pocket, pulled out his notebook, and was shocked to see what he had written. He said, 'That's the answer I've been searching for! That's the solution to the problem! The invention is now complete!' " And he built his huge earth-moving equipment, and that's how the breakthrough came to him.

Mine your mind. Get in touch with God. He made your mind and He can tell you how to mine it! When He does, look out!

## Mom's Hot Apple Pie

My mother was a remarkable woman, and the most powerful encourager in my lifetime. She was also my favorite cook and my chief critic. She was married for fifty-three years to my father, a simple Iowa farmer. And many times she probably felt she led an obscure and unimportant life. Often she failed to see the significance of her human existence. The most important accomplishments of her life were to raise her five children, take care of her husband, and find pride in one special talent—baking apple pies. (That talent plagued me with a weight problem for many years, and I no longer eat apple pies!)

Twelve years ago, I received a phone call. "Bob," said the strained voice on the other end of the line, "your mother is very sick." I immediately boarded the first available plane and flew to northwest Iowa. But before the plane touched down in Sioux Falls, my mother had already passed away. I talked to the pastor who was with her shortly before she died. He shared with me her final request: "Read Isaiah forty-three, verses one through four," she said, "Fear not. . . ." "Yes," her pastor replied, "I know the passage: Fear not. For when you go through the waters, they will not over-flow you. When you go through the fire, it will not consume you. For I am your God. I have redeemed you. I know your name; you are mine. I will be with you." And she was com-forted.

Recently I received a simple little letter postmarked IOWA, and inside was a check for $68,400.00—the second-largest unsolicited check we'd ever received. I called the lady to make sure that we should accept this donation, because the shaky handwriting was obviously that of an older woman. We didn't want to leave someone destitute. When I got her on the phone, it quickly became apparent that she possessed a keen mind. We had a very exciting conversation. "You know," I said, "I'm from Iowa. I grew up in a little town you probably never heard of; it's called 'Alton'." "I know," she replied, "I was born in Alton." "You were born in Alton?" I asked in astonishment. "Yes," she said, "As a young girl, I left to become a schoolteacher. When I started teaching, I began a little savings account and put some of each week's salary into that savings. Now I'm getting on in years and I'm alone; I never married. I've got a wonderful, tiny little house—I call it my dream house. It doesn't cost anything to keep it up.

"And you know," she continued, "I suddenly thought about the savings account. I hadn't looked at it for years. When I checked up on it, I discovered it had grown these many years to $68,400.00—just out of a schoolteacher's salary. Isn't that incredible?" "It sure is!" I exclaimed. "Since I don't have a family or anyone close," she explained, "I've decided I want to give this money to the Crystal Cathedral."

"You say you were born in Alton," I interjected. "Did you ever know, by any chance, my mother, Jenny Beltman Schuller?" "Oh, I sure did," she replied. "I'll never forget her. In fact, I'm so grateful to her. One time my sister got sick, and your mother came over and gave her an apple pie."

When God delivers us from evil, He turns us into beautiful people. He gives us a calling; maybe it's making apple pies or giving gifts of money, love, or services. But remember, any fool can count the seeds in an apple, but only God can count the apples in a seed. If you ask God to save you, He'll save you for eternity. And He'll use you in ways you won't even know about. Believe me, God will do something wonderful with the life you give to Him!

# A Boost From Pope John Paul II

When I was in Rome, one of my most wonderful experiences was watching Pope John Paul II receive his audiences. Thirty thousand people from all over the world—Japan, South America, England, Ireland, Italy, America, and Poland were assembled in Saint Peter's Square. A fence separated the masses from the pope as he sat on his throne with secretaries on either side. To his right were the cardinals, some visiting bishops and a few chairs for a small number of honored persons, among whom I was included.

Since I was sitting in the front row about fourteen feet from the Holy Father, I was able to observe his face and eyes very clearly as he received his audiences.

Finally the group from Poland was recognized. The pope looked at them and smiled as he read something to them in Polish. The secretary was about to announce another group, thus signifying the end of the audience. But the Polish group was not about to be cut off. Without invitation or approval, they began to sing a song—their national anthem.

For the first time during the entire one and a half hours the pope was receiving people, he dropped his head—I suspect, to hide his tears. What must he have been thinking? Was he remembering his ties to Poland, his homeland? Or was he reminding himself of his new loyalties to his own state, the Vatican? Whatever he was thinking, it was clear that he was deeply moved. For halfway through the anthem he raised his head and sang the rest of the song with his countrymen. I must admit, a tear or two rolled out of my eyes. He showed his loyalty to his roots. He gave his own people the boost they needed.

# The Parthenon

I remember the first time I saw the Parthenon in Athens. I've always considered it one of the most beautiful works of architecture in the world. When I stood looking at the smooth, white marble columns, however, I had the most sickening feeling. There, in one of the columns, was a rusty old bridge spike, about eight inches long, wedged into a crack. It was ghastly. "Who did that?" I asked my guide, as I pointed to the spike. "Some vandal?" "Oh, no," he replied, "that was driven in there when the barbarians took over. They hammered nails into the columns and hung ropes between them. That's where they dried their laundry."

A truly beautiful person helps us become sensitive to the

wonders around us. He helps us appreciate our own potential and encourages us to become all that we can be. He enables us to worship God in the beauty of holiness by helping us to become whole and complete ourselves.

# Give It All You've Got

Not long ago I checked into a hotel back East. It was late in the evening, and the lobby was empty except for the desk clerk. I checked in and began to unpack quickly, so I could get some rest. As I reached for my toothbrush, I realized that I had forgotten to pack my toothpaste. "Well, no problem," I thought to myself. "There's a dispenser down the hall." So I walked down the hall and stood before the machine studying the contents. Enclosed behind the glass were all kinds of goodies—razor blades, pocketbooks, combs, and little tubes of toothpaste! All I had to do was insert two quarters into the slot and my problem would be solved. I had no change, so I went to the desk and got four quarters. When I returned to the dispenser I dropped in the first quarter . . . *cling*. Then I inserted the second quarter . . . *cling*. I pushed the red button below the tube of toothpaste and waited. Nothing happened! It didn't work! So I pressed the coin lever, and my quarters returned.

*Okay,* I thought, *let's give it another try.* I dropped the first quarter in . . . *cling*. Then the second quarter . . . *cling*. (I even used the other two quarters for good luck!) I pushed the button—again nothing happened! Still no toothpaste! I paused for a moment staring at all the things behind that glass—just out of my reach. "Think positive," I said aloud. So I pressed the button again. Nothing!

A little frustrated at this point, I pushed the coin-return lever, recovered my quarters and stood in front of that stubborn machine. It had what I needed but it wouldn't release what it had to offer! I was willing to cooperate. I had a positive attitude toward it. I was willing to pay the price, but it just would not release the valuable contents it held within.

Some of you are like that dispensing machine. Deep within yourself, you have a lot to give, but you don't know how to give it. You have a lot to offer, but something keeps you tied up—feeling timid, shy, retiring, bashful, and inferior. I challenge you to begin to believe that you have something beautiful and positive to give—it's stored up inside of you.

# You're Never Too Old

One day I read about a remarkable woman named Eula Weaver. Her picture was in the newspaper and she was in her jogging suit! Now that's not so unusual, except that this woman is eighty-eight years old. Now, what would happen if you were seventy-seven years old and were paralyzed? What thoughts would be going through your head? Perhaps: *Well, this is it, I'm at the age when people die.* Or, *It must be God's will for me to pack up. I'm only three years short of eighty. This is it!*

Not Eula Weaver! She had a stroke at seventy-seven years of age and was paralyzed, but she didn't give up. "I could hardly walk at all," she said. "Doctors gave me two choices. One, to spend the rest of my life as an invalid; or two, get out of bed and start walking—no matter how much it hurt!" That's when she decided to get out and start walking. And today, eleven years later, and two years short of ninety, she's running a mile every day.

# Montezuma's Treasure

Down in old Mexico, they jailed a peasant who had lived in a tar-paper shack but had recently built a cinderblock house on the beach for his wife and children. Everyone wondered where he got the money. They checked it out and found that he had sold two gold bars to a jeweler. The jeweler had paid him fifty-eight hundred dollars for these two twenty-four-carat gold bars. They had an actual market value of over one-half million dollars! More of the story began to unfold as they checked out the gold bars, until finally the chief archeologists in Mexico affirmed that these two gold bars are part of Montezuma's lost treasure. Now some of you may know that the greatest lost, undiscovered treasure today on planet earth is Montezuma's gold. At the end of the sixteenth century, this Aztec ruler (who had acquired the greatest amassed fortune in gold bars in any civilization) saw his fall coming—and indeed, his empire was abolished by Cortez. Now what we don't know is what happened to Montezuma's gold. But suddenly a peasant had found a few of the gold bars. Does this mean now that we're close to discovering the whole treasure?

I'm not suggesting you go look for Montezuma's treasure. What I am suggesting is this: The greatest discovery yet to be made is the discovery of the opportunities that you have in living—the undeveloped, nonactualized potential within you that waits to be discovered like a lost treasure.

# The Devil's Plan

*I will not quit!* I say to you that these four words are God's antidote to man's biggest emotional problem. And what is that? Man's biggest emotional problem is *discouragement.*

A purely mythological and legendary story has been created to prove this point. It was fabricated to tell a very authentic illustration. When Satan got all his cohorts together and saw that the Christians were doing a lot of good in this world, and that Jesus did make a lot of difference, he said, "Look, we've got a problem. Jesus Christ has created a big problem for us. What are we going to do?" One of the devil's cohorts said, "I've got a good idea. We'll get into the brains of all the Christian men and women and we'll fill them with lust. That will really knock them out." They had a big discussion, but they couldn't make a decision. Another devil said, "No, that isn't going to work because these Christians love each other. And people who really know how to love never give in to lust. People who are used to quality are never going to buy something that cheap. That won't work."

Then another devil came up with this idea: "Let's get all these Christians so filled with selfishness that we'll tell them to love money, and they'll be so hung up on money that they'll go to hell." They talked about it and decided it was a great idea to appeal to the materialistic instincts. They thought about it a little more and Satan said, "I don't think it will work. These Christians will just go out and make all the money they can, and then they'll give away all they can. That's what's going to happen. If you get them thinking about money, they won't be against it. They'll be for it. They'll make a lot and give it away, and the movement will spread because they feed it. That's a lousy idea."

Finally one little devil came up with the best idea. "Let's fill them with discouragement! If we get them discouraged, we'll just get them thinking and looking at all the rest of the deviltry and sin going on in the world. They'll look at all the people who don't follow Jesus. We'll get them discouraged. If we get them discouraged, we've got it made. Because if we get them discouraged, they'll become cynical. When they become cynical, they won't believe in hope anymore. And when they don't believe in hope, they will be despairing.

And once they're despairing, they'll be defeated." And all the chorus of devils applauded and said, "That's the key. *Discouragement* is of the devil!"

I WILL NOT QUIT! is in the heart of every winner. And if you could look into the heart of a defeated person, you will find the words *I quit.* Great people are common people committed to uncommon goals.

## You're Twice My Boat

Once there was a little boy who made a sailboat. He carefully carved it; sanded it; painted it; and made a beautiful sail. When he finished it, he couldn't wait to see if it would sail, so he took it down to the lake. He found a nice grassy spot by the edge of the water, got down on all fours and gently set the boat in the water. Then he blew a little puff of air and waited. The boat didn't move. So he blew a little harder, until the wind caught the sail and the boat started moving. "It sails! It sails!" he cried out, clapping his hands and dancing along the side of the lake. But then he stopped. He realized that he had forgotten to tie a string onto the end of the boat. He watched it going farther and farther away, until it was out of his reach.

The little boy was both happy and sad. He was thrilled that it sailed, but saddened because it was now out of his reach. He ran home crying.

Sometime later he was wandering through town, when he passed a toy store that sold both new and old toys. And there in the window was his boat! He was ecstatic! He ran in and said, "That's my boat! That's my boat!" The shop owner looked down at the little boy and said, "I'm sorry, I bought the boat. It is for sale, though." "But it's my boat," the boy cried out. "I made it, I sailed it. I lost it! It's mine!" "I'm sorry, the shop owner exclaimed, "I bought it. If you want to buy it, you may have it." "How much is it?" the lad asked.

And when he found out how much it was, he went home very sad.

But this little boy was very determined. When he got home he went to his room and counted his pennies, nickels, dimes, and quarters. He still needed a little more money before he could buy back his precious boat. So he worked and saved, until finally he had just the right amount. He ran back to the store, hoping the boat would still be there. There it was sitting in the window, just as before.

He ran into the shop, dug into his pockets, and placed all of his money onto the counter. "I want to buy my boat," he enthused. The shopkeeper lifted the little sailboat out of the window and placed it into the excited boy's hands. He grasped the boat, holding it tightly to his chest, and ran home proudly, saying, "You are my boat. You are my boat! You're twice my boat. First, you are my boat because I made you; and second, you are my boat because I bought you!"

If you were the boat, you would know that you were loved. It's a choice, not a chance. The news I have, my friend, is this: You are that sailboat! Jesus Christ is the little boy. And the cross is the price! You are God's child twice over. First you were God's child because He made you; and second, you are God's child because He bought you on the cross of Calvary!

# Prosperity Through Possibility Thinking

As I've mentioned before, these days I'm raising fish. Actually I have been for some years. I raise Japanese carp known as koi fish. Several years ago I bought a bunch of little teeny ones for three dollars apiece. Since then, they've grown and reproduced. Today I have a few hundred of these beautiful Japanese koi fish. They're friends of mine, each with a distinct personality. Some are nice; some aren't so nice. In a way, my fish remind me of people.

If I sit at the edge of the pond and watch a leaf fall into the water, I notice that most of the fish will scatter and flee in all directions, as the leaf hits the surface. But there are a few—only a few—who will not flee to hiding places when something hits the water's surface. They are the big fish who make a slow curve around the new object, inspecting it carefully and cautiously. They know that what they find might not be an enemy, but might, in fact, be food.

These are the fish who always find the food. That's why they're the big fish. Frightened fish stay skinny. And a frightened society will soon become an impoverished society. Productivity will stop, and the inevitable conditions of recession and inflation will degenerate into economic depression. There is nothing we need more in the United States today than *possibility thinking.* Possibility thinking works wonders because people dare to take some risks on the odds that if they make it, they can do a lot of good for a lot of people.

## "We Call Him Schuller"

We live on a few acres in what was "the country" when we bought it several years ago. During the time I've spent in our home there, I've enjoyed many hobbies. I have several ponds on my property and so, at one point I decided to buy some ducks. Unfortunately the ducks flew south for the winter and never returned. Then I bought three beautiful snow-white geese. They were gorgeous creatures, but also messy and disagreeable in temperament. Two of them came to an untimely end when they decided to tangle with the dogs and lost. That left one beautiful white goose. About a year ago, I decided to give him to an electrician who did some work on our house. He took the goose to his ranch home. Just the other day the man came back to visit and showed me a picture of the goose. "Boy is he big!" I exclaimed when he showed me the picture. "He sure is," the man replied. "He dominates the farm. He runs all over the place, flapping his wings, and honking incessantly. We call him 'Schuller'."

## Make the Ending Glorious

When I was a little boy, I studied piano, and my mother was my teacher. When it came time for a recital, my mother made me go over the conclusion again and again. I had to get it down perfect! "Keep on practicing the conclusion, Bob. Learn those last measures!" she used to say. "Look, Bob, you can make a mistake in the beginning; or you can make a mistake in the middle; the people will forget it—if you make the ending glorious!"

*Make the ending glorious!* I don't know what kind of childhood you had. I don't know what kind of life you had. I don't know where you are now! But where you are now, Jesus is present. Take Him into your life now, and I can tell you the ending will be *glorious!*

# How to Be an Extraordinary Person in an Ordinary World

*It is an honor for me to be able to dedicate this book
to the most extraordinary person I know:
my wife, Donna Michelle Schuller.
Without her this book would not exist.*

# Contents

# Introduction by
# Robert A. Schuller

What has the charm or the power of a story? For a child, the world is created anew every time he hears those magic words, "Once upon a time. . . ." And adults? How many of us live vicariously, even model ourselves and our attitudes on "Dallas" or "Dynasty" or the personal stories on the "Hour of Power"? Stories aren't neutral. In a very real sense the stories we choose become the stories we live.

I was a privileged child: there were good stories in our house, stories of adventure and excitement. Some of my fondest memories are of my father holding me in his lap just before bedtime while he read the Bible to me and my sisters or told us stories about people he knew—real people who overcame great odds, did good works, or just took the little gray corner of their world and painted it with the glorious color of love for all the people around them.

My father's stories did more than excite us. They motivated us at a deep and profound level. They showed us that there is no ordinary world if you have the grace to see that God is in it. And there are no ordinary people . . . each and every one of us is extraordinary because God made us. (And, as that child says in a wonderful little story my father often tells, "God don't make no junk!")

Robert H. Schuller is an extraordinary man. Not because he's the pastor of the Crystal Cathedral, or the author of best-selling books, or seen nationally on the "Hour of Power." He's extraordinary because he's grasped this simple truth: Jesus Christ taught in stories and parables . . . and He must have had a good reason. Stories stick with you. They stuck with me. What I have learned of love, generosity, honesty, and the love of God I learned from my father, and the stories he told. The life he lives exemplifies those stories.

The people you will meet in this book are life changers. They are heroic men and women who took their defeats, infirmities, disasters, and depressions and turned them into works for the Lord. They changed their lives for the better, and their stories will change your life if you allow yourself to believe and adopt their powerful remedies for "ordinary human existence."

Here they are as my father has captured their extraordinary character and spirit in story:

Let Penny Cotton show you how to overcome illness.

Learn from Katherine Grant's unique ministry.

Live the experience of Allen Phillips, whose life was spared through his faith.

Love the world around you like Sara and Norm Rasmussen and watch it respond, grow, and be transformed.

Let these people show you that you too can Be an Extraordinary Person in an Ordinary World.

# EXTRAORDINARY EXAMPLE

# How to Handle Your Foes: Keep On Shining!

A judge was campaigning for reelection. He had a reputation for integrity. He was a distinguished and honorable gentleman of no small charity. His opponent was conducting a vicious, mud-smearing, unfair campaign against him.

Somebody approached the judge and asked, "Do you know what your opponent is saying about you? Do you know he is criticizing you? How are you going to handle it? What are you going to do about it?" The judge looked at his counselors and his campaign committee and calmly replied, "Well, when I was a boy I had a dog. And every time the moon was full, that hound dog would howl and bark at the bright face of the moon. We never did sleep very well those nights. He would bark and howl at the moon all night." With that, the judge concluded his remarks.

"That's beside the point," his campaign manager impatiently said. "You've told us a nice story about your dog, but what are you going to do about your critic?"

The judge explained, "I just answered you! When the dog barked at the moon, the moon kept right on shining! I don't intend to do anything but keep right on shining. And I'll ignore the criticism, as the moon ignored the dog. I'll just keep right on shining! Quietly, calmly, beautifully!"

Remember that! It might give you courage to sail—to strive for the top and not worry about what people say whether you succeed or you fail.

# Called to Greatness

Recently I was in the Hawaiian Islands. I stopped at the Punch Bowl and looked at those acres and acres of little white crosses where the best and the bravest were buried. And I thought of this: Why did they step forward? Why did they say yes? Why did so many of them volunteer? Why did they not resist the draft? Why did they put the uniform on and wear it proudly? Why wasn't there a mass protest against the war? Why didn't we just say, "We're our own country here. Nobody's burning people in ovens in America. And sure, they dropped a bomb on Pearl Harbor, but that's three thousand miles away. Just let them have the island." Nobody said that. Why not? Why did the Americans rise up? What motivated them? What spark was ignited within them?

I think I know part of that answer. I was born and raised in Iowa and every Sunday morning we went to the little country church. And what I'm about to tell you is indicative of the social structure of the United States in the '20s, '30s, and '40s.

At that time everyone regularly attended church. And in the two hundred to three hundred thousand little churches all over the United States, fathers and mothers went to church and dedicated their children to the Lord. In that dedication the parents would pray that God would take the little child and make him do something beautiful for God, become a Christian, and maybe even go into the Lord's service. The greatest honor that could come to a father and mother would be if their child grew up and said, "Dad, I want to be a missionary. I want to become a doctor and build a hospital in Japan or Arabia or India."

Let me tell you, in the '20s, the '30s, and the '40s our heroes were called missionaries. And when they finally got through college, seminary, and medical school, they packed their bags and set off for the remote parts of the world before there was penicillin. The odds were that they might die of a tropical disease. They knew that.

Why did they go? They had a call—a call to greatness. It was the same for the many men who went to battle in World War II. They had a call to greatness. And after being at the Punch Bowl I have a message for all people: Do not pity the person who was killed in war. Rather, pity the person who's alive but doesn't have anything he'd die for, for the person who's never had a call to greatness. Greatness starts when you become aware of your mortality, when suddenly it dawns on you that you're going to die. You don't know when, and you don't know how, but the fact is—you're not immortal. With that consciousness comes a thought like this: *I want to make a mark—somehow, someway, somewhere."* Greatness comes when you are consumed by a call to make a commitment that may mean your very life.

No person is truly alive or totally human until he makes a commitment to something that he will gladly die for. That is a chariot of fire. It lifts you above the earth. It transcends the flesh and brings you into the realm of the spirit. Don't feel sorry for those who are buried under white crosses. Feel sorry for those who are alive and have nothing today that they would gladly die for.

# A Very Bad Impression

A bus driver in Chicago had a female passenger who was really irritated by something. She let loose with a string of unrepeatable words. Everybody was ashamed. And then the bus stopped, the profane passenger got ready to disembark, and the bus driver said, "Madam, you left something behind." She asked him what it was and he said, "A very bad impression."

# One Day in Seven

One day in seven. Now let's take this commandment. The Sabbath day. The Moslems set a day aside. It's Friday. The Jewish people set a day aside. It is Saturday. Most Christians set a day aside. It is the first day of the week, to commemorate the Resurrection of Jesus Christ. You need one day in seven. It is not an ordinary day if you know how to use it. I'll share with you how to use it, because Americans have given it up for the most part.

Traditionally, Sunday was a very great creative day of quietness for faith, for fun, for the family, for the church, and for the community. Something happened—and I make this statement here and now based on research that I have done—and that is, in the past fifty years we have seen a growing, deepening sense of depression in the widespread epidemic of emotional ailments such as anxiety and stress, with its effect upon the human organism. This emotional epidemic of negative, mental, and spiritual problems in our country has risen sharply in proportion to our forsaking of that one day in seven as a useful day for healing.

How can you use it? It's not an ordinary day if you know how to use it. Use it as a day of *rest*. You need one day in seven to rest the heart, the system, and the body. The Bible says, "In quietness and confidence shall be your strength" (*see* Isaiah 30:15). I try to work hard but I take Mondays off. My Sabbath, as you might expect, is not Sunday, and it's not the Jewish Saturday, and it's not the Moslem Friday. My Sabbath is Monday. I do not go into my office on that day, because if I can't get my work done in six days, I'm disorganized. Simple. And I would rather live longer and do more than try to accomplish a lot in a few years and die too young. We need one day. Use it for rest. And then use it for a day of retreat. Retreat from the tension-producing inputs that you have to be exposed to the rest of the week.

I'm eternally, profoundly indebted to Richard Neutra for the doctrine of biorealism. I never learned it in theology. But it's embedded in psychology and profound theology. His doctrine of biorealism is that the human being is created with a built-in tranquilizing system, with eyes to see the trees and the hills and colors of the flowers; ears to hear the singing of the birds and listen to the rustle of the leaves and the whisper of the wind; the nose to smell the fragrance of the flowers and the new-mown grass; the skin to feel the caress of the sun and cool breezes. It's a biological reality, and the biological reality is that God created this in order for these to be channels of tranquillity entering your system.

And so when God created Adam, he put him in a beautiful lush, green garden filled with the exotic fragrance of wild flowers and the melody of singing birds, not in an ugly parking lot where his senses would be assaulted by the wailing of sirens and the exhaust fumes from cars and buses. And that's why when you are in the mountains, you feel the closeness with God. Of course, the bird was designed to fly, the fish was meant to swim, and you were designed to live in a garden. You were not designed to live in a concrete jungle.

So Richard Neutra said, "What can we do? We can't demolish our cities and bulldoze all the asphalt. We need the cars and we need the buses. What can we do? We have to design for emotional survival." You bet! So we design places where you can hear the birds sing, where you can look out and see the clouds drifting through the sky. And we try to create a garden retreat from the tension-producing sounds and sights of the world. That's why we need one day in seven. Now many of you live in cities. You don't live in a house. You don't live in a place where you're protected from those sights, so what do you do? I've got news for you. You go to church on Sunday. That's right! And that's why many churches are designed with stained-glass windows and solid walls. Because without them you'd look out on a parking lot with electric power poles. But in those beautiful retreat places called churches, the sounds and sights that would fill you with negative emotional tensions are released and the stress goes.

So it is in our family. Let me say something: We have a great family—I mean my wife and me and our five children. We have always kept Sunday as a day to rest; as a day to retreat—to retreat from the normal pressures of the week. I remember when our oldest daughter, Sheila, was about four years old, and her neighborhood playmate came to the house one Sunday asking if Sheila could come out and play. I wasn't prepared for that, and I said, "No, not today, but she can play tomorrow and the next day and every day the rest of the week, but not on Sunday." I wanted that one day completely different so that she was exposed to just the family and friends in the church—retreat. Let it be a day of rest. Let it be a day of retreat. Let it be a day to regroup. I mean regroup your thinking and get your act together.

# The Introduction

I was in New Orleans to participate in the City Prayer Breakfast. It was a great, big, exciting event. The mayor of New Orleans was there along with twelve hundred other people. I had the honor of delivering the prayer-breakfast talk. Only minutes before I was to speak I got word that Jesse Jackson had decided to attend. He had flown in from Los Angeles, and would be arriving any minute. Suddenly, I saw him enter. When he made his entrance, everybody knew he was in the room.

Although I have been friends with Jesse for many years, his presence created a problem for me. I had been carefully briefed on protocol as to whom I should recognize by name before I started my speech. I had the introductions of the mayor, the senators, and the archbishops, all written out. But I did not have an introduction for Jesse Jackson. How could I recognize Jesse without appearing to personally endorse his candidacy?

When it was time for me to speak, I made a little announcement. I said, "Does anybody have a copy of the book *Tough Times Never Last, But Tough People Do?* Surely, someone came here this morning carrying a copy of that book. Would you please give it to me?" Some generous person in the crowd came up and handed me a copy of the book. With the book in my hand, I said, "Jesse Jackson, stand up!"

Jesse stood, and I said, "I've got a book for you. You are going to need it." I handed him the book and said, "Anybody who runs for president from any party is going to go through tough times."

Jesse took the book and accepted the gesture of friendship in the spirit in which it was intended. He laughed with everyone else, for he knew it was true—anyone running for president would be subject to tough times. They would have to face criticism, distortions, misinterpretations, and accusations. I tell you, many of the best people never run for political office because they don't want to go through the toughness of the campaign.

# Think of All You Know

I have a grandson, Jason. Now with all modesty, I have to say Jason is a gifted, exceptional child. Yet when he was six months old, he couldn't do much. He couldn't take a spoon in his hand and dip it in a bowl of cereal, aim it at his mouth and hit it. He couldn't say "grandpa" or even his own name. He couldn't hold a pencil or control the movement of his own tiny fingers. He didn't know the difference between red and blue, and furthermore, he couldn't stand on his own two feet.

So if you find me an independent human being who has learned to stand on his own, speak proper sentences, button buttons and zip zippers, and write real letters, then you have found someone who is a borderline genius. Stop and realize all you have already learned in your lifetime. With so much going for you, you can do anything you set your mind to do. You are a brilliant human being. Some of the biggest goals you now have, along with the biggest problems you need to solve, are nothing compared to what you have already accomplished.

# A Loss of Dignity

One day my wife and I were invited out to breakfast. It was held in a beautiful dining room. We were very impressed with the restaurant, and then we noticed a distinguished gentleman who came and sat in the booth next to us. He was elegantly dressed. His choice of clothes, shirt, tie, and hairstyle made him stand out as an impeccable gentleman. He was barely seated when he uttered a sentence that included about five words which I can only describe as the kind of language even an angry farmer wouldn't use in his barnyard. His style of dress and his bearing contradicted the words that came from his mouth. Suddenly the perspective we had of the gentleman was completely changed. He demeaned himself. He robbed himself of all dignity. When he first made an entrance into the dining room, he attracted attention because of a nobility in his bearing, an elegance in his manner. He wiped out all of his gain in one sweeping, careless, crude sentence. Words are powerful things, and you can't play lightly with them.

# Ever Changing

I learned something interesting from Richard Neutra, one of the great architects of our century. When we retained him to build our first church building he said, "You know, one of the problems with buildings is, buildings are things, and things go out of style. Why? Because they don't grow, they don't change. They are static and people are bored with them.

"But," he added, "I have a solution to that problem. Dr. Schuller, people will never get bored with the buildings I'll build for you, because they'll see right through them. They'll see the sky and the trees. Some days, when they look out, the sky will be a drab gray. On other days, it'll be a bright blue, and some days it will be awash with splashes of white clouds. If they come in the nighttime, they may see a star or the moon. The building will be dynamic, exciting, and always changing."

# A Great Attitude

Jesus Christ was the most positive Person who ever lived. Nothing is greater than meeting positive people. One summer I was in China and I met a vivacious eighty-three-year-old lady from Arkansas. She was a charming, delightful, positive person. I commented on how enthusiastic she was. "Oh, yes, Dr. Schuller," she said. "Ever since I began watching 'Hour of Power,' I've become so positive. You should know that at my age I have four boyfriends." She continued, "I begin my day with 'Will Power,' then I take a walk with 'Arthur Ritis,' come back with 'Charlie Horse,' and I spend my evening with 'Ben Gay.' " Now that's what I call positive thinking!

# The Innermost Sanctum

Recently it was my joy to be invited to the home of Gregory Peck in Los Angeles, because Mr. Peck was doing the narration for the Glory of Easter which was to be staged in the Crystal Cathedral. Mr. Peck has always been my favorite actor. He is so elegant, so intelligent, so suave, charming, very honest, and kind.

Well, I had never been to his home before and like many of the homes in Bel Air or Beverly Hills, it's a marvelous place. Since it is hidden behind steel fences and steel gates, you can get only a glimpse of the house from the road. We announced our arrival, the gates swung open, we were admitted, and there was the beautiful house. We entered into the lovely home and were led into the living room. From there you could overlook the garden and the lawn.

I could have left that place and said that I was in Gregory Peck's private place. But I would have made a mistake. I was only in the living room—the front room of the main house.

It is at that level, however, that many of you people probably judge this ministry and the message that we're trying to get across. If you see the possibility thinking, that's only part of it. That's like saying, "Oh, I understand what he's trying to say," when you've only been in the living room. That's because possibility thinking is only the centerpiece of the message. The story, the essence of Schuller and what he believes, doesn't end there.

Just before I left Mr. Peck, he said, "Bob, would you like to see where I do my work?"

I said, "Yes, I'd love to!"

As some of you know, Gregory Peck is recording the entire Bible for us. I had assumed he was doing the recording in the studio in Hollywood. Instead, when I asked him about it, he said, "Oh, I do it right here. I have a studio set up in a little log cabin here on my grounds. Let me show it to you."

So, we took a trip through the garden on the four-acre estate. We wound our way down the hillside until we came to a very secure, very secluded, very private ravine. There sits his log cabin. For all the world it is a log cabin like the one that Abraham Lincoln might have lived in. It was one room with very unpretentious furniture.

That's where Gregory Peck does his work. That's where he researches his roles and memorizes his lines, and that's where he is recording the Bible for us. Now that's the innermost sanctum where the work happens.

Today, I want to take you down a narrow little road to the log cabin where Schuller is really at. When you get there, we'll end up in a Bible verse. It is my favorite Bible verse. It is, "By grace are you saved, through faith, and not of yourself. It is a gift of God" (*see* Ephesians 2:8).

# A Very Obvious Contradiction

Life is full of contradictions. Perhaps you have felt like the victim of an injustice. If so, you are not alone. There is much more of that in our society than we'd like to admit. I felt it myself recently. My publisher had sent me on a book tour, which means I had to fly around and meet the press at different points of the country. So it was that I found myself in Miami Beach. Since I was scheduled to be there only one night, I decided to call my friend Eddie Balestero. I called him and said, "Eddie, this is Dr. Schuller. What are you doing tomorrow?"

He said, "Not much, why?"

"Well," I said, "my publisher has rented a Lear Jet to take me from Florida to Washington, D.C., and we've got a couple of empty seats. Have you ever flown in a Lear Jet?"

"No."

"Well, then, why don't you come along with me tomorrow?"

The next day, Eddie and I were about thirty-five thousand feet up in the air in this Lear Jet. I said, "Why don't you give your wife a call?"

So Eddie called his wife. By this time he was having quite an exciting day. We landed at the airport. Waiting for me there was a huge limousine, again at the publisher's expense. Eddie got in the backseat of the limousine. He said, "This is the first time I've ever ridden in a limousine."

It was about noon. I said to the driver, "Louie, can you recommend a good place to have lunch?"

Louie said, "Oh, yes, Dr. Schuller, there's a restaurant I think you'd like. It's private and people won't bother you there."

I said, "Let's give it a try."

The day had been exhilarating until we ran into the snobbish maître d' in the restaurant. I said to him, "I'd like a table for two, please."

"Do you have a reservation?"

"No, but—"

"I'm sorry, we just don't have any space."

Just then I felt a hand on my back and a gusty voice said, "Bob Schuller, how are you?"

It was Fritz Mondale!

I said, "Oh, fine, Mr. Vice President. How are you? Meet my friend Eddie Balestero."

By this time, Eddie's head was spinning. We had a wonderful conversation. The maître d' said, "Your table is ready, Mr. Vice President."

And then he looked at me and said, "Oh, I just noticed that we do have another table."

So Eddie and I had lunch. Contradiction—one moment no tables at all. The next moment, we had a table.

# An Enormous Success

When he was forty-six years of age, Oscar Hammerstein had worked with thirty different composers. Nothing took off. There was no successful song. It was a despairing, dispiriting time for him. Finally, Oscar Hammerstein tied in with Richard Rodgers. The following year they wrote the musical *Oklahoma*. He was a success. In fact his success was so enormous in its impact that he went out and bought a full page ad in *Variety* magazine. To keep himself humble, he bought this headline: "I've done it before and I can do it again!" He then listed every single one of his failures.

# A Fictitious General

I love the story of the man who was very insecure. One day he was promoted from major to colonel and was ushered into his new office. He looked proudly at his new surroundings and sat in the chair. Suddenly there was a knock at the door. He said, "Come in." In walked a corporal. The colonel said, "Just a minute, I have to finish this phone call." He picked up the receiver, pushed the button, and said, "I'm sorry about the interruption, General. Now, where were we? Oh, yes sir, I will take care of it. Of course I will, sir. It's true we are close friends. Yes, I'll call the president immediately after I finish talking with you, General. You're welcome, sir." The colonel ceremoniously put the phone down, turned to the corporal, and asked, "What can I do for you?" He answered, "Well, sir, I just came in to connect your telephone."

# One of My Biggest Mistakes

I attended a tiny country high school in Iowa. I never took geometry. When I started my undergraduate studies at Hope College, Michigan, I discovered that everyone was required to take eight hours of science. Math courses are applicable to that requirement.

Consequently, I was put into a math course. The first week the professor rattled off some statements. He was referring to geometric principles. Because I'd never had geometry, I didn't know what he was talking about. But I noticed that the other students were nodding as if they completely understood. I did as they did, thinking, *I'll pick it up later.* The next week it was the same. I didn't have the foggiest notion what he was talking about, but I pretended that I understood it as clearly as my fellow students did. The truth of the matter showed on my first test. I didn't get a good grade.

My professor approached me and kindly asked, "Are you having problems, Bob?" I said, "Oh, no. I'm doing just fine." That was a lie. If I were completely honest I would have admitted that I had an enormous gap and lack in my precollege work. But I didn't want to admit it because I didn't want him to know how dumb I was. That was one of the biggest mistakes I ever made.

If I had only known what I'm trying to teach you now— that if there is a gap, a lack, or a need, have enough spirit to admit where you are poor—I could have gone to him for help. I could have pulled an *A* instead of a *D*.

# What's Your Need?

I remember years ago, when E. Stanley Jones used to conduct *ashrams,* as he called them. *Ashram* is a term used in India. It means a time of spiritual growth and expansion. Dr. Jones always began his ashrams by passing out pieces of paper with this introduction: "No one will see what you are about to write on this paper. I want you to write what your need is today."

It happened at every ashram. While people were thinking and praying and writing, someone would say, "Brother Stanley, I don't have a need. What do you write down, if you don't have a need?" And Brother Stanley would say, "If you think you don't have a need, then *that's* your need!"

# EXTRAORDINARY
# ATTITUDE

# The Power to Control

Not long ago I had an unforgettable experience. I have a friend who recently bought a new Cessna Citation jet airplane. When he invited me to lunch I jokingly said, "Good, let's go have lunch in Cabo San Lucas."

He took me seriously! So the other morning we left at 6:30 A.M. for Cabo San Lucas, at the tip of Baja California. Now, on Cabo San Lucas, there's the beautiful Finistera Hotel that lies on the ridge between two huge rocks. As we approached our destination, my friend said to his copilot, "Will you trade places with Dr. Schuller?" I must tell you that I am not a pilot. I've never had my hands on the controls of a plane.

My friend said, "Bob, you're a possibility thinker." I said, "Yes."

"Okay, I want you to take the controls of this jet, and in a few minutes you'll fly us right in to Cabo San Lucas. Come in low, and go right between those rocks. Then curve and go over the bay, where we'll dip the wings over the boat waiting for us."

I gulped and said, "Sure, I'd love to do it." I put my hands on the controls and followed his instructions. It was incredibly simple. As easy as putting melted butter on a hot bun, I flew that plane right over the hotel and cleanly between the rocks. It's a tremendous feeling, having the power to control the direction of such a plane.

Similarly, you have the power to control your life and your prosperity. You even have the power to turn your poverty into prosperity. You can get what you really need, and want, if you'll do it God's way.

This morning, I want you to imagine that you are in a jet airplane. You're putting your hands on the controls for the first time, and you're steering this magnificent flying creature. What potential you have!

# Beginning Is Half Done

Some of you may be afraid to begin. You don't think you can finish. You're thinking, *Can I make it all the way to the top?* Here's a great concept: Just decide to begin and then decide to keep going. Don't worry about the top—just decide to keep going past the point of no return. That's all you do. That's the way I do it.

A couple of days ago I knew I had to run. I wanted to run. I knew I should run. But I wasn't in the mood for running the six miles I usually run. My home is six miles from the church, so I got into my running suit and decided, "I'm only going to run halfway from the house to the church." When I got halfway from the house to the church, what could I do? I couldn't hitchhike home. I had to finish; there was no other way.

I use this principle a lot in my life. When I know there is something that I should do but don't want to do the whole thing, I only make the commitment to go as far as the point of no return. Then I'm trapped. I have to complete the job. The key is in deciding to begin.

# A Desire to Succeed

Dear Dr. Schuller,

Last year I made a decision to return to college. I'm thirty-four years old. I have four children. I really doubted my decision because I had been dismissed from another college at the age of nineteen for poor grades. I was especially afraid of algebra, which I had failed flat. But in May of last year, having moved to Texas many years ago, I heard that you were speaking at the American Renewal Series in Dallas. I was once a member of the Garden Grove Community Church and thought your message might give me a lift. Perhaps I could even make a new resolution and follow through if I got motivated. So I drove into Dallas and heard the story you told about the man who failed college and went on to become a doctor who was the attendant of Bobby Kennedy.

Dr. Schuller, I know I was not the only person in that convention center, but that message was for me. I decided that, despite my terrible academic record, I would go back to school. I did, and I completed the year with a 4.0 average, including two algebra classes. That's pretty good for somebody who flunked out of Fullerton fifteen years ago. Thank you, Dr. Schuller.

# Floyd Baker's Faith in Teaching

Floyd Baker, a friend of mine, teaches physics and astronomy at Fullerton College. It was many years ago when Floyd started coming to our church. He began listening to the lectures and messages on positive thinking and self-esteem psychology. As he heard the principles on faith and positive programming, he wondered, *Will this work in my college classroom?* At that time, every year 50 percent of the students who took the Introduction to Physics for Science Majors course at Fullerton College flunked, and consequently, every year in his first lecture he'd say, "I want to be honest with you. This is probably the toughest course you'll ever take. Fifty percent of you will flunk. It happens every year." He was right. Fifty percent of them always flunked.

However, after listening to the messages in our church he decided to try a most audacious experiment. He stood before his incoming class and said, "Students, I have to tell you something. This introductory course in physics is very difficult. In fact, fifty percent of the students have failed this course every year. But I've been checking your records and I'm impressed with you. I am amazed at what an unbelievable class this is. You are all tremendously bright. In fact, I predict that for the first time in the history of this school, all of you will pass. None of you will flunk."

Later he confessed to me that it was terrribly frightening to make such a claim. However, he reported in a paper the following results: "I did not change my testing procedures one bit. And that year, every student in that class passed.

Not one failed. I know I worked harder as a teacher, and the students did also."

I can do all things if . . . I am programmed positively. The Bible calls it faith. We call it possibility thinking. Even Jesus said that you could move mountains, on one condition: you must have faith.

Nobody can begin to understand the power of faith. We don't know how it works, but once you have a positive picture in your mind and you hold it before you, unseen, unmeasurable, and undetectable forces are released. These forces—call them determination if you will—can bring success to anyone who believes. I can do all things if . . . I have the faith. That is the first condition.

# The Best Man for the Job

There once was a king who needed to hire a carriage driver. He decided to test the applicants for the job by asking them to drive the carriage as fast as they could, and as close to the edge of a cliff as they could, without endangering the life of the occupant. He watched as some sped by only three feet away from the cliff. Each applicant, trying to outdo the other, drove closer and closer to the edge. Finally, it was the last man's turn. He surprised everyone by slowly driving down the middle of the road.

When the king made his choice, whom do you think he picked? He chose the man who drove down the middle of the road. Why? When the king asked the last driver, "Why did you drive down the middle of the road?" the carriage driver said, "I believe in staying as far away from danger as possible. That's the way I'll drive if you hire me."

How do you handle life's temptations? Avoid them. Avoid the spills. But what if you've already made one big mistake? You still live above your circumstances and not under them.

# Turn Your Problem Inside Out

A psychiatrist once told me about a counseling session he had had with a certain patient. He said, "After listening to the patient for a long time, I told him, 'I noticed that there are two words you use all the time. Those two words are the cause of your emotional depression. Wipe those two words out of your vocabulary and you'll never have to come to me again. The two words are: *if only.* Wipe them out. They make you sick. In their place substitute these two words: *next time.*' "

Don't curse your hurts. Don't nurse them. Don't rehearse them. Disperse them. How do you disperse them? As Max Cleland, author of *Strong at the Broken Places,* stated, you can disperse your hurts by looking for another open door. When you look for the open doors, your back is to the closed door. And every time one door closes, God opens another one. You disperse your hurt when you reverse it. Reversing it means you turn it inside out. You turn the problem into a partner. You turn the scar into a star. You turn your frustrations into a fruitful experience.

# Consider Tomorrow

Recently, while in New York to deliver a message, I took a cab from downtown Manhattan to Long Island. During the hour-long ride I worked on the message I was to give. I took out my daily itinerary for the three-day visit to the city and began to make notes on the back.

I looked over the notes I'd written. I was dissatisfied with them. In my frustration I tore the page off, threw it down, and started over. I wrote down new thoughts on the next page of my itinerary. My new efforts were better.

When I reached my destination I began to get out of the car. Suddenly I remembered the piece of paper I'd crumpled and thrown on the floor. That paper contained my itinerary for the next day. I said, "Hey, I've got to keep that." As I retrieved my itinerary I added, "I almost threw away part of tomorrow."

# Shoes for Africa

Life is a matter of perspective. Consider, for instance, the story of the two shoe salesmen who were sent to Africa to check into the potential international market there. Like the two spies who returned to Joshua in the Old Testament after reviewing the Promised Land, the salesmen returned to their shoe company with their report. One salesman had a negative report. "There is no market there," he said. "Nobody wears shoes in Africa." The positive salesman reported, "On the contrary, it's a fantastic opportunity—no one has bought shoes yet!"

Life is a matter of perspective and life's perspective is a self-fulfilling prophecy.

# Build a Bigger Island

I've made six trips to Japan in the past fifteen years and on one of those trips I said to a group of pastors, "You need a larger piece of property on which you can build a bigger church."

But they replied, "Dr. Schuller, you don't understand. When you live on an island, you cannot grow." Their answer sounded so profound at the time, but something about it bothered me. Finally I figured out why that statement bothered me. I know from having visited the Netherlands that any country that borders on the ocean is expandable. In Holland, they just built the dyke and siphoned off the water. The ocean was pushed farther back, and today they've got a bigger country without going to war or threatening a neighbor.

Here's what you can learn from this: As a human being, you are an island of consciousness with boundaries of awareness that limit your knowledge and understanding. However, you can move the island until it is bigger.

This business of expanding your consciousness is not an option. Either you are expandable or you are expendable. What do I mean? When you stop growing, you start dying—intellectually, spiritually, emotionally, and professionally.

# Give It Your Best

Dr. Herman Ridder was with me at West Point one day and the cadets were so enthusiastic. They were getting ready to win their five-hundredth game in hockey. Can you imagine? But Dr. Ridder had a marvelous observation. He said, "If you have five hundred straight wins you're in the wrong league."

It's true. If you keep winning, winning, winning, then you're really losing, because you're not facing an adequate opponent.

Some people handle contradictions by simply resisting them. In Birmingham, Alabama, they tell the story about a great football game. The teams were really unequally matched. One was made up of little guys and the other had big guys. It was a scary game for the little guys. As you might guess, they were losing, but miraculously, only by one touchdown. With only a few minutes to go, the coach called them all together. He said to the quarterback, "Loo, we can win this game. We're little, but Calhoun can run faster than anybody. Give the ball to Calhoun."

Back on the field, it was time for the first play. Calhoun did not get the ball. The coach, on the sidelines, was very upset. On play two, Calhoun still didn't get the ball. The game ended. They lost. The coach said, "Why didn't you give the ball to Calhoun?"

The quarterback said, "Calhoun wouldn't take the ball!"

Is your name Calhoun? Mine? Do you look at the big guys, at the mountains, and hope they'll go away if you ignore them?

Perhaps you don't dare to sell your product because you

don't want to be rejected. Are you so afraid of failure that you never try?

Remember, truth is the center of the intersection. The truth is that you won't succeed until you've had a failure. Only then will you know you've given it your best. Really, that's what success is all about.

# "Hit It to Me!"

I don't know anybody who practices possibility thinking better than Tommy Lasorda.

I remember asking him once, "Tommy, how can you constantly keep your enthusiasm up? You lose some, you win some. How do you keep your enthusiasm up? How do you keep ringing the bell, getting a dream again?"

He said, "Oh, I just constantly welcome ideas that challenge the impossible."

I asked, "How do you inspire your guys?"

He said, "Let me give you this illustration: One time we were really doing pretty poorly. I noticed the guys weren't fielding very well. Too many hits were getting by. So I did something we had never done before. I gathered the players together in the locker room and I said to them, 'Let's pretend it's a tight game. We're ahead four to three. It's the last half of the ninth. We're still leading by one run. Bases are loaded. There are two outs. Suddenly a heavy hitter comes to bat. You are all out there in the field. Question: What do you think?' They all said, 'Tommy, we think, *I hope he doesn't hit it to me!*' "

Tommy's reply? "That's the trouble! In a tight spot, you go back out there and you think, *Hey, hit it to me! I want it!*"

# Anything's Possible

Recently I lectured in Seattle, Washington, where I met a fellow who was six feet four inches tall and broad-shouldered. He was grinning from ear to ear and had a lovely wife at his side.

He said, "Dr. Schuller I can't begin to thank you. That stuff you dish out every Sunday really works. I didn't believe in Christianity but my wife did, and she made me watch the 'Hour of Power.' I started watching, then I started listening, and finally the things you were saying really seemed to make sense. To make a long story short, today I'm a Christian!"

Then he said, "That's not all. After I became a Christian, I decided to practice faith—or as you call it—possibility thinking. And I've gotta tell you—it works! You won't believe what it did for me. I had read in the paper here in Seattle that there was going to be a fishing tournament. They tagged a few salmon and whoever caught the tagged salmon would win the jackpot of one million dollars!"

He continued, "Dr. Schuller, I caught the salmon with the tag! However, before the tournament was ended, one other guy caught a tagged fish, so I have to split the million with the other guy. But, I'm getting twenty-five thousand dollars a year for the next twenty years!"

He was so excited. He added, "It would not have happened if I hadn't become a possibility thinker and thought that it might be possible to catch the fish."

# Get Set for a Long Life

Rene Dubos, a great scientist who died not too long ago, said, "The human being has an infinite capacity to adjust downward," to which I replied, "Adjustment is always a downward movement. The upward movement is never an adjustment—it is always a commitment!" That commitment comes through self-esteem, pride, and human worth.

To my knowledge, the last article written by Rene Dubos was in the December issue of *Omni* magazine. It was called "Survival," and in it he said what I'm trying to say. If you lose your pride in being human, you lose your self-esteem. When that happens you'll no longer believe that it's possible to solve the problems. Self-esteem produces possibility thinking. Remove self-dignity and you remove self-confidence. But adopt the faith of your Father's possibility thinking, and then get set for a surprise.

# Take Another Look

A while back I was at Knott's Berry Farm. I hadn't been there for years. They still sell a complete chicken dinner for $6.50. I read the menu and was reminded of their inspiring story. It was during the big depression. Walter Knott, his wife, Cordelia, and their four children could not make ends meet. So Cordelia started making a couple of extra jars of jelly. She'd make extra pies and put them out on a rickety card table by the road. She'd wave down passersby who stopped to buy her wares. This worked so well that she added a couple of pieces of chicken. She put up a sign, offering a chicken dinner for only a couple of dollars.

Through such efforts, Cordelia kept that family together. She turned the depression into a launching pad. Be positive. Take another look. There are always possibilities.

# Play With Your Dream

It's amazing, when you take the attitude of fun, how often you can perform so much better. I was excited when Debbie Armstrong won a gold medal in the 1984 Winter Olympics. I think the secret of her success was her attitude. Kristin Cooper, her teammate, said, "Debbie and I were up at the top and she was laughing and babbling away. She kept saying, 'We're just going to have fun. We're just going to go down that mountain and have fun. You have a good run, Cooper, but just have fun.' And when she stomped out of that chute, I couldn't believe her."

Let's just have fun! In talking about her success later, Debbie said, "I always knew that if I got my head in gear, and just got up there on that mountain and was happy and had fun, I would do well."

I must confess—most of my dreams started out as jokes. There was a time when I said, "We're going to build a new church. Let's just make it a great big glass box." A lot of us laughed about it. Play with your dream. Have fun.

# The Best Way to Start a Day

One morning I was sitting in a restaurant with my wife, having an early-morning cup of coffee, away from home, away from the telephone, where we could put ourselves together and plan our day. An elderly man came and sat in the adjoining booth. The waitress came and poured him coffee. As she poured him his first cup of coffee she said, "That's the best way to start a day, with a good cup of coffee." And he said, "Oh, no, the best way to start a day is not with a good cup of coffee, but the best way to start a day is with a—"

He stopped, smiled, and his eyes twinkled as he said, "The best way to start a day is with a good morning." And I was so proud to observe that he was a member of our church. A Christian is basically positive instead of basically negative. Yes, the best way to start a day is with a good morning!

# "You Really Gave Me a Boost!"

I received a telephone call one morning just before I went into the pulpit. The call was from Vince Evans, quarterback for the Chicago Bears. Vince came to Jesus Christ one Easter morning while watching the "Hour of Power." He called to ask me to pray for him and his team. They were playing one of the most important games of the season. "Dr. Schuller," Vince began, "today we're playing Tampa. Tampa's good. Some say nobody can beat them. I want to do the very best I can. Will you pray with me?"

"Of course I'll pray with you, Vince," I said. And I began by thanking God for the beautiful human bodies He created. I thanked God for Vince's clear mind—a mind that was unpolluted by drugs or chemicals. And I thanked God for the dynamic spirit that was shaping Vince's life. As we came to the close of our prayer together, I prayed, "Oh, Lord, when he takes off the football helmet and steps into the shower, may he have the wonderful feeling that comes with knowing he played straight, honest, and the best he could."

"You really gave me a boost!" Vince said after we prayed. "You know," I answered, "you gave me a boost, too!" "I did?" he asked. "How did I give you a boost?" "Well," I responded, "for years, I've been sitting in my office on the twelfth floor of the Tower of Hope. For years I've sat at this desk and looked at the wallpaper. The designs are shaped kind of like parachutes. But as I was talking to you I suddenly realized that they're not parachute-shaped after all—

they're shaped like football helmets!'' ''But how does that give you a boost?'' Vince persisted.

"From now on, every time I sit here pondering a problem, formulating answers to questions, making decisions, climbing mountains, and overcoming obstacles, I'll look at those helmets and think of you and the other great football players I know. I'll think of how you 'Go, go, go,' and 'Win, win, win!' "

# Freedom From the Bayou

A group of women who lived on the bayou were complaining because they didn't live in the city and didn't have luxurious homes. One of the women was a positive thinker. She got so tired of the other complainers, the faultfinders, and the criticizers that she finally looked at them and said, "Look, you live on the bayou. The bayou flows into the ocean. You've got a boat. You can go anywhere from where you are."

When you begin to believe in God, it's like having a house on the bayou, because God, like the bayou, flows into the gulf, and the gulf flows into the river, the river flows into the ocean, and there's no end to it. So there is no end to God's power and God's possibilities to do something within you. And when you touch faith with God, it's like living on the bayou. You can go anywhere from where you are.

# Labor Made Easier

Two laborers were watching a new computerized steam shovel at work in an open pit mine. The shovel took in a truckload of dirt in one big bite. After just a few bites the truck was full. One laborer said to the other, "Man, that machine has put five hundred of us out of work. It's our enemy!" The other man said, "Yes, and if we got rid of our shovels, we could create a million jobs for people to dig the mine with spoons."

# You Choose to Succeed or Fail

I talked to a businessman who said, "I've failed but it's not my fault." And do you know why he said that? Because he blamed his failure on everybody else! He attacked the unions, governmental regulations, the tax structure, and competition. And I had to say to him as friendly and yet as firmly as I could, "Sir, in the final analysis you threw in the towel, they didn't. You said, 'I give up.' You decided to quit." And at that point he finally admitted, "I guess I did."

I suspect that at the end of my life somebody may say,

"Schuller was a big failure . . . in golf!" And that's true! I used to play golf but I was so terrible I gave it up! I quit! Someone might also say that I was a failure in tennis. And that would be true, too! But I have chosen to be a failure in these sports. Instead, I have chosen to divert my time and energies to other areas. You succeed or fail based on the decisions you make!

# A Matter of Outlook

I've been on university campuses and I've seen a lot of young people, eighteen, nineteen, and twenty years of age. Many of them walk slowly. They move in a fatigued way. They slouch in their chairs. They have an extremely low level of energy. Yet, I can show you people in our church, like my Uncle Henry, who is in his ninetieth year, who has a spring in his step. He's difficult to keep up with.

It's not a matter of the calendar. It's a matter of outlook. The energy you have depends upon your mood, and your moods depend on the thoughts you entertain.

# You Have Wisdom

There's a story about a man from the Orient who traveled around the world in search of the smartest guru. He was told that the wise old man lived in a cave high up in the Himalayas, so that was his final destination. He loaded his horse down with supplies and set off across the mountains and deserts to find this man of wisdom. After months of traveling, he came to the foot of the Himalayas. He led his horse up a narrow path until he came to a cave. "Are you the guru who is known for his wisdom around the world?" he called out.

He waited and waited until finally the old man walked out into the light, so that he could be seen. "Old man, how can I become brilliant? Where can I find wisdom?" the weary traveler asked. The wise old guru raised his head and looked into the anxious man's eyes. "Where can you find your horse?" And with that he turned and walked back into the dark cave.

His horse was with him all the time! Brilliance and the capacity for wisdom were with him all the time. It's right there deep inside of you. Jesus said, "The kingdom of God is within you" (Luke 17:21). God is sending ideas to you that can take the form of dreams, but you don't believe it! You have that ability! You have that gift!

# Teamwork

No one can operate successfully in isolation. Dare to share the credit and glory with a winning team. History is inveterate in its teaching. Ultimately only teams will succeed.

Zig Ziglar once said, "If tomorrow you got a call from your boss and he said to you, 'Hey, I have good news for you. I have free tickets for you and your wife to Acapulco. You leave two weeks from today and we will provide full air fare, all your meals, rooms in the best hotel, and a five-hundred-dollar bonus to make sure you have plenty of tipping money,' what would you do? You wouldn't say, 'Sorry, sir, I wasn't planning on it.' You know what you'd do. You'd get organized in a hurry and rearrange your schedule. You'd do everything in your power to make it possible for you to go. You would begin to delegate some jobs that yesterday you thought you, and you alone, could do. You would start giving somebody else some of the power and glory that you possess today."

I am a success in my life, my marriage, my family, and in my career simply because I am surrounded by better, wiser people than myself. Those of you who watch the "Hour of Power" on television may know only me and my son, but in this church there are a thousand or more laypersons who make this program possible.

# Eliminate Your Negative Thoughts

One winter I took a trip up the Nile River to Aswan Dam. In the old tomb of the kings there are sketches of the pharaohs. It was fascinating to learn that every representation of pharaohs in the temples depicted the pharaoh with a bird and a snake around his head. The bird is a vulture, and the snake is a wrapped cobra. The vulture eats rotten food and the cobra attacks and kills.

These symbolized that the pharaoh had to guard the thoughts that went on in his head. If rotten thoughts came, the vulture would consume them, and if poisonous thoughts came, the cobra would kill them.

We're taught from childhood that you don't hit, you don't kill, you don't steal, and you don't lie. In the same way, we should teach children from infancy on that you do not allow negative thoughts to enter your head and when they do, you should, like a cobra, kill those thoughts.

# Turn the Dial on Your Crummy Moods

Every morning before my children left for school, my family and I would repeat the lines of Ella Wheeler Wilcox: "I'm going to be happy today." How you are going to feel today is a decision you make. As our children were growing up we taught them a cybernetic reality, and that is, the brain is like a radio dial. All of the ideas that bombard you are like sound waves. You can switch the dial and pick up music, or you can pick up propaganda, or you can pick up some tension-producing message. We say to our kids, "Turn the dial." If they get depressed or cynical or crabby or grumbling, we tell them, "Come on, turn the dial." Make the choice that is positive. Choose to feel good today.

Now, if you think that's too simplistic and unsophisticated, consider the findings in a recently published book by David D. Burns, M.D., Professor of Psychiatry, at the University of Pennsylvania. His book is called *Feeling Good*. What is he talking about? He is stating that the most important thing in life is to feel good and have emotionally healthy feelings on a day-to-day basis. Feelings will control everything. You can bury a stick; you can bury a tin can; you can bury a stone or a bone; you can bury a piece of glass—but you cannot bury a worm. And you can't just bury your feelings. That is a psychological impossibility, because feelings will either peek out or shriek out. You can't ignore them. You have to deal with them.

It's a lot harder to harness the exit of an emotion than it is to control the entrance of an emotion. It's much more difficult to control your temper than it is to prevent yourself from anger in the first place. It's much easier to feel good on a daily basis when positive emotions are fed upon every day.

# "My Name Is Phideaux"

The story comes to mind of the two sophisticated, snobbish French poodles who ran into a mongrel on the corner. The mongrel said to the poodles, "What are your names?"

One Poodle said, "My name is Mimi, M-i-m-i."

And the other said, "My name is Fifi, F-i-f-i."

And the mongrel said, "My name is Fido, P-h-i-d-e-a-u-x!"

Contradictions. They are in all of life. The trick is to combine them creatively. When we do, then we make the lion lie down with the lamb.

# Your Key for Success

A psychologist and I were talking about a person we were both interested in trying to help. This person's whole life was one set of problems—one failure after another—and each failure reinforced the future failure. That's why you call people like him "born losers." The psychologist hit it right on the head. He said, "The trouble is this person has never had a peak experience." He's never had an experience in really succeeding. So he's convinced that he was born a failure. This young man failed in school, failed in teenage relationships, failed in sociological relationships, failed in his first job, got fired from his second job, and landed in a reform school. And that's basically his life-style. His last peak experience was when he learned to walk!

How can you have a peak experience? There is no way it can happen without the kind of dynamic, religious experience we call "establishing a relationship with God." And that is the key.

# EXTRAORDINARY
# HUMOR

# King of the Jungle

A lion was king of the jungle. One day as he paraded through the jungle he met a rabbit. He said, "Who is the king of the jungle?" The rabbit said, "You are." Next the lion came to a deer and asked the elegant creature, "Who is the king of the jungle?" The deer said, "You are, Mr. Lion." So he walked on and met a tall giraffe, towering higher than all of the creatures in the jungle. The lion looked up to the giraffe and roared, "Who is the king of the jungle?" The giraffe bowed his head, bent his neck, until his eyes were even with the lion, and said, "You are, Mr. Lion."

Proudly, the beast went on his way until he ran into a huge bull elephant with tusks six feet long. He looked up at the monstrous creature and roared, "Who is the king of the jungle?" The elephant, without saying a word, swung his trunk back and forth, wrapped it around the lion's body, lifted him up, whirled him around, then slapped him against the side of a mountain. The lion, dazed, struggled to his feet, staggered over to the elephant, and said, "Just because you didn't know the answer, you don't have to get so mad."

# A Three-Legged Chicken

Bob Hope tells a story about a fellow who was riding along at fifty-five miles an hour when he looked out the window. He couldn't believe his eyes! He saw a three-legged chicken running right alongside the car! He increased his speed to sixty miles an hour but the chicken kept right up with him. At seventy miles an hour, the chicken took off and left the man behind in a cloud of dust. Dumbfounded, the man pulled over and stopped in a farmer's yard. He rolled down his window and asked the farmer who was sitting there, "Did you see that?" The farmer said, "Sure, I saw it. I've seen plenty of them."

The man said, "What was it?"

"That was just one of our three-legged chickens."

"Three-legged chicken! What do you mean a three-legged chicken?"

"Well," the farmer said, "there are three of us in the family: my wife, my boy, and myself. We all like drumsticks. So we decided to breed a three-legged chicken. That way, we all get a drumstick."

# Plan Ahead

When I was in Washington recently, President Reagan made an interesting comment. He referred to Abraham, who lived to be nearly 150 years old. His wife was only a few years younger. The president said, "Can you imagine how rich he would have been if he'd opened an IRA account?"

# Mixed-Up Messages

Recently I heard about a florist who was going out of business. Someone said the reason he failed was that he always got his messages mixed up. You see, a terrible thing happened one time. He was told to send flowers to a newly married couple. The florist also had an order to send flowers for a local funeral.

Well, he got the cards mixed up! The people who were getting married got the message "Our deepest sympathy to both of you." At the funeral, they got the message "Good luck in your new location."

# The Spanish Monk

I remember the story of the monk who went into a monastery in Spain. One of the requirements of the religious order is that the monks must maintain perpetual silence. Only after two years are the monks allowed to speak, and then only two words. And then, after two years of additional silence, they're allowed two more words, and so it goes every two years. There was a young man who had spent his first two years at the monastery and then was called by his superior to make his first two-word statement. His first two words were, "Bed hard." Two years passed and he got his second chance. His next two words were, "Food bad." Two more years passed. His two words were: "I quit!" The superior looked at him and said, "It doesn't surprise me. All you've done since you've been here is complain, complain, complain."

# A Local Call

There is a humorous story making the rounds in Washington about the time Menachem Begin met with President Reagan. He was curious about the three telephones on

President Reagan's desk. Reagan explained, "Well, the silver one connects me to the USSR, the platinum one connects me to the Republican headquarters, and the gold one connects me to God." Begin said, "Really? What does it cost to use the gold phone?" The president replied, "Ten thousand dollars. But it's worth it." Not many weeks later, when Reagan visited Israel, guess what he saw on Begin's desk? Three phones: one silver, one platinum, one gold. When Reagan asked what they were for, Begin answered, "The silver one is for the head of the Israeli political party, and the gold one is my line to God." Reagan said, "Yeah, what does it cost to call God?" Begin exclaimed, "Oh, just ten cents—here it's a local call!"

# Sister Theresa's Travels

I heard a cute story recently. God decided to send one of the righteous women to check out some of the problem spots in the world. He said to a nun, whose name was Sister Theresa, "I want you to go to New York City. Reports are that it's pretty bad. I'll give you a call and you can let me know."

She said, "Okay, I'll be at the Waldorf Astoria."

After a few days the Lord called her. She said, "Lord, it's worse than You've been told. The city is as decadent as Rome was at its worst."

God said, "I was afraid of that. Now I need you to go and check out Las Vegas."

She went to Las Vegas. She said. "You'll be able to reach me at the MGM Grand Hotel."

The Lord called her after a few days and she said, "Lord, it is worse than You've been told. It's like Sodom and Gomorrah."

God said, "Sister Theresa, I want you to check out one other place: Hollywood, California."

She said, "Okay. Try to reach me at the Beverly Hills Hotel."

After a few days, He called the Beverly Hills Hotel. The phone rang in her room. A tape recorder came on. "Hello, this is Terry, fer sure. I'll be back in thirty minutes."

# Good News and Bad News

I recently heard the story of two great ball players—Dodgers, naturally. The two men made an agreement that whoever died first would return to communicate to the living friend whether or not there was baseball in heaven. The inevitable happened—one of them died shortly afterward. The surviving player sat in the dugout during a game one day, and suddenly in the third inning he felt himself surrounded by light. He knew immediately that it was his fellow teammate who had died. There in the dugout, the player heard a voice speaking to him: "Hey, it's me. I've got good news and bad news. The good news is there is baseball in heaven! I'm playing with Ty Cobb, Babe Ruth, and all the greats. It's fantastic! The bad news is I noticed you're scheduled to pitch next Tuesday!"

# The Secret to Success

I have a story about a sea captain, a very successful sea captain. Everybody wanted to know what his secret was. They noticed that every morning right after breakfast he would go up to his cabin, draw the drapes, lock the door, and spend some time alone. He would then come out confident with intelligence, capable of coping with all of the pressures that a captain has to handle. And the second officers often wanted to know what he did that made him so strong, wise, and confident. Finally they devised a scheme so they could peek into the privacy of his cabin.

After breakfast the officers watched the captain go into his cabin, unlock the safe, and pull out an envelope. From the envelope he took a piece of paper which he put on the table and with his hand on his head, he read from the piece of paper. He looked and looked and looked. Then he put the paper back in the envelope, put it back in the safe, spun the cycle, locked it, came out confidently, and gave his commands. The ship sailed magnificently.

They checked on him day after day; every day it was the same routine. The drapes would be drawn, the door locked, the safe opened, and the envelope pulled out. That same piece of paper folded on the table. He would look and look and look.

The day came when the captain died. The officers rushed into his cabin, opened the safe, pulled out the envelope, looked at the paper, and saw his secret. There were the words: "The right-hand side is the starboard side."

# EXTRAORDINARY PERSEVERANCE

# A Thrill That Fulfills

Our daughter Carol is a skier. Last year she tried five times to qualify for the National Handicapped National Ski Championships. But she failed to ski fast enough without falling or something. Last week she had another opportunity to qualify. In order to do so you have to make the race in a certain time. In the first race she was disqualified because she lost her outriggers. In the second race, she felt she was too slow. And in the third race she went so fast that she ended up sitting down on the ski as she came across the line. That eliminated her from that race.

Assuming she had failed at all three attempts, she didn't wait for the results. She and her coach were in the locker room when they heard over the public-address system, "The winner of the second race, setting a speed qualifying her for the nationals and winning a gold medal, is Carol Schuller." She made it! But I must say, she really paid a high price for it.

I'm not talking in terms of dollars. I'm talking about one word: *effort.* You've got one life to live—don't spill it. Don't settle for a cheap thrill. Don't buy the frills. Sharpen the skills necessary to make your dream come true.

With that kind of character, you'll be on top of the circumstances, not under them. If you want to see it through, it is up to you. If you want to go from now to the end of your life, healthy, happy, and successful, then I say, if you want to see it through, it's up to you. Right now I ask you to do one thing. And that is this: Turn your whole life over to Jesus Christ. Your sins? He'll forgive them. Ideas? He'll give you some fantastic ones. If you follow them, you'll find a thrill that will really fulfill.

# My First Dream

Do you know what my first dream was? The first dream I ever had came to me when I was a little boy and I began to scheme how I could accomplish it. I had the dream that I wanted to be a minister. And then I had to develop the scheme—it meant eight years of school, four years of high school, four years in college, and then three years in theological graduate school. That's nineteen years of education. And at the age of five I made that commitment.

Anything can be accomplished if you're willing to pay the price, prepare for it, and stick with the scheme: How much will it take? What will it cost? What kind of resources will I need? What kind of help will I need?

# The Help of Rosie Gray

Our interest in the handicapped is not new. Actually, the ministry of the Crystal Cathedral was the result of one disabled person. Twenty-six years ago, when my wife and I came to California to begin a church, all I had was four hundred dollars and a dream. We couldn't find a chapel, empty hall, or school building to rent for Sunday worship. Finally, in desperation, we used a drive-in theater that stands only a mile from the Crystal Cathedral. From the platform of the snack bar roof, I preached to a few curious people who came in their cars. I prayed that the months would quickly pass and we could raise money, find land, build a chapel, and worship in a "civilized" Christian way.

Unknown to me, on the first Sunday at the drive-in, there was a totally paralyzed woman in the audience. Her husband, Warren Gray, had seen the ad in the local paper which was placed there by this twenty-eight-year-old minister: "Starting Sunday, March 27—Worship as you are, in the family car!" And the old rancher lifted Rosie, his seventy-two-year-old, paralyzed wife, carried her to the car, and drove her to that drive-in theater because it was the only church she could attend.

Years before, Rosie had had a stroke. She could not walk or talk or control her actions. By any indication, Rosie was totally out of it. The truth was, she had a clear mind and understood what she heard. Although the Grays came regularly, I never met Rosie and Warren until our congregation bought land and built a small chapel. We were ready to make the move out of the drive-in and into our new home, when Rosie's husband Warren asked me to call on them. Meeting me at the front door of their ranch home, he said, "Reverend, before you meet Rosie I must tell you that you may not think she has a brain. She can't walk. She can't talk. She had a stroke years ago, but she is actually smart. She and I have been attending the drive-in every week and we'd like to join the church." After this introduction, I met Rosie.

As I knelt by her bedside, I asked, "Rosie, do you love Jesus?" Without nodding her head or blinking her eyes, she answered my question as one small tear rolled down her cheek. The following Sunday she and her husband were received as charter members of the church. Meanwhile the congregation prepared to move into the little chapel with the new carpeting, upholstered pews, stained-glass windows, and beautiful woodwork.

Finally, after so many years, we would be out of the drive-in. Yet suddenly we had a problem—what would we do with Rosie Gray? She couldn't sit in a wheelchair. She either had to be strapped to a bed or to the seat of the car. So twenty-five years ago, confronted with the reality of the handicapped, we decided to conduct two church services each Sunday. At half-past nine we worshiped in our new little chapel. Then, following the first service, I dashed out to the nearby drive-in. I preached there to Rosie and Warren and the others who came in their cars.

The doctors said that Rosie would not live long, yet as the months went by she did not die. Another rainy winter came and I had to buy a new umbrella. Still Rosie did not die. Summer came and Rosie was doing exceptionally well. Another winter came and went. And I continued to stand in the open sky in the cold or rain, preaching to Rosie Gray and the others who gathered to worship in their cars.

After six years, God gave us the idea of selling our beautiful building. That's when I learned never to fall in love with a building, but to look beyond it. We bought ten acres of land and built a large building with open doors so that I could talk to people seated inside and talk to people outside in their cars at the same time. This church has always realized that although a person may be handicapped, he has great possibilities. "Out of your weakness shall come strength" (*see* Hebrews 11:34). If it had not been for Rosie Gray, this ministry would never have become what God intended it to be.

# "You Made It!"

Let me share with you one of the most inspiring sights I've ever seen. It happened on the slopes of Squaw Valley at the National Handicapped Ski Championships. The skier was about eighteen, and blind. She was being led down the giant slalom. She made it through forty-four gates, until she was lined up straight with the finish line. Her guide behind her said, "Straight ahead, go for it!" She dug in, and was flying when she hit a rut. Her poles flew out of her hands. She fell flat on her stomach. She knew she'd have to get her body across the finish line or be disqualified. She looked beaten but she didn't stop. She reached out for her poles. When she couldn't find them, she started swimming over the snow straight ahead until she crossed the finish line.

The judge said, "You made it!" But she didn't hear him. She just kept swimming another five, ten, fifteen feet with all her heart.

The judge kept saying, "You made it! You can stop!" She still didn't hear. Finally it sunk in. "You made it!"

She stopped, flat on her belly, heard the applause, jumped to her feet, and danced for joy.

# A Very Persistent Boy

I recently read the story of a little boy who went with his mother to the toy department of a store. A big sign read, "Children are not allowed to play with the toys or on the toys." Ignoring the sign, the little boy climbed on the hobbyhorse and started rocking back and forth. His mother said, "Come on, you've got to get down, you cannot play on that horse." He pushed her away and held on to the neck of the horse, even though his mother scolded and tugged at him. Finally, a clerk approached and said, "Sorry, but the sign says, 'No Children allowed on the toys.' But if your mother wants to buy it. . . ." The boy ignored him, so the clerk called the assistant manager, who grabbed the boy's arm and repeated, "Sonny, you're not allowed to play on that horse unless you buy it." The boy pushed him away, so the assistant manager called the manager. He also gave the youngster a lecture, explaining in very rational terms, "Sonny, if everybody came and played on these toys they would soon be broken and we could not sell them. We'd lose money. Now it's time to get off the horse." The little boy hung on tighter. Frustrated, the store manager called in the staff psychologist, who proceeded to go through all the various behavior-modification techniques and strategies to get the boy off the horse. But the kid wouldn't budge.

Finally, a tough, burly old man, who had been watching the entire scene, approached the frustrated motivators and said, "Let me talk to him." He went over and whispered something in the boy's ear. Immediately the boy jumped off the horse and said, "Okay, Mama, let's go home." Surprised, the mother asked, "What did that man say to you?" The youngster replied, "He told me, 'You get off the horse or I'll break every bone in your body!'"

# Never Give Up

My friend Ralph Edwards once asked psychologist Joyce Brothers and myself to do some counseling on a television program called, "So You Think You've Got Troubles." On one program, we faced a woman who by her own admission was overweight. She said, "You may think my problem is my weight. I tried to lose weight. I went on diets, but kept gaining weight. Finally I decided that I am doomed to be fat. I decided to quit fighting it and just stay fat. But I also decided that I was going to enjoy being fat."

We asked her, "So what's your problem?" She said, "My

problem is that society is down on all fat people. I want to start a national organization to treat fat people nice. But I can't get people to take the idea seriously."

I can't condone the idea that anybody should ever give up the battle of their self-discipline. We didn't encourage her to accept her condition as final. The same may be true for you.

# The Greatest Peacemakers I've Ever Met

I must tell you about the interesting time I had in Squaw Valley, California. Only a few weeks earlier I had lunch with the queen of England, and attended a dinner hosted by Bob Hope, but neither of those experiences compared with my visit to Squaw Valley. At that beautiful snow-covered mountain resort, I met the greatest collection of peacemakers I've ever met anywhere, including high-level meetings in Washington and around the world. The people I met in Squaw Valley topped them all.

They had gathered—hundreds of them—to compete in the Twelfth Annual National Handicapped Ski Championships. They had chosen for the site of their competition Squaw Valley, the 1960 home of the International Olympics.

I had carefully planned my week to include a trip to the Handicapped Nationals because my daughter Carol was skiing in them. As you may recall, Carol lost a leg in a motorcycle accident some years ago. When she became acquainted with the handicapped ski program, she decided to become a skier. She's been training hard for each of the twelve regional contests in America. All contestants must qualify in the Regionals before they can compete in the Nationals.

My heart was in my throat because I had never seen Carol ski before. She was scheduled to ski her first race on Thursday. I was to speak in Louisville on Wednesday, lecturing to the Christian theologians at the Southern Baptist Convention. My flight was to get me from Kentucky to Squaw Valley in time for the first race on Thursday. However, when the weatherman announced a blizzard was on its way, the first race was moved up to Wednesday. I missed it. I was terribly disappointed because that was her best race. She won the gold medal, first prize in the junior division in the downhill. I am very proud of her.

I missed that race, but on Friday the second races were to happen. My wife and I were there for those. Never had we seen so many one-legged people in one place. There were the triple amputees, with no legs and one arm missing. There were races for the blind—even a sightless race in the giant slalom.

The course is as long as the one that Olympians ski. They show no favoritism to the handicapped. There are forty-seven gates through which they have to maneuver coming down that mile-long, steep hill.

The blind were the first to ski. I'd never seen that before. They ski, followed or led down by a sighted person, who shouts directions, such as, "Turn to the right. Now to the left. Straight ahead. Quick, quick, to the right!" This is the way they ski and race. It's an amazing sight.

Then there are the three-trackers. Carol is a three-tracker. The three-trackers ski without a prosthesis, with a ski on their one good leg. They are aided by outriggers—poles with mini-skis on them.

In the first three-tracker race, which we missed, Carol related to us, "A funny thing happened. When the one-legged men skiers were coming down, one of the guys fell, and his leg became detached, not from the ski but from his knee, so that the leg and the ski came all the way down the hill and crossed the finish line! The judges didn't know whether they should award the leg or the body up on the hill!" These people have a fantastic sense of humor.

The athletes I met at Squaw Valley have made peace with themselves and with God. I'm talking about people who have lost legs, arms, sight, or mobility. They might have become bitter and angry at the world, but they didn't. They are at peace with themselves. They look in the mirror, they see what they are, and they've accepted it. They're not blaming God or anybody else. They are not fixing the blame, they're fixing the problem.

# Snatched From Destruction

I was born and raised in an Iowa family where we always had bread with lots of butter. There was always an abundance of pie and desserts. Consequently, I was a fat butterball when I was a child. I had to struggle with my weight problem all my life. I tried diets. I counted calories. I still do. But the weight accumulated through the years. Finally I decided that I would eat only lean meats, vegetables, and fresh fruit for dessert.

One night I was taken out to dinner. The bread was passed. My host said, "This is fantastic. Feel it." I felt it—it was soft and warm. The fellow next to me was already spreading the butter, which was melting into the warm, fragrant bread. My host continued to tempt me. He said, "You must try the steak with the bearnaise sauce." I followed his advice. When it was time for dessert, I was feeling a little guilty. I was coaxed again, this time with, "They make the best pie here. It has a chocolate crust. You can't pass it by. Go on a diet tomorrow." I took the pie.

When I walked out of there, I calculated that I'd had three thousand calories. That night I went to bed filled with guilt and remorse. I woke up at two or three in the morning. I felt a total sense of futility because frankly, it was one time when possibility thinking totally failed me. I could build churches, towers, and a cathedral. I could write books, but I could not get rid of my fat. I could raise millions of dollars for God's work, but I couldn't turn my back on a piece of chocolate pie.

I remember praying out one simple prayer: "Dear Jesus, I don't know if You're dead or alive. I don't know if You're even real. I have believed it and I have preached it, but I couldn't prove it by my weight control. If You're there, can You help me?"

I was poor in spirit. I admitted my lack. I asked Him, and instantaneously, in my mind I saw the old Floyd River in Iowa. It was flooded way up to the grassy slopes. There in the middle of the stream was a great, gallant, strong, uprooted tree being carried away by the current. My body was that tree. The sloping hillside where the water lapped appeared harmless. It didn't look wild and it didn't look rough. It was safe. That was what butter, ice cream, and cake were for me. I was being destroyed by the seemingly harmless. Instantaneously, I heard the message. It was in the past perfect tense: *I have snatched you from destruction.*

I knew then that I had been liberated from subconscious forces that kept me addicted to sweets. I had an internal transformation. I still have my little ups and downs but never have reverted to what I was.

You have a problem. Admit it. There are people who would love to help you, starting with Jesus Christ.

# A Successful Bean

I received a letter from a friend, Ansley Mueller, who lives in Pleasant Plains, Ohio. He sent me a little plastic case with a seed in it. There's a story behind it. You know, for years I've been teaching the principle "Any fool can count the seeds in an apple. Only God can count all the apples in one seed." Well, Ansley Mueller had been listening to this principle and one day he gave me the little seed with this true story. He said:

It was 1977, Dr. Schuller, and I lost half my crop. It was a bad, bad year. It was so wet, I couldn't get half of it harvested and it didn't develop. So, at the end of the year, in October, I would walk through the fields and try to pick up a bushel here and a piece there. Then, I saw standing by itself a most extraordinary, unusual looking soybean plant. I walked over and I was shocked by its size and its good looks. I went and carefully picked off the pods. There were 202 pods and I opened them and counted out 503 soybeans. I took them home. I kept them in a pan all winter and they dried out. The next spring they just seemed special to me. In 1978 I took those 503 soybeans and I planted them in a little plot behind my house and when October came I harvested thirty-two pounds! Thirty-two pounds! I dried them out in the winter and in 1979 I took those thirty-two pounds and I planted them on one acre and when October came, I harvested. I had 2,409 pounds and I planted them on sixty-eight acres, which was all the land I had available. In October, just a year ago, I harvested twenty-one hundred bushels and cashed it out for fifteen thousand dollars! Now, Dr. Schuller, one plant, four years later, fifteen thousand dollars. Not too bad, is it? So, Dr. Schuller, here's your bean. Good luck!

# A Close Call

Not long ago, my wife and I were in Washington. Our return flight from Washington hit a squall. They kept us on the runway for forty minutes as a hurricane wind buffeted the plane. When we landed in Dallas, we had missed our connecting flight to California. It was crucial that I return to California in time to give the Sunday message.

As we landed in Dallas, we knew we'd missed our flight, but one of the attendants said, "There is a flight leaving for San Diego a few minutes after we land. Maybe you can get on it."

So just as soon as the plane landed, they buzzed us over on an electric cart. My wife and I weren't the only ones who had missed the flight—there were three others who were with us as they raced us to the boarding gate. But before we got halfway down there, we met others coming back. They said, "We've missed it! It's gone!"

The amazing thing is that I did not believe them. I practiced what I preached. I decided not to surrender to the first negative thought that came. Consequently, we didn't give up and we didn't turn back. Instead, we went on ahead. Sure enough, the accordian canvas had been folded back, leaving a great gap from the gate to the airplane. We had apparently missed the plane. Or had we? It was still there. It wasn't in the air. And anything's possible, right?

What would you have done if it had been you? Well, here's what I did: I walked to the edge and, holding on to the accordian canvas, I caught the pilot's attention. I called, "Hey!" He merely waved good-bye.

I said, "Open the door!"

He smiled again, then he saluted me. Just as I was beginning to think that it might be a good idea to try getting a train to California, a miracle happened. You talk about the Red Sea parting for Moses? Well, let me tell you, when the door of the airplane slowly and grandly opened, it was just as dramatic. The ground crew rolled the accordian back, my wife and I got on the plane, and so did three other people. The airlines made money on it. I think everybody was happy.

# Robert Picking

I have a friend whom I met for the first time a few years ago when he was in his mid-nineties. At the time, he worked every day. He is Robert Picking, president of the Picking Company. His grandfather founded the company, his father propagated it, and the grandson is running the company today. The company was founded in 1874 in Cyrus, Ohio, and was called D. Picking and Company. It is the last of the old copper shops in America still making their original products primarily by hand.

I was thrilled to receive one of their products recently as a special gift from Bob Picking. It is a beautiful little shovel made out of solid copper. I treasure it not so much for what it is but for the labor and creativity that it represents. It was made by Bob Picking himself.

He was at work one day, as he is every day, when he noticed some cast-off pieces of copper piled in the trash. They weren't big enough for a skillet or a pot, and they weren't big enough for a kettle. Bob asked the workers what would happen to the odd-sized pieces of copper. They reported that it was waste, and that it would be melted down and disposed of. He said, "Nothing should be wasted. Nothing."

To prove his point he picked up one small piece and shaped it to form the scoop part of a small shovel. Then he took a long, narrow piece and rolled it to make a handle. He soldered the two pieces together into a beautiful work of art, and then he autographed it, "Robert Picking," and gave it to me. He never misses a day's work, and he never stops creating. Do you know how old he is now? He is 101 years old.

# EXTRAORDINARY
# VALUES

# "Look for the Stars"

There was a woman who moved to the desert with her husband and found that life there was not happy at all. She wrote to her mother, saying, "I'm going to leave my husband. I can't stand living in the California desert. It's awful. There is only desert sagebrush and Indians. They don't seem interested in me and I can't really relate to them." Her mother wrote back these two lines: "Two people sit behind prison bars. One sees mud, and one sees stars." She continued, "Honey, look for the stars." So the woman did. She decided to get interested in the Indians. She got interested in the desert flowers and the desert stones and it became the most enriching time of her life.

# "I Cut the Coal!"

This story is dedicated to people who are not at the top of the ladder but are nevertheless making America hum. I'm dedicating it to farmers, truck drivers, waitresses, retail clerks, and people dealing with the public (who are sometimes unnecessarily difficult). Yes, I'm dedicating this story to the people who are on the bottom rung of the salary scales in this country—to the janitor, to the gardener, and to the dishwasher in the back of the kitchen. The power of the simple, common person! It was Abraham Lincoln who said, "God must love the common people, because He made so many of them."

During the Second World War, Winston Churchill, a man respected and admired, was going up and down his scarred country trying to marshal the moral will of the people to withstand the assault of the enemy. He visited troops and factories and then someone suggested that he call on the coal miners. "If you could just stop in one of the little coal-mining towns, Mr. Churchill," one man pleaded. "They feel that they are doing nothing for the war effort. They don't get their pictures in the paper and they never receive any credit."

So Winston Churchill went down to visit the hardworking coal miners. He gazed at the greasy faces of these tough miners as they gathered (shocked that Winston Churchill would come to talk to them!). And the words he spoke that October day will never be forgotten. Standing before them, he said, "We will be victorious! We will preserve our freedom. And years from now when our freedom is secure and peace reigns, your children and your children's children will come and they will say to you, 'What did you do to win our freedom in that great war?' And one will say, 'I marched with the Eighth Army!' Someone else will proudly say, 'I manned a submarine.' And another will say, 'I guided the ships that moved the troops and the supplies.' And still another will say, 'I doctored the wounds!'" Then he paused. The dirty-faced miners, with their caps pushed back, sat in silence and awe waiting for him to continue. "They will come to you," he shouted, "and you will say, with equal right and equal pride, 'I cut the coal! I cut the coal that fueled the ships that moved the supplies! That's what I did. I cut the coal!'"

# The Most Valuable Possessions

I remember calling on a very rich woman who had suffered a great personal tragedy. She had vases from the Ming Dynasty; she had jewels and many other beautiful and valuable things. She greeted me and said, "Dr. Schuller, I once heard you say on television, 'Trouble never leaves you where it found you.' That is so true."

She said, "These things don't mean nearly as much to me now. Oh, I still love them. I'm not going to throw them away. But if there were a fire, I wouldn't take that Chinese vase as I would have before. Do you know what I'd take? The family pictures."

When tragedy hits, values change. The family becomes important—the husband, the wife, and the children. When your values change, your life changes.

# I Believe in Success

I recall a dear friend I went to school with many years ago. He was a socialist. I am not of that same economic persuasion, so we often had friendly debates about the implications of the philosophy. Once, after talking some minutes, I finally said, "You keep saying that managing to make a profit is a sin, a social irresponsibility. I respect your opinion, but I view the situation a different way. I say to manage to obtain a profit is not wrong in and of itself. Profit is only wrong when handled in a socially irresponsible manner. To me, the great crime against society is to manage for a loss."

I believe in success—the alternative is failure. When you or I fail, we can be sure that someone down the road is missing an opportunity for employment because of that failure.

# Stop and Smell the Roses

At Easter I am reminded of a time many years ago when I had a touch from Jesus Christ that was most meaningful. It was early in our church's history. We had started a drive-in, and then we got the dream of building a walk-in, drive-in church and turning it into a Garden of Eden with fountains and waters and flowers and birds and beautiful pieces of sculptured architecture. I presented the ideas to my small band of people, about three hundred members. Of the three hundred, almost half of them thought it was a crazy, wild, awful idea. The others thought it was fantastic. I was in the middle.

When you're a pastor of a congregation and it's split down the middle, with half of them totally enthusiastic and the others dead set against it, you have what's called a problem. This was my problem. And it got worse.

Unknown to me, a dissonant element in the church hired an assistant minister for one specific purpose: to meet with them privately and secretly to see how they could possibly have me fired. Meanwhile, I was saddled with an unavoidable commitment to the church board to give leadership to this church. I had a problem that had no apparent solution and which became a pressure that I couldn't run away from. My dream became a depression.

Thank God my major in undergraduate work was psychology. If it hadn't been for that, I don't know if I could have survived. But even then, in spite of my intellectual, rational knowledge of the emotional processes that were at work within me, I was unable to sort it out. I was so depressed that the will to die was stronger than the will to live.

About that time, *Life* magazine came out with a cover picture of the back of a minister's head and his robe. You couldn't see his face. But the headline read: "Why Protestant ministers are cracking up." I thought, *Oh boy, I'm next.*

That night I was unable to sleep. Hour after hour I tossed and turned. The sheets became hot. I began to perspire. Panic approached me. I thought *Schuller, you're cracking up.* As I became controlled by the fear that I was having a nervous breakdown, I desperately prayed a prayer more sincere than any prayer I'd ever prayed. I said, "Jesus Christ, are You dead or alive? I've been preaching it every Easter. But are You a myth? Are You a legend? Or are You really alive? Do You care?"

What happened next I shall never forget so long as I live, and even as I retell it now I feel shivers under my robe. I felt a finger go through the skull bone deep into my brain, like a surgeon's finger probing at flesh that has been anesthetized. I could feel that pressure but no pain. The finger went deep and it slowly withdrew, and as it did it took with it all anxiety, all depression, and all fear of failure. Peace flowed from the top of my head over my body. He touched me and made me whole. He was alive.

I knew then that He would not let me fail. I fell into the deepest sleep and awoke the next morning, walked out the door to go to my office, and stopped in my tracks, startled by the beautiful roses. I turned quickly and said to my wife, "Honey, the roses are blooming." She said, "Oh, Bob, they've been blooming for three months." They had been blooming, but I never saw them. I was totally unaware of them. My anxieties had paralyzed my perception of beauty around me.

# Scale It Down

When we started in the drive-in theater, many years ago, I began to dream of a church of my own. My first dream was for a forty-acre plot on Katella Avenue. I was sure that we needed forty acres. And I was sure that Katella was the best location. However, when a forty-acre parcel on Katella became available, we couldn't afford it. I negotiated; I compromised. I decided that we actually needed only ten acres. That was all we bought. Later on, we added another ten acres; now we're up to twenty. Better half a loaf than none!

People who never change their minds are either perfect or stubborn. You're not perfect, you don't want to be stubborn, so be willing to occasionally change your mind. Scale down, if necessary.

# Don't Exaggerate Your Problems

Recently I visited Mainland China. My uncle and I went inland from Amoy to Changchun with the official guides of the Communist regime. While in Changchun we went to church and returned to our hotel for lunch. As I was about to go out for a little stroll, I was told I could not leave the hotel. I was under virtual house arrest for four hours!

Now I've been in the Soviet Union three times and this was my third trip to the People's Republic. But this was the first time in all my international travels that I was confined to my hotel without my approval.

The People's Republic guide, a lovely, young girl, tried to explain. She said, "You don't understand, Dr. Schuller." To which I replied, "I do understand. I understand what freedom is—you don't. If you came to the United States of America you could travel freely from state to state. There you don't need papers to go from city to city."

See your problems in their proper perspective. Don't exaggerate. You're still in the United States of America, and you can go anywhere you choose.

# Commitment for Energy

Not long ago I read in the newspaper about the newest fads in the Los Angeles area. It detailed what was "in" and what was "out." Designer jeans are now out, and old Levis are in. Certain restaurants are now out, and other ones are in. Tennis is out, and racquetball is also going out. Golf is coming back in. (Not that golf impresses me, though. I used to play golf until I tried applying my principles of possibility thinking to it. When it threatened my religion, I gave up.) Anyway, the article surveyed the cities and lifestyles of America. One exciting thing it pointed out is that living together before marriage is going out, and marriage is coming back in. In other words, commitment is in.

Answer this question: What commitment would you make this morning if you knew it could not fail? Maybe it is marriage. Are you willing to make the plunge of commitment? If you are, here's what will happen. Commitment will produce energy. Energy will produce enthusiasm. Enthusiasm will produce a whole new way of living.

# Don't Miss the Sunset

An artist was teaching his students how to paint. On a special occasion, he took them on an all-night trip to a hill because the sunsets were so beautiful there. They were all painting the sunset. Just as the colors broke (purples and reds and pinks and oranges and yellows, golds, greens), the teacher walked around the students and he noticed that one student was very busy painting the shingles on the barn in the valley under the sunset. There he was, tediously painting the shingles!

The teacher told him to paint the sunset and forget the shingles. "If you don't forget the shingles, the sunset will be gone and you'll have missed it," the teacher said.

What's the point? The point is, don't miss the positive that's passing. You can get so locked up on the shingles that you miss the sunset. You can concentrate so much on the negatives that you don't notice the positives.

# Do as Lincoln Did

At the height of the Civil War, Lincoln and his secretary of war visited the battlefield home of General George McClellan. They waited in the parlor of McClellan's home for the general to return from the front. Finally the door opened and in walked the general. He saw the president and the secretary of war but never acknowledged them. Instead he walked by them and on up the stairs to his room. They assumed he would be down very soon, so they continued to wait. When he did not appear they sent the maid to inquire. She returned and said, "I'm sorry, Mr. President, but the general asked me to tell you that he is tired and has gone to bed."

The secretary of war was shocked and said, "Mr. President, that's unacceptable. You must relieve him of command." Lincoln thought about it for a minute, then said, "No, I will not relieve him; that man wins battles. I would hold his horse and wash the dirt from his boots if he could shorten this bloodshed by one hour."

# A Value Problem

A recent issue of *Time* magazine had on its cover a face of someone distorted in agony. The headline read, "Anxiety; How Are We Going to Deal With It?" As I keep up my studies in psychology and human behavior I can tell you that boredom, depression, and anxiety, as well as other emotional and mental problems, are epidemic in America. The interesting phenomenon is that they are no longer restricted to the poverty pockets of our country. They are also rampant among the affluent. What this means is that your depression or your anxiety is not necessarily related to your state of employment or unemployment. The depression and anxiety epidemic is not a money problem. It is a value problem.

We don't need money. We need to get a dream, a desire for something we'd die for. Some of you are teenagers and some of you are in college. Some of you have been out of college for years, yet you still don't know what you really want to do with the one life you have to live.

# The World Is Throbbing With Life

I will always remember Asa Skinner. He was a member of my first church in Chicago, Illinois. He was a fine executive who was always active. He underwent brain surgery for a tumor, and I wondered how he'd be able to tolerate the long recovery period at home. I called on him shortly after he was discharged from the hospital. His wife met me at the door. I said, "How is Asa doing?" She replied, "Oh, very good." I asked, "How are his spirits?" She answered, "They're fantastic. Come on, you can see why."

I found him in his tiny backyard, sitting in a chair with his bathrobe on and his head bandaged in white. His wife told me he was studying. As I approached him I noticed that he was looking at the ground through binoculars. When he saw me, he said, "Oh, Dr. Schuller, look at them!" He was watching the ants build a home and transport material. He said, "I've been noticing the wasps. Look at the nest they built." Then he pointed in the far distance where there was a tree. He said, "See, in that tree a robin is building a nest."

The ants, the wasps, the robin. He said, "Dr. Schuller, this world is throbbing with life and all of life is so beautiful; it's a pity that a single insect has to die."

# Nothing Is Ordinary

William Wolcott, the great English artist, came to New York City in 1924 to record his impression of that skyscraper city. After a week of beginning to feel it, one morning he found himself in the architectural office of a colleague for whom he'd worked years before in England. And now suddenly the urge and surge to sketch came over him. And he quickly said to his colleague, "Please, I need some paper." And seeing some paper on a desk, he said, "May I have that?" The architectural colleague said, "That's not sketching paper, Mr. Wolcott. That's just ordinary wrapping paper." Wolcott, not wanting to lose the inspiration, reached out and said, "Nothing is ordinary if you know how to use it." And he took that drawing paper and made two sketches. One sold for one thousand dollars and the other sold for five hundred dollars. The principle: Nothing is ordinary if you know how to use it.

# Not Necessarily Lazy

You know, Henry Ford once hired an efficiency expert to go through his plant. He said, "Try to find nonproductive people, tell me who they are, and I will fire them." The man returned and reported that he definitely found such a person. "Every time I walk by his door," he said, "he is sitting with his feet propped up on his desk. When I go in, he stands, shakes hands, we exchange a few words, and when I leave he props his feet up on his desk again. The man never does a thing." When Henry Ford learned the name of the man he said, "Well, I can't fire him—I pay him to do that. I pay him to do nothing but think."

You need one day in seven when you can have an experience in a church to do nothing but think. Get another shot of rejoicing and recharging and renewal power, and your dreams and your ideals will be resurrected.

# Coming or Going?

I remember a time when we were rushing to catch a hydrofoil. It was in Naples, Italy, where the hydrofoil runs to the island of Capri. There is also a ferry that runs back and forth. One man came running alongside the pier. He took a running leap, jumped three feet, and landed on the moving ferry. He breathlessly exclaimed, "Wow, I made it!"

The deckhand said, "What's your hurry? We'd have been along the pier in another minute." Some people don't know whether they're coming or going.

# "If You Don't Know . . ."

I have a favorite story of a wise professor who was so learned and had so many credentials that he could teach whatever he chose. He could teach biology, history, or astronomy. One day he decided to motivate one of his young students by planning an all-day canoe trip in the wilderness. He hoped to show him how education is meaningful in human existence.

The day was just dawning when the student and the old professor started out in their canoe. As they drifted downriver, a leaf fell into the quiet water and the professor picked it up and handed it to the student. "Now tell me, do you understand the leaf?" The boy answered, "No." The wise old man said, "See, my son, if you do not learn biology, you will miss out on twenty percent of life's potential joy."

As the canoe rounded a bend, rocks that hovered above the water's edge revealed markings of Indians from many years ago. The old professor said, "See those markings? Do you know what Indians made those markings, and how they lived?" The boy said, "I don't know." "My son," said the professor, "If you do not learn history, you'll miss out on another twenty percent of life's enjoyment."

As they maneuvered through the shallow waters, the old man's wrinkled hand reached down and scooped up some pebbles. He handed the stones to the boy and asked, "Of what geological period is this rock?" The boy said, "I don't know, what kind of rock is it?" The professor said, "If you don't know geology, you're missing out on another twenty percent of life." Shortly after, darkness fell, and the first star came out. The old man pointed to a constellation and asked, "What star is that?" The boy again said, "I don't know."

"My son," the professor said, "if you do not understand biology and history and astronomy, you are missing out on sixty percent of life. You will only be living life on a very shallow level." Suddenly they heard a loud roar and realized their canoe was rapidly being carried along by the swift current. The roar ahead of them grew louder and the student asked, "Professor, do you know how to swim?" The old man said, "No." As the boy dove into the river and swam to shore he yelled back, "Then you're missing out on one hundred percent of life!"

# You Can't Kid Nature

As many of you know, I was born on an Iowa farm. Adjoining my family's farm was a river, which thrilled me because I loved to fish. I remember one time when a city kid came to visit the neighbors across the road for a few weeks. The city kid was our neighbor's nephew. His uncle had welcomed him but warned that he would have to help out with the work.

One day Uncle Harry gave his nephew a can of beans to plant. He explained, "Just dig a little hole, put in a couple of beans, and step it down. Do it all the way along the fence, 'til you get to the end."

Unaware of the task that had been assigned to this city lad, I invited him to join me fishing.

He replied, "Uncle Harry said I have to plant these beans. He said I have to dig a little hole, put in three beans, and step it down."

I said, "Oh, that's too bad. I wish you could go fishing with me. Ever been fishing?"

"No. I'd like to go fishing with you, but I've got to finish these beans." From the looks of the full can it appeared that he'd just started. Suddenly, directly in front of him was a stump. "Uncle Harry will never know," he said, as he dug a hole, dumped in all the beans, and covered them with dirt. He turned away from his task and said, "Let's go fishing!"

We had a grand time. We caught a good number of fish. Coming home with bullheads, we ran into Uncle Harry.

He said, "I see you've been fishin'. Did you get all the beans planted?"

His nephew said, "Sure did, Uncle Harry."

"That's great. Glad to hear it. And you still had time to fish?"

"M-m-m, yeah."

"I'm surprised you were able to plant them so quickly."

He answered, "I work fast."

Uncle Harry seemed to accept his word for it. Soon it was time for the boy to return home. Months passed. The summer was drawing to a close. The city kid returned for a last visit before school started.

Uncle Harry said to him, "Hey, would you like to see those beans you planted?" They walked out behind the farmhouse. There was a neat row of beans for about fifty feet. Suddenly there was a stump of a tree covered with uncontrolled vines.

The lesson is this: You can't kid nature and you can't play with God. You can't avoid principles and you can't tamper with natural laws. This is a natural law: If you treat people nicely, they'll treat you nicely. It is the law of proportionate return, and there's no way of getting around it.

# Real Quality

I recently read a fascinating story by John Dart in the *Los Angeles Times*. In it, he described how Johann Gutenberg, who died in 1468, took with him his publishing secrets. The Gutenberg Bible, unlike all other known print on paper, still has jet-black ink after five hundred years. There is no seepage through the paper and the edges of letters are perfectly sharp. Twenty-four people, headed by Dr. Schwab and Dr. Cahill of the University of California at Davis, have been using the cyclotron to find the secret of Gutenberg's ink. They have finally discovered that Gutenberg used unusually high lead and copper content. In essence, the ink he used was closer to paint than it was to ink.

Gutenberg's secret? No frills. He went for real quality. If you want to succeed in life, don't go for cheap thrills.

# EXTRAORDINARY
# GENEROSITY

# God Protected Us

There's a man alive today enjoying life and health who probably would have died from lung cancer if he hadn't listened to one of my messages and made a decision. He and his wife left church that morning and decided they were going to tithe. They looked at the money they had left and they said, "There's no way we can get by." But then he looked at his wife, and she looked at him and said, "If we tithe, the only way we can get by is if we cut something out of our life that we're spending money on now." He replied, "But there's nothing we're spending money on that we can cut out." She said, "Unless we quit smoking."

It was true, if they quit smoking, then they could afford it. He said, "I guess it's not right to take God's money and buy our tobacco." They quit smoking and he later shared with me, "I believe that God has prospered me by tithing, and He has probably protected both my wife and me from lung cancer."

# A Gift From the Heart

Recently, I donated my Good Shepherd medallion to our charity auction. Prior to the event, I had announced on television my plan to make this donation. A lady in New York City, who has watched the "Hour of Power" faithfully, heard what was going to happen and decided she would buy the medallion regardless of the cost. She flew to California to attend the auction and was prepared to bid any amount.

The medallion was worth only one thousand dollars, but she bought it for sixty-four hundred dollars. All of the money went to our mission project. The day after the auction she stopped to see me before her return to New York. Enthusiastically she said, "Dr. Schuller, the real reason I bought the medallion was I felt you should always have it." Then she gave me back my medallion as a gift!

# Surrender to Compromise

Albert Schweitzer built a hospital in the African jungle. One day he asked one of the natives to carry some wood. The native, who had been learning to read and write, replied, "I'd like to, sir, but it's beneath my dignity. I am a scholar, an intellectual."

Albert Schweitzer chuckled and said, "I've always wanted to be an intellectual, too, but I never quite made it, so I'll carry the wood!" And he went out and carried the wood.

# A Beautiful Gift

I'll never forget the young girl who came to me. She was pregnant, and she could not marry the man. She wanted to know whether she should get an abortion or not.

I said to her, "Look, I can't make your decision for you. I can, however, share with you a principle that will help you make the right choice. I want you to think of one thing—there is a negative and positive solution—and then let your conscience be your guide."

It was many months later when I next saw her. She looked so happy. She said, "I just gave a beautiful gift to a beautiful couple."

I asked, "What gift did you give?"

She said, "A baby. They told me that my baby was an answer to prayer." Then she added this: "Dr. Schuller, you often say that the bottom line in giving is being unselfish. Giving is living, and I'll always know that I gave the world something beautiful."

# The Best That I Had

Some years ago there was a play called *Eagerheart*. It was the story of a beautiful, eager, young peasant girl named Eagerheart, who lived in a simple little country hut. The news reached the town and the surrounding farming huts that the king of England would be coming through the territory. That meant that he could knock on any door and hospitality would be extended to him.

Eagerheart couldn't wait for the day when the king was expected to pass through town. She cleaned her little hut, swept the floor, and pressed the curtains. Everything was clean, fresh, and sweet-smelling.

Just as she was ready to rush to the village, so she wouldn't miss him, another peasant woman with a shawl over her head and a baby in her arms, came to her door and said, "I am tired from a long journey. May I come in for rest and water?"

Eagerheart said, "I must go to the village to meet the king, who is coming to town. But, yes, you may come in. You may rest, you may have water. But I can't stay. Good-bye." With that, she rushed off to the village.

As she made her way to the village, she met three Oriental men, bearing what looked like expensive gifts. They asked her directions to the countryside and she pointed them down the path that she'd just taken. She wondered what those strange, rich-looking men would be doing near her place. One of the men, noticing the question in her eyes, said, "We are astrologers. We read the stars and the stars tell us a king is coming."

Eagerheart said, "I know, that's why I'm going to the village."

They said, "But our stars tell us we can find him in the country."

She did not challenge them but thought that was strange. She kept going until she got to the village. Suddenly she saw many villagers streaming out of the town. She asked one, "Where are you going?" He replied, "The king is coming, and the word is that he's out in the country."

So Eagerheart followed the crowd, and lo and behold, the parade led to her own little hut. She said, "He can't be in there, that is my place!" But she ran up and opened the door and there was the old woman whose head was covered with a shawl, the woman who carried a simple, little child, whom she had admitted to her home so casually and left when she went to the village. Now the woman stood, the shawl was removed, and Eagerheart recognized the old woman as the queen mother of England and the baby as the new king. Eagerheart dropped to her knees, and she said, "Oh, had I stayed home, I could have spent the time alone with him!" But then she added, "At least I gave him the best that I had."

# Give Someone a Lift

There is a story of a man who had a dream one night. He dreamed that he died and found himself in a large room. In the room there was a huge banquet table filled with all sorts of delicious food. Around the banquet table were people seated on chairs. They were obviously hungry. But the chairs were five feet from the edge of the table and the people apparently could not get out of the chairs. Furthermore, their arms were not long enough to reach the food on the table.

In the dream there was a solitary large spoon, five feet long. Everyone was fighting, quarreling, and pushing each other, trying to grab hold of the spoon. The man reached out, picked up some food, and turned it to feed himself, only to find that the spoon was so long that as he held it out he could not touch his mouth. The food fell off.

Immediately, someone else grabbed the spoon. That person reached far enough to pick up the food, but could not feed himself. The handle was too long.

In his dream, the man who was observing it all said to his guide, "This is hell; to have food and not be able to eat it." The guide replied, "Where do you think you are? This is hell. But this is not your place. Come with me."

And they went into another room. In this room there also was a long table, filled with food, exactly as in the other room. Everyone was seated in chairs, and for some reason they, too, seemed unable to get out of their chairs.

Like the others, they were unable to reach the food on the table. Yet they had a satisfied, pleasant look on their faces. Only then did the visitor see the reason. For exactly as before, there was only one spoon. It, too, had a handle five feet long. Yet no one was fighting for it. In fact, one man who held the handle reached out, picked up food, and put it into the mouth of someone else who ate and was satisfied.

That person then took the spoon by the handle, reached for the food from the table, and put it back to the mouth of the man who first gave him something to eat. And the guide said, "This is heaven."

If you want to be fed, you have to feed someone else. If you want happiness, you have to forget about your own happiness and look for someone who needs the lift that only you can give.

# Caring Is Carrying

In the villages in the Bahamas today, they still do something that has been a tradition for years.

Before I tell you what it is, let me tell you about the kind of family I came from. In our little Dutch ethnic community in Iowa, it was a custom that if somebody became ill, my mother would bake a pie, or cookies, or a loaf of bread, and take it to the neighbor. It was the natural thing to do when someone was sick. But I never before heard of what they do in the Bahamas. You go to the villages in the Bahamas and about suppertime everybody cooks their food. As you walk down the street you can smell the delicious fragrances in the air. Everybody seems to eat about the same time, but before they sit down in their home to eat, the doors open and the people walk out of their front doors with plates. They have made more than an abundance of food. So they take a plate of home-baked food and carry it across the street to share with a neighbor. Soon another neighbor comes to their house and shares his food.

It reminds me of the times when my wife and I go out for dinner and I order a different entrée than she does. If mine is very good, I want her to share my taste of joy. So I say, "Would you like to taste my entrée?" And she says, "Yes." And I cut a piece and share it with her. And she gives me a portion of hers. Caring is carrying. It's a law of life.

# A Touching Scene

I've been to many of the world's most beautiful Christmas pageants, including the Glory of Christmas that is held every year in the Crystal Cathedral. But nothing has touched me more than the scene in the Christmas pageant that was held in a little country school in Iowa.

The star of that pageant was a young fellow named Howard who was big and rather awkward. He was given the role of the Innkeeper. He was so excited that he rehearsed his one line until he could say it perfectly. His line was, "There's no room in my inn." When Mary and Joseph came to him on stage, he was to face them gruffly and say, "There is no room in my inn."

When the pageant finally took place, on opening night, Joseph came with Mary, who was almost stumbling, tired, in distress. They came up to little Howard, who was playing the role of Innkeeper, and Joseph said, "I'm looking for a room for my wife." And Howard, who had memorized his lines, suddenly saw Mary, and felt terrible. A tear welled up in his eye, rolled down his cheek, and he said, "Oh, come on in, you can have my room!"

# Give Something Back

How do you handle debt? That's the big question. I like George Kennedy's attitude. This esteemed actor not too long ago said to me, "Every time my wife, Joan, and I sit down to a meal, we always begin with the same little prayer. We look at the food we're about to consume and we say, 'Oh, Lord, help us to give something back.' " What a fantastic prayer! We all should learn how to give. Most of us don't know how, you know.

Take, for example, the average college alumnus. Most alumni give very, very little to their institutions, even though they're making money based on their education. Here's why: They think they don't owe any more to their school. They've paid their tuition, which was high, so they feel they've given back all that was expected. In reality, they haven't given a thing. They only paid their bill. Giving doesn't start until you've paid what you owe.

# The Beautiful Hazel Wright

I have never met anyone whom I consider more beautiful than Hazel Wright. As my wife and I have come to know her, we have learned the secret of her beauty. What is it? She knows how to give. She's not selfish.

Selfish people are not pretty people. They are cautious, conservative, security-conscious people who are dominated by worry and fear. On the other hand, giving people are dominated by joy, love, faith, and hope. It's really true. The measure with which you give will be reflected in your personality.

Many years ago Hazel's husband began to prosper in his enterprises. He would buy her little gifts. She said to him one day, "I don't need things. I thank you for your love—that's enough for me." So Hazel's husband, rather than buying her jewelry or other pretty things, gave his wife some stock in the company. The stock accumulated because she never spent it on herself.

Hazel never was a mother. She remained childless until she saw great institutions and organizations that were threatened. Because she is a caring, compassionate woman, she decided to adopt and support these floundering projects. Then when her husband died, she decided to keep his love alive to some degree by continuing to give whatever she could to those who really needed it.

As a result, if you're ever in Palm Springs at the Eisenhower Memorial Hospital, you will see three large buildings. One carries the name The Wright Building. Hazel Wright had that building constructed for the sick and the suffering.

# A Way of Saying Thanks

I recently called Kathy Gill. Kathy is one of our staff people. She's in Seattle undergoing a bone marrow transplant because it's the only thing that can save her life. What powerful faith! She said, "Oh, it's wonderful just to look outdoors and see the sun shining." Kathy is a young mother, not more than thirty years old. She is so grateful just to be alive. *Alive.* If you are given the gift of life, my friend, and the gift of health, and if you're not living under a death sentence right now, you should be so grateful to God. A tenth is almost nothing to give as a way of saying thanks.

# Go for the Touchdown

One day years ago when I was at Western Theological Seminary, a guest lecturer came and spoke, of all things, on money. He said, "Students, you will soon be going out as pastors of churches. If you do a good job you're going to need money. If you fail, you won't need anything. But if you succeed, you're going to need money and a lot of it.

"Then, how can the church get the money to do the job? The Bible has an answer: God's way is to convince people to give one-tenth of their income back to God. It's called tithing. In Malachi 3, the Lord says, 'Bring your whole tithe into my storehouse and prove me and see if I will not open the windows and pour out such a blessing there will not be room enough to receive it' " (*see* verse 10).

I raised my hand and said, "I am a seminary student earning twenty dollars a week cleaning toilets. Are you telling me that I'm supposed to give ten percent, or two dollars, in the offering plate each Sunday?"

He said, "Yes."

I said, "I don't think I can afford that."

He replied, "You can't afford not to. If you trust God, He will give you the wisdom to make your eighteen dollars go further than the twenty dollars would." That was the toughest decision I ever made. But at the close of his lecture, he said, "I think we all ought to pray about this."

Then he did something that I had never seen before. Normally, I would have found it repulsive and manipulative. But, in his closing prayer, he said, "God, I sense that somebody here needs to believe what You have promised us in the Bible. I pray that this person will make a decision now to practice tithing all his life. If you want to make such a decision, will you now raise your hand?"

I found my hand going up. When I had it in the air, I thought, *Oh, dear, what have I done? Lord, have I promised You that I'll give You 10 percent?*

I was absolutely astounded that I'd done such a thing, because I'd had it tough, financially. My family had just lost everything in a tornado. Then a fire burned my dormitory. I had to buy new clothes. I don't think anybody was poorer than I was. Yet, I had just promised God I would give Him 10 percent of all I had.

However, it was the greatest decision I ever made in my life, because I heard a little voice deep down that said, *Schuller, if you don't have enough faith to grab that idea from God, you won't have enough faith to grab hold of some of the bigger ideas He wants to throw your way. If you can't catch a short pass, how do you think you can jump and catch the big one and go for the touchdown?*

Well, I went for it, and six years later I received the call to begin a church from scratch. My denomination had promised me a salary of $375 a month for six months. After that, I was on my own. I also received a gift of $400 from the little church that I'd served in Chicago.

On our way to California, my wife and I stopped and saw a friend who was in the music business in Sioux City, Iowa. I said, "I'm going to California to start a new church. I don't have any members yet. I don't own any property, but I do have four hundred dollars in my pocket. I have a wife who is an organist. I'd like to buy an organ. Can you sell me an organ?"

He replied, "I'll sell you this Kahn electric organ for eighteen hundred dollars. I'll take your four hundred dollars as a down payment. The balance will be thirty-six dollars a month for thirty-six months."

I said, "It's a deal." Since I was a tither, I knew that for six months I would be getting $375 a month. Ten percent of $375 is $37 a month. Consequently I knew I could make the monthly payments on the organ. If I hadn't been a tither, I wouldn't have purchased the organ.

That was just the first step. If I hadn't had enough faith to try tithing, I would never have had the nerve to grab hold of all the bigger ideas that God was getting ready to send my way.

# In Appreciation

Recently in Florida, a husband and a wife, both about sixty-two years of age, took my hand and with tears in their eyes, told me their story.

They said, "Dr. Schuller, we want to give all our property in our will to your ministry."

I said, "Wait a minute. Thank you, but you know, you must remember your children first."

They said they had no children.

I said, "But you must have dear friends who have helped you."

They said, "We have no friends dearer than you. Eight years ago we had decided to end our lives together. We researched it. We had scientifically planned how we were going to kill ourselves in a suicide pact. And the day that we planned to do it, we turned the television set on to find out how the weather would be affecting our plans. We were flipping the dial and we saw you. All we saw was a smile. And it stopped us cold. And then you told us about Jesus, that He was alive." By this time they were weeping openly. They said, "Reverend Schuller, that was eight years ago. Everything is wonderful now."

# A Unique Ministry

Not long ago I received a letter from a charter member of our church, Clara Landrus. She wrote me about her mother, Katherine Grant, who just recently passed away at the age of ninety-three. Mrs. Grant lived as a shut-in for the past eight years up in the small town of Clarkston, Washington. According to Clara, her mother began every Sunday morning with the "Hour of Power." October 25 was her last Sunday with this television ministry, for on November 1 she went to be with Jesus, where there is no sunset and no dawning.

As a shut-in, Mrs. Grant had a unique ministry. She had people come and visit her, and when they did, she would give them a lift. Clara's mother kept a diary and recorded her daily events. In the past ten months, Mrs. Grant had a total of 357 visits by 81 different people. Those who visited her left feeling better. One person summed it up to Clara: "Your mother put a bloom on so many days for so many people."

# EXTRAORDINARY
# FAITH

# When Proof Is Possible Faith Is Impossible

One summer I was in Tokyo for an evangelism event. I was to speak to a few thousand Japanese people who claimed to have no faith at all. Before I talked to them, I visited with several of them at great length, trying to understand where they were coming from.

I asked them, "What would you call yourselves?"

They replied almost unanimously, "We are atheists."

I said, "Why are you atheists?"

The combined answer was, "We are very scientific. We do not believe in something that cannot be proven."

My answer to them came from my subconscious. I heard myself say it before I thought it, therefore, I know it came from God. The answer was, "That's a contradiction, for the truth is, when proof is possible, faith is impossible."

If you know all of the answers, you don't need any faith. If you have absolute conclusive proof of any position, it requires no trust to move forward.

Faith is a behavioral human response when you're challenged to make a choice and you cannot be certain of either of the options. That's what faith is.

So then the question arises, "If there is a God, why didn't He prove it to us?" The answer is simple: If He proved Himself to you (and it would be easy for Him to prove Himself) you could never be a believer—you would simply be a follower.

# Moses: A Great Possibility Thinker

Moses was a great possibility thinker. When he was urged to take the children of Israel out of Egypt, he left, even though he had no way of knowing how he would get those people across the Red Sea. If he had waited to leave until the solution to his problem was apparent to him, God would never have parted the waters.

At the heart of the meaning of faith is a very important principle: God never performs a miracle until you've committed yourself to something beyond your ability.

# God's Biggest Job

As I left my house one day, I was enthusiastic about going to work. I rushed into the garage, threw my briefcase into the backseat, started the car, and backed out of the garage. But something didn't feel right. I jumped out of the car and discovered I had a flat tire. Have you ever had the experience of a slow leak? Or have you ever had the experience of a blowout? Have you ever had the experience of feeling self-confident, beginning to believe you were an attractive person made by God? Then someone gave you a rebuff or a rejection, and what happened? It was like a self-confidence blowout.

Maybe your work doesn't go well. You aren't receiving the recognition you deserve and you don't believe that people appreciate you. What is that? That's like a slow leak. And one day you wake up and the tire is flat. The self-confidence is gone.

God's biggest job is to keep you believing. He made you. He's planning your life. You're great! That's His biggest job—to keep your self-confidence up day after day.

# Eternal Life

I recall the wife of a congressman from Orange County in California. She had two children, a son and a daughter. Both of them were killed when they were teenagers. Her husband also died at a fairly early age. She was completely alone. You know, it's easy to go to someone and say, "Don't look at what you have lost, look at what you've got left." But here was a case where she had no one left.

I said, "Where do you find comfort? What gives you the strength to keep going?"

She said, "I live in Long Beach. I used to go to the beach every day. Often I just sat there, numb. I could not think. I could not feel, but I could see. And I watched the waves as they built into a curl of foam as they washed up onto the sand and retreated. I did that, day after day, week after week, month after month, and year after year. One day, as I watched the waves curl, break, foam, and sweep across the sand, I was struck with a message from God. I heard a voice within me say, *There is nothing but eternal life.*"

And she said, "I knew where my son was. I knew where my daughter was, and where my husband was."

# A Telegram for Humphrey

I remember sending a telegram to my friend Hubert Humphrey, before he went to the hospital for major surgery in New York City. I was in the music department when my secretary buzzed me and said Hubert Humphrey was on the phone. When I picked up the receiver he said, "Hello, Bob, I'm so glad I got hold of you. I'm going into major surgery in a few hours and I wanted to thank you for your inspiring telegram. My staff just brought in a large stack of telegrams and letters, neatly pressed and sorted. I was browsing through a few of them and guess whose was on top!"

I said, 'The president of the United States?" He laughingly said, "No, Bob, yours was! I have it before me now and I'm drawing so much strength from it." (The telegram read: "Dear Mr. Humphrey, God wanted me to send His Scripture to you. 'I have a plan for your life, it is a plan for good, not evil. It is a plan to give you a future with hope!' Jeremiah 29:11.")

Every person listening to me needs that inner strengthening that can only come from God, who is bigger than you or me! Now when heartache hits, difficulties block your path, or progress seems retarded and you wonder if you should pack up and quit—hang on! We will never know how many people failed because they gave up on faith. Don't ever quit!

# Laguna Canyon

Many years ago, before the area was developed, a friend of mine from Orange County was riding through the hills of Laguna Canyon with another Orange County resident. They passed a large herd of cows grazing on a hillside. My friend Chuck said, "You know, John, I am worried about my cows. It's been a dry summer. I sure hope they get enough water to drink."

John looked at him and said, "I didn't know you owned these cows and that ranch. I thought it was Irvine property." Chuck said, "Oh, no, John, I own all those cows, I own all those hills, and I own this road. You know what, John? So do you. Every night I look down at all the twinkling lights in Laguna Beach, and I say, 'I own it all. I'm just glad I don't have to manage it!' " He said, "Sure. You know, John, it says in the Bible, 'The cattle and the fowl of the hills are mine.' God owns everything and we are His children. *We* own it all. But the truth is, John, we are just stewards. He trusts us with it."

# No Problem Too Big

Recently I entered the Crystal Cathedral with Bob Jani and pointed out to him that the entrance to this cathedral has the lowest ceiling of any chapel or church in the United States. The ceiling in my home is eight feet, six inches high. I cannot touch it with my fingertips. But the ceilings under the balconies in the cathedral are only seven feet high. I can lay my hands flat on the ceiling, it's so low. So it is thrilling to step from under the low balconies into the awesome expanse of the main sanctuary. It's like a reminder that nobody is too small to touch God. And no problem is too big for His power.

# Prayer Talk

I remember a time when I was going down a mountain, flat on my back, in an ambulance, with broken bones and bleeding kidneys. I had had a fall in the mountains and I was hurting. I began to pray. I used two-way communication, saying, "Lord, why in the world did I fall, anyway?" And I heard Him say, *Schuller, it's your own miserable fault. You shouldn't have sat on such a rickety ladder.*

"That's right, Lord. That's right. It's my own fault. Lord,

I hope I'm not too badly injured." I heard Him say, *Don't worry. You've got two kidneys and only one is hurting. You'll be okay.* And so it went all the way down the mountain, over an hour in the ambulance. The attendant said to me, "Don't you want a shot?" And I answered, "No, I'm having too good a time talking with God."

# Your Most Important Decision

I've been in churches where I have heard ministers preach the toughest sermons I've ever heard. They scold people, they rebuke people, they slap their hands and pound their fists; they give them verbal crucifixions from the pulpit. I've thought, *How can these people take such a verbal whipping? This minister is just tearing the people down. How can they take it? They're going to walk out any minute. They're going to hate that preacher!* And you know what? I was totally wrong. I lingered in the back and heard the people say to the pastor, "Oh, that was a great sermon, Reverend." I couldn't get over it!

Then I began to analyze it. I looked at the faces of the people, and do you know what I saw? I saw people who do not understand what the grace of God means! They have to earn their forgiveness. They want to pay for their own sins. They want to be verbally spanked so they won't feel guilty anymore. They don't understand that Christ died on the cross and paid the whole deal! All we have to do is accept!

Man's biggest problem is that he hates himself. God's toughest job is to make you believe that you can be a beautiful person. Your most important decision is in choosing— choosing to accept God's forgiveness and choosing to take God into your life.

# Trust the God Who Loves You

It happened January 6, 1982. He was driving through the Grenalla Pass, going from his home in Bailey, Colorado, to Georgetown, Colorado. His name was Allen Phillips. He could easily make the trip at the 11,665-foot elevation. He was expecting the road to be clear, so he had no chains on his tires. Suddenly an enormous storm struck, and Allen found himself in a blizzard. He was hopelessly stuck. Darkness fell and he knew the road was closed. There was no way he could get out. He didn't have enough gas to keep the car running, and he knew that by morning he would be dead. Then a thought came into his mind—a crazy, impossible thought.

He remained cool. He did not panic. Here was the idea: He would use the headlights of the car to signal an S.O.S.—three shorts, three longs, and three shorts. Even though he was surrounded by trees and mountains, maybe somebody would see.

A Rocky Mountain Airline commuter flight happened to be flying high overhead and one passenger, the local deputy sheriff, who knew the Morse code, just happened to be looking out the window. He thought he saw three shorts, three longs, three shorts. He went to the pilot and said, 'I think I've seen a Morse code in headlights.'' The captain then made a swing around and indeed, he saw three shorts, three longs, three shorts. The captain radioed the Federal Aviation Administration. The FAA called the Clear Creek sheriff's station. They sent out two snow vehicles and they rescued the stranded man!

# Understanding Christianity

Sigmund Freud came to America in 1908. He was very distressed that the Americans mistranslated his words. But after his visit, he went back to Germany and made this profound statement: "Psychoanalysis will survive unless it is accepted without being understood." And I say the same thing about Christianity. Christianity will survive unless it is accepted without being understood.

What do I mean? Christianity is accepted by many people as a good way of life; a nice philosophy; an interesting set of ethics; a basically wholesome moral system; culturally quite refined. It is accepted, but not understood. Do you want to understand it? If you want to understand it, this is what is involved: I say to Jesus Christ, "I'm willing to sacrifice myself; my pride; my glory; my honor; my name. And I want You to live in me and through me. I will die. Jesus, you can live in this brain, thinking my thoughts; in this face, smiling at people; in this heart, loving the lonely; and I will never expect any credit." That's understanding Christianity and that's power!

# Always There

I'll never forget when I took my oldest daughter, Sheila, to the airport. She left home to go to college. Then my second child, my son, finally had to leave home. I took him to the airport; he flew to Holland, Michigan, to go to Hope College. Then my third child, Jeanne, left. She took the plane to Chicago. She chose Wheaton College. Recently Carol, our seventeen-year-old, left home. She's got a few medals in her room that she picked up at the National Skiing Championships in Colorado. When she saw the movie *Chariots of Fire* she said, "Dad, I want to try to make the handicapped Olympic team." And she explained, "You know, every time there's an Olympics, there's also a division for the handicapped. And the next international Olympics happen in 1984."

So, all by herself these past months, she was thinking and praying. She thought she had a shot at making the team in 1984, but she said, "In order to do that, Dad, I really have to start training. I have to spend a few hours every day, five days a week, on the slopes with a good coach." She said, "Dad, I've lined up a coach in Winter Park, Colorado. And I've written to Sacramento so I can be released from high school and can continue my courses through correspondence, and not become a dropout." She had solutions to all the problems.

"And so," she said, "I've been calling around and I think maybe I can even find a room I can rent." And, well, you know, we believe in possibility thinking at our home, so we didn't discourage her. We took her to the airport. Three suitcases. Her skis. Her outriggers. We kissed her good-bye. And she left home for Winter Park, Colorado.

I called her before church one morning. She was getting ready to go to church, herself. I asked, "Can I tell the people what you're doing?" She said sure. I said, "Of course if I tell them, then you can't come home in two weeks."

Let's face it, she wasn't gone twenty-four hours and she called up and said, "I miss you, Mom and Dad." I told her, "Well, most of the time you were in your room and the door was closed. You never talked that much." She said, "No, but I knew you were there all the time."

I said, "That's a little the way it is with God, isn't it?"

# A Promise

There was a Scottish lassie who was dying. When somebody came to her and asked, "Lassie, where are you going?" she replied; "I'm going to heaven."

"How can you be so sure you're going to heaven?" She said, "Oh, He promised. He said, 'I will not leave you.' That's good enough for me." The person asked, "But what if He forgets His promise?" The lassie said, "He'd lose more than I would. I'd only lose my soul, but he'd lose His honor."

"I will not leave you comfortless"—that's a promise of Jesus!

# Break Away From Defensive Holding

I was in Washington recently and I talked to a father who had two daughters in high positions on Capitol Hill. I said to the father, "How did you ever manage to have two daughters in such powerful positions on Capitol Hill?" And his answer was, "I used to take them to the capital when they were little girls so they could see the seat of power. One daughter graduated from high school and I wanted her to go to college. But she said, 'I'm going to get a job— I'm going to become secretary to a great senator!'" The father said, "I didn't want to let her go. I didn't dare let my two daughters leave home and go to the city without having chaperones or protection."

I asked him who gave in and this is what he told me: "I'm a football fan, Dr. Schuller, and about that time I was watching football and I saw my favorite team get a red penalty flag. They were penalized for defensive holding. It was like a message from God saying, *Father, don't be penalized for defensive holding. Don't hold your daughters back! Let them go! Let them fly like birds! Let them be what they were designed to be!*"

Some of you are being penalized for defensive holding. God has a plan for your life. God has a dream for you. His ideas come to you and they are always big. They are always beautiful, but they always seem to be impossible. So, because they threaten your success, you hold back. Because there's a possibility of failure, you don't move ahead.

What would you be trying to do today if you knew you

could not fail? The difference between a person at the top of the ladder and a person at the bottom of the ladder is that the person at the top never penalizes himself for defensive holding.

# A Special Evening Walk

I made a return trip to Mainland China a few years ago. My son led a tour of people who were invited to be a part of that mission. One night I tapped on my son's door. We were in Shanghai. It was rather late, but Bob was not in his room. Someone said, "He went out for a walk."

I immediately went out into the street to see if I could spot him. I saw a crowd, almost a mob, gathered on the bridge. I cautiously approached the large group of Chinese who surrounded the six-foot-four-inch-tall American. It was my son. Bob was talking to two of the leaders of this great crowd. I could see that he was excitedly sharing with these two.

Afraid of intruding, I quietly retreated to the hotel. Later that night he told me what happened. He was on the bridge when the group came up to him. There were two bright students who spoke English. They asked him, "Who are you? Where are you from? What are you doing here?"

He said, "Have you ever heard about Jesus Christ?"

"No."

"Well," he said, "I'm a Christian."

They asked, "What's a Christian?"

He told them, and he led them through the spiritual laws. He explained that it is a law that God wants us all to be beautiful persons. It's a law of life that we all have our sins, our internal tensions. We all need salvation. And then he said, "Jesus came to save us."

He asked them if they'd like to accept Jesus as their Friend. To his amazement, they said, "Yes."

So Bob prayed with them. There on the street in Shanghai, Bob and the young Chinese students prayed together. Bob had told them about the Bible, so in response to their request he later sent them Bibles and continued corresponding with them.

# That Floyd River

I was born on a little farm in Iowa and I remember fishing in a river near the house. When I look at rivers I usually find myself asking these questions: Where's the source of the river? What is the course of the river? What is the force of the current?

You know that Floyd River of Iowa doesn't realize it, but it flows into the big Sioux. And the big Sioux doesn't know it, but it flows into the Missouri. And the Missouri flows into the Mississippi. And the Mississippi creates a massive fruit-bearing area called the Delta—the fertile farmland of the South. Someday I wish that profitable, fruitful, superproductive Mississippi Delta could stand up and with a warm southern drawl say, "Hats off to you, Floyd River, Iowa!" They may not realize it in the Delta, but they owe something to the Floyd River in Iowa.

The little stream flows into the big stream. You need the same Christ in you that I have in me to be your Source, to set your course, and to be a Force in your life.

# "Walk Humbly With Your God"

I think everybody who attended the 1984 Presidential Prayer Breakfast in Washington, D.C. had wet eyes at one point. It was not the remarkable and beautiful talk by our president, Ronald Reagan, and it was not the address given by a marvelous speaker, Barbara Jordan. But it happened when Senator Jacob Javitz read the Old Testament lesson.

Senator Javitz is suffering from ALS, or as it is most commonly known, Lou Gehrig's disease. I happened to have a table up in front. I was able to see the sparkle in his eye.

There were pillows propped behind his back and he had a breathing apparatus with a plastic tube that allowed him to breathe.

Between gasps of breath, he read: "What does the Lord require of you but to be just, to love mercy, and walk humbly with your God."

Then he said, "My favorite chapter in the Bible is Psalm 23":

The Lord is my shepherd, I shall not want. He makes me to lie down in green pastures. He leads me beside the still waters. . . . Even though I walk through the valley of the shadow of death, I will fear no evil, for thou art with me. Thy rod and thy staff, they comfort me. Thou preparest a table before me in the presence of mine enemies. Surely goodness and mercy shall follow me all the days of my life and I shall dwell in the house of the Lord forever.

Senator Javitz knows it. Jesus has a way of coming into our lives and He deals with our contradictions. Somehow He integrates us, consolidates us, takes the opposing movements, and creates the cross out of them. We rise with a life so amazing, so divine, so abundant, so eternal.

# What If?

A while back, I was in San Francisco riding on a cable car. Halfway up the hill the cable car lost power. Everybody had to get out of the car and walk the rest of the way up the hill. Many people fear this in their own lives. They don't dare to make a commitment. They're thinking, *What if the power runs out before I get to the top of the hill?*

Not long ago, I was flying with a friend of mine. We were in his private plane, coming back from Cabo San Lucas. The pilot and my friend, who is also a pilot, were up front, and I was in the back with my son. It was a nice, relaxing plane ride. The weather was beautiful. The Sea of Cortez below us was a gorgeous turquoise and green. There was nothing but sea to the right, to the left, ahead, and behind us. I was studying and reading and doing a lot of work. As I lifted my eyes, I saw the pilot suddenly throw some switches. Then I heard him say, "Would you see if the owner's manual is in the glove compartment?"

I got nervous. My friend opened it and said, "Yeah, here it is." The pilot said, "Check this problem out. What do we do if—I think it's on page fourteen." I interrupted, "How far are we from land? What if the motor fails before you are over the landing strip?"

What if the power stops halfway up the hill? What if the motor goes before the landing strip is below you? What if the top rung of the ladder breaks before you've reached the roof? What if the sound system fails before you've finished the sermon?

Strength to see you through to the end. That is what God promises and that's what God provides. Be confident of this one thing: that God, who has begun a good work in you, will complete it. That is how God carries us—with a dream, with a decision, a desire, and finally with the determination never to stop trusting Him, even if the motor may be misfiring.

# A Very Positive Statement

I did some traveling one summer, and it was amazing. I was not able to escape the Crystal Cathedral. First, I went through Germany and opened *Sterne* magazine (which is like *Life* magazine in the United States), and there was the Crystal Cathedral. Not long after, I found myself flying Japan Airlines. I pulled out their monthly magazine and saw a picture of the Crystal Cathedral. I found myself, not too many weeks later, in Shanghai, downtown in the heart of modern communism. And I made contact with a very important Chinese official who is best left unnamed and unidentified. We met privately on Sunday in my hotel room, and he shared many things with me that cannot be repeated. But he also said, "Would you like to go to church with me tomorrow?"

He explained, "A church has just been opened—it has been closed, you know, for twenty-seven years. Actually it's just around the corner from the consulate—a very important location." I said, "I'd love to attend." And I went with him.

As we approached the church, my friend said, "You know, they may recognize you here." I said, "Oh, really?"

"Yes," he replied. "Your picture is up on the wall. I'll show you."

So we walked past the consulate where our government had erected a large, glass-covered poster on the wall that encircles the consulate offices. There were pictures and scenes of the United States which the consulate felt would make a great impression upon the millions of modern Chinese who walk down the street. Included was the largest picture of yours truly standing in the Crystal Cathedral. I asked my friend, "What does it say under the photo?" He said, "It says, 'Americans are happy people—they believe in God. Faith is very much alive.'" He continued, "'In fact, not long ago, one of the most beautiful churches built in America was erected and made out of ten thousand, six hundred, sixty-eight windowpanes.'"

The Crystal Cathedral was used by the federal government of the United States to hopefully make a positive statement of faith to China.

# The Lord Is Alive

A dear friend of mine was the president of Hope College in Holland, Michigan, when I was there in my undergraduate days. Many years ago, he and his young son were taking a trip from Michigan when an accident happened. As my friend tells it, suddenly the icy roads caused the car to flip over into a ditch. He lost consciousness. It was very cold and snowing heavily. He wondered if he'd even survive. He awoke and found himself being held in the arms of his little boy, his own heavy body resting against the child's tiny chest. The boy was crying—crying and praying. He said, "Dear Jesus, don't let my daddy die.

He's a good man, and does a lot of good for a lot of people. Dear Jesus, don't let my daddy die." And then my friend saw a Presence. He said, "There, next to my son, as clearly as I saw my son I saw Him, the Lord. And I wanted to go with Him so badly. I wanted to rush to Him and be with Him forever. And there was my little boy begging me to stay."

He said, "Bob, the skeptics can say what they want, the doubters can say what they will, the unbelievers can make their speeches. Me, I am an educator, I am a rationalist, I am a humanist, I am a scientist, and I have to tell you, I know I saw the Lord. And He's alive!"

# Never Say Lost

Many years ago, when my friend Doris Day's husband died, I said to her, "I am so sorry that you lost your husband." Boy, did she straighten me out. She said, "Bob, don't ever use that word *lost!* That is a negative word. When you hear the word *lost* the subconscious thinks of all kinds of nonrecallable experiences. I lost a coin, I lost a job, I lost this, I lost that. Never use that word *lost*. I have not lost my husband. I have agreed to let God accept him in faith."

# My Best Friend

I remember when I made a speech a few years ago in Saint Louis, Missouri. I came to town and was in my hotel at five o'clock in the afternoon. I was scheduled to go on the stage at half-past six to deliver a speech at a big, important convention. I unpacked my suit, which I hadn't worn in four months. I had lost thirty-eight pounds in those four months. My waist had dropped four inches. The trousers required a belt, and I had neglected to pack one. Possibly I could have made it through the lecture if I'd been the kind of speaker who never raised his arms.

I looked for a big safety pin which, of course, I couldn't find. I looked for a wire clothes hanger, thinking I could open it up and use it as a belt. That idea did not work. I called the front desk and asked, "Is there a tailor in town?" They said, "The tailor in the mall might still be open." I quickly trotted there and went in with my pair of trousers. He looked at me with that "We are about to close up" look. I said, "Can you take my trousers in for me?" He said, "Sure, but it will take a couple of hours."

I said to him, "They told me at the hotel that you are the greatest tailor in town. Is that true?"

"Well, I have been at it a long time."

"I have a friend in Orange, California, who could do this job for me in twenty minutes. You say that it'll take you two hours?"

He said, "Your tailor can do it in twenty minutes? We can do it in eighteen!"

He fixed the pants for me while I waited. They fit great. I said to him, "I knew you could do it! I've got faith."

He said, "You sound like a religious guy. In fact, haven't I seen you someplace?"

I said, "Could be."

"Are you a minister?"

"Yes."

"What's your religion like, anyway?"

I said, "Well, first of all, it's not really a religion in the sense that most religions are—made up of rules and regulations—don't do this and don't do that. It's not restriction, don't go here, don't go there. And it's not just a ritual where we recite the same memorized prayers. If it's not regulations, restrictions, or rituals, then what is it? It's a relationship that I have with Somebody who's become my Best Friend. His name is Jesus Christ. I believe in Him."

# It's the Regularity That Counts

Not long ago I was running and my path crossed with a man whose name many of you know. His name is George Romney. He was once the governor of Michigan. We ran together for about a mile.

I said, "When did you get into physical fitness so seriously?"

"I was in a physical-fitness program up in Wisconsin and there was a banner in the athletic center. The banner said, 'It's not the amount, it's the regularity that counts.'"

Then he added, "You know, Bob, that's true in prayer life. It's true in your walk with the Lord. It's not how many minutes you spend praying every day. It's not how many chapters of the Bible you have read. Yes, we have to pray every day. Yes, we have to read the Scriptures every day.

But it's not how many hours we spend on our knees. It's not the amount, it's the regularity that counts. If you're regular and faithful in your prayer and in your walk with Him, you'll know what God's will for your life is. You'll know what He wants you to do."

Play with the dream. Pray about the dream constantly, then pay the price. God isn't going to call you out of the security corner only to see you fall flat on your face. Rather, He calls you out of the corner to take a chance, but then He expects you to pay the price.

If you're in business, you pay the price through excellence of product, excellent service, and excellent treatment of people. It's easy to succeed if you treat people nicely.

# God Is Sometimes Silent

An amusing incident happened to me recently. I lectured on Tuesday at the University of Berkeley and on Wednesday I was scheduled to speak to the Lutherans at the five-hundredth anniversary of Martin Luther's birthday in Arizona. On Thursday, I was to be at Northwestern University of Iowa, and on Friday I had to be at Johns Hopkins in Baltimore. As you can see, it was really a tightly scheduled week. Everything was carefully timed and planned. If I missed a connection, I would really be in trouble.

Everything went smoothly until I got to Phoenix to catch my eastbound plane. I was first at the check-in desk, to make sure I would not be late. Soon there was a line of about thirty or forty people behind me with all their suitcases, waiting to check in. The plane was scheduled to leave in thirty minutes. Eventually a lady came to start the check-in. She looked harried. Trying to be understanding, I said, "You look like you have troubles."

She didn't even look up to see my face. She just mumbled, "Boy, have I got troubles!" She said, "I suppose you're here to check on this flight to Denver."

I said, "Yes."

She said, "Well, I just got word that that flight's going to be canceled, and I suppose you are now going to want me to help you, which I'm obligated to do, but I don't know what I'm going to do!" And then she looked up and said, "Oh, Dr. Schuller!" And she took hold of my hands and said, "Say a little prayer for me. I'm in trouble. I don't know what I'm going to do. Let me talk to the computer a minute."

She began to type on the keyboard. She stopped and looked at the computer. Her face registered dismay and frustration. Frantic, she picked up the phone. "Ben! Help! The computer's dead! Nothing! It's just looking at me. You say we have a line problem? I don't care if it's a line problem. Make it come alive, please!" She hung up.

The point is this: Before you complain because God is silent, remember, every once in a while, the computers are silent, too. However, you don't stop believing in a computer because there's a line condition. And we don't stop believing in God because there's a line problem.

# "Help! Is Anybody Up There?"

One day I was in a distant city when I met a man who told me how he had been converted. His life had been completely and totally changed. "I can't tell you the kind of dirty, unclean, demeaning life I was living," he said. "I just want to tell you that since I've become a Christian, my whole moral life has changed. I am a different person. In fact," he said, "I was converted listening to one of your jokes."

"What was the joke?" I asked. And he told me the story of a fellow who had dropped off a cliff and was plummeting toward the rocks below when he managed to grasp the twig of a tree that was growing through a crack in the granite cliff. Hanging there, hundreds of feet above the sharp granite rocks and swirling white water below, he looked up into the clouds that hid the edge of the cliff from his sight and cried, "Help! Is anybody up there?" And out of the clouds came the words, *I am here*. "Who are you?" he questioned. *I am your God,* the voice replied. "Can you help me?" the man asked in a voice tinged with desperation. *Have faith,* the heavenly voice commanded. *Let go.* The man looked down at the jagged rocks, then looked up toward the clouds and shouted, "Is anybody else up there?"

# Fannie May's Advice

I will never forget the time I was in the airport in Chicago, Illinois, and I stopped in the Fannie May Candy Store. My wife likes candy; I don't eat it. I actually think it's bad for your health. It's against my religion, but not hers!

I went into the store and there was another customer there—an old lady with a bag, a bunch of gifts, and a little suitcase. She looked very disorganized and somewhat ruffled. She was looking at the counter and since the clerk was waiting for her to decide what she wanted, I said to the clerk, "Do you have chocolate-covered nuts in one-pound boxes?" Before the clerk could respond, the little lady answered, "Oh, sure, they have chocolate-covered nuts in one-pound boxes; they also have them in two- and three-pound boxes, and they are very good." The clerk said, "Yes, that's right. We do have chocolate-covered nuts in one-pound boxes.''

Turning my back to the older lady, I asked the clerk, "Do you by any chance have turtles? You know, the caramel and walnuts with chocolate over them? My wife loves those caramel turtles.'' Again, before the clerk could answer, the busybody said, "Oh, sure, they have turtles in one-, two-, and three-pound boxes.'' The clerk appeared somewhat annoyed, and then the old lady said, "I'd advise you to buy a one-pound box of the Colonial assortment. It has chocolate-covered nuts, the turtles, and the creams, too.'' I answered, "My wife doesn't like creams.'' She said, "Oh, I think she'd like these creams. These are delicious.'' I tried to ignore her, but to no avail. She really persisted. It was a very awkward situation until suddenly the woman said, "I have to go or I'll miss my plane.'' She quickly gathered her bundles and suitcase and walked out. I breathed a sigh of relief and so did the clerk. Then she turned around and shouted to the back room, "Okay, girls, you can come out now. Fannie May is gone!''

I said, "Fannie May! That was Fannie May?'' She answered, "Yes. Her name is not really Fannie May. Her husband died and left her with a candy store. She decided that instead of feeling sorry for herself, she would invent some new chocolates. So she made up all of these recipes herself, opened more stores, and today she has one hundred seventeen stores. All she does is fly around the country and check on her stores. She calls them her one hundred seventeen children.''

I was looking at the clerk as an authority, when the real authority was right there! How sad. You know, some of you, in the same way, look to Dr. Schuller or some other minister to interpret the Bible. Let Jesus Christ be the Authority. Don't look to me—look to Him. If you really want to feel good about yourself, Christ says you must value life most highly in yourself and in others. You look upon every seed as a tremendous potential. Then you'll love life. You'll love the Lord, your God, your neighbor, and yourself. With that much love, what a beautiful community of human beings we can become.

# "Take Me to Christ's Church"

I once said to Dr. Viktor Frankl that even meaning is meaningless unless it feeds my self-esteem because the deepest need (deeper than sensuality, deeper than status or power, deeper than significance) is self-esteem. I have to feel as if I am worth something and so do you. Don't let people put you down and say you're on an ego trip. Look, if a person has no ego needs, that person is sick. The ego needs stem from our deep need to feel worthy, and Jesus Christ does this. That's why He's still the most popular Person in the world today.

I was told that somebody came out to California recently and picked a cab. The man said to the cabdriver, "Take me to Christ's church," so the cabdriver took him all the way to Orange County and dropped him off at the Crystal Cathedral. The man said, "I said Christ's church!" (There is a Church of Christ in Garden Grove). You know what the cabdriver said? "If He's in town, He'll be there!"

# Don't Carry the Truth Too Far

If you have the faith of a grain of a mustard seed you can say to this mountain, "Move," and nothing will be impossible to you. The philosopher George Santayana said, "Anytime somebody has a truth, somebody else will come along and carry it too far." I have been in this work for about thirty years, and I get letters, I meet people, and I know there are people who carry possibility thinking too far.

Not long ago I read a tragic story of people of another faith who believed that if they had enough faith, nothing was impossible. They interpreted that to mean that when a loved one died, if they prayed and had faith, the dead person would come to life. So when their child died, they did just that. Days passed while they prayed. Finally the body was decomposed and the officials moved in. How tragic.

A man once told me that when someone suffered the amputation of a limb, we need to pray, and believe that the limb will grow back. I totally disagree. That kind of faith does not glorify God! It insults the intelligence of His brightest creatures—you and me. God is not glorified through human insults.

# EXTRAORDINARY COURAGE

# Break Your Record

I recently took time for rest and renewal. After a grueling schedule I went to Hawaii with my wife. When we go there, we always run. For many years, I have run from the Kahala Hilton Hotel to Diamond Head and back, which is four and one-quarter miles. If I run from the hotel to the lighthouse on Diamond Head and back, I've run precisely five miles.

That's as far as I ever run in Hawaii. That's because if I wanted to run farther I would have energy and power that I never tapped before and never knew was there. This time, my breathing didn't go half-cycle—it went full-cycle with every breath. It was magnificent to feel the body working like a marvelous, finely tuned machine.

I felt like a million bucks. I was running and I was only about a half mile from the hotel. Now I had gone six and a half miles and I had set a new record, and broken through what had been a mental barrier in my life for twelve years. I found a tennis ball in the gutter, picked it up, and started dribbling.

At that point, I met a crusty, old, retired army general who is well known in Hawaii. He was riding his high-speed racing bike. He saw me and recognized me. Knowing that I'd had some problems, he said, "Don't let them get you down, Reverend."

What a lift he gave me. Don't let anybody get you down. Don't let anything get you down. Don't let any problems, don't let any obstacle, don't let any difficulty get you down. Break into new dimensions. Set the record. Let me give you a line right now: "If it's going to be, then it's up to me."

# Saved by the Mystery Doctor

A dear friend of mine, Algetha Brown, is a beautiful singer. In my opinion, she's one of the great black women singers in America. Algetha is married to an air force career man. Right after the Second World War, they were assigned to Germany.

The Nuremberg trials were happening. As Algetha said, "At that time there were many scared German citizens, because the word was out that if you were a Nazi or if you were a close friend of the Gestapo or if you were a good friend of a Nazi, the odds were that you might be called in for questioning. You might be arrested. You could be put on trial, sent to jail, and even to death if you were involved in the Holocaust."

She said, "Dr. Schuller, my husband and I met so many good, beautiful, wonderful German people who weren't Nazis, but they knew the wrong people so they were in hiding."

At the time, Colonel Brown, his wife, Algetha, and their two sons were living on the fourth floor of an apartment building. One day, her oldest son came down with the mumps. Algetha kept him in his room. Since it was a warm day, his window was open. Soon the little boy got restless, walked over to the window, sat on the sill, and watched the changing scenes on the street below.

Suddenly a gust of wind came and slammed the shutter, throwing the boy off balance. He fell four floors, ripping through a balcony iron railing two floors below, and landing on a cobblestone street. In a matter of minutes, the ambulance picked up the unconscious boy and brought him to the nearest civilian hospital.

Because he was a military officer's son the military doctors came and examined the boy, finding multiple compound fractures on the right arm. Even though he was not conscious, they could find no internal injury. Everything seemed to be okay, but they said that the arm would have to be amputated. There was no way it could be saved.

When the doctors left the room Algetha cried at her little boy's side and looked at the arm that would be coming off in twenty-four hours. The nurse, a German woman, walked up to Algetha, put her arm around her, looked at the beautiful little boy, unconscious on the bed, and said, "I probably shouldn't say this, but I know a German doctor who might be able to save that arm. I don't know if he'll come. He's in hiding. He had the wrong friends during the war. I do know where he's hiding."

Algetha said, "Would you ask him?"

Late that night Algetha was almost asleep at the bedside of her little boy, praying for his surgery in the morning, when a stranger in shabby clothes entered the room, looking furtively around. Seeing no one other than Algetha, he walked up to the bedside. Algetha looked up and asked, "Who are you?"

Whispering, he said, "I am the doctor the nurse talked to you about."

"Oh, thank you for coming!"

The doctor said, "I'm just going to check him. I must leave quickly before people find out I'm here." He checked the arm and said, "Mrs. Brown, that arm could be saved. I could save it."

The distraught young mother said, "Oh, would you, please?"

To her dismay, he said, "I can't. I'm awfully sorry."

She said, "Is it because I'm black?" He didn't even answer her. He merely turned and left the room.

The next morning, as the boy was being prepared for surgery, the nurse came in and said, "Mrs. Brown, I just got a call from the doctor. He said that he can't let them take the boy's arm. He said he would come out of hiding to do it, but we must keep it a secret."

An hour later he was scrubbing up. Two hours later, with the military surgeons standing back, the German doctor went to work. It was the first of seven operations that took out every little piece of stray splintered bone. The arm was saved.

But the news got out about the miracle surgery. Headlines read, "Black American Boy's Amputation Saved by Mystery Doctor."

Investigators read it. They said, "There's only one doctor who could have pulled that off. It's the one we've been looking for." They found him, of course. They arrested him and brought him to trial. He received a sentence of five years in prison.

As he was being led away, handcuffed, Algetha said, "Why did you do it?"

He answered simply, "You always have to do the right thing, no matter what the risk is, don't you?"

That's how to live life and be proud of yourself. Then when you die, you can meet your God, with pride behind you, love around you, and hope ahead of you. Say yes to God. Fantastic things will happen to you. "Blessed are they that hunger and thirst after righteousness, for they shall be satisfied" (*see* Matthew 5:6).

# Miss Terry

I dropped into Milwaukee to give a speech recently. When my friends picked me up at the airport, they said, "Dr. Schuller, you've got to stop and see Miss Terry in the hospital." My schedule was very full, but I consented, so we quickly made a hospital call.

I am so glad I decided to stop and see Miss Terry. I will never forget her. She is a beautiful, young black mother of two children. But her heart is not strong enough to keep her alive. Her only hope of survival is a heart transplant. I prayed with her that God would give her as many years as He could to spend with her children. She hugged me and said, "Dr. Schuller, the program every Sunday morning keeps my hopes up. Thank you for what you're doing."

Miss Terry is only one of a few million people who are counting on me and on you. Jesus said, "Unto whom much is given, much will be required" (*see* Luke 12:48). There are a lot of people who need to be treated friendly, fairly, frankly, firmly, and faithfully. It has to start with me. And it has to start with you.

# The Five Principles of Success

Any success I've achieved in my life I owe to five principles. Before I give them to you, I have to tell you that I learned them from someone wiser than me.

His name was Dr. Henry Poppen. I was only a young boy growing up in northwest Iowa when he came with his dashing tales of derring-do in Mainland China. This brave missionary captured my respect and admiration as he told about the adventures he had with bandits, and his near escape from death on mountain trails as he shared the Good News of Christ with the people of China.

Then came the great conflict between Japan and China, when half a million Chinese refugees escaped to an island without shelter or food. The English government appointed Dr. Henry Poppen to be the governor of those five hundred thousand refugees. I asked him later, "Dr. Poppen, how did you dare to face up to the Japanese general who came to the shore demanding surrender? Instead of being frightened and intimidated by him, you courageously declared, 'I will not surrender.' In fact, you told him to bring you and your people boatloads of soybeans. How did you dare to talk to him that way?"

He said, "Bob, I merely spoke to that Japanese general the way I talk to anybody. I have five words that I live by, and communicate by. They are: First . . . be friendly; second . . . be frank; third . . . be fair; fourth . . . be firm; and fifth . . . be faithful."

# Take the Offensive

Recently, when I was visiting Guatemala, I was escorted by a brilliant young man in his early thirties who holds a dual passport to Guatemala and the United States. He shared with me his concern for the country. He said, "Dr. Schuller, Christianity is losing the battle in Guatemala because they're fighting defensively. All of the missionaries have fled. They are afraid of being kidnapped and held for ransom by the Communists, or of being shot down by terrorists. There is no way we can win the fight without changing our tactics from defensive to offensive."

He continued, "Did you know that I served in Vietnam?"

I answered, "No. I was not aware of that."

Then he shared with me this fascinating story. He was an officer in Vietnam, assigned to keeping one area clear of the enemy. Every day he and his men would have to go into the jungle. Every day he saw a casualty or two, even though he approached all battles cautiously.

One day his commanding officer, a colonel, visited. He

said, "Lieutenant, how are you doing? Are you keeping the area clear of the enemy?"

My young friend replied, "I think I'm doing quite well, sir."

The colonel took a look at the lieutenant's casualty count. He shook his head and said, "There are some losses here." Then he looked at the lieutenant and said, "Do you know what you're doing wrong?"

"No, sir."

He said, "You're trying to hold and clear the territory, but you're trying to avoid all contact with the enemy."

"That's correct, sir. I don't want to lose my men. Every life is very valuable, sir."

The colonel said, "Don't tell me that. I know that! Look, you're trying to *hold* the territory, you're not trying to *conquer* the territory. You're fighting defensively. I'm giving you a command right now to go out there and contact the enemy at any time and any point you can."

My young friend looked at his commander and said, "Sir, with all due respect, may God help my men. I don't know how many lives I'd lose."

But the colonel only looked firmly at the young man and said, "That's a command!" With that he got into his helicopter. The blades whirled slowly, then faster and faster. As he took off, the lieutenant looked at his staff sergeant, who had heard the whole conversation. He said, "Sergeant, did you hear that? That colonel must be a crazy man. 'Go out there and contact the enemy!' How many bodies will I have to count tomorrow night?"

The sergeant said, "Sir, may I say something? With all due respect, I think the colonel is right. Look at how many casualties we've had this past month."

The lieutenant said, "Well, if you think he's right, and if the colonel is commanding me, I guess I have no choice but to change my strategy."

The next morning they went on the offensive. There were several casualties. The second day they plunged deeper and took more casualties than they usually had in an average week. But on the fourth day there were no casualties. The fifth day they went deeper into the jungle.

Again there were no casualties. The sixth day they penetrated as far as they could, and still there were no casualties. On the seventh and eighth days they couldn't even find the enemy. The lieutenant said to the sergeant, "What happened to the enemy?"

The sergeant replied, "Sir, I think the enemy has gone off to fight somebody who's fighting on the defensive."

# Pebbles Make Up the Beaches of the World

Penny Cotton, a young woman who attended the National Women's Conference at the Crystal Cathedral recently, suffered a stroke when she was twenty-seven years old. It almost killed her, and left her paralyzed. Because of the paralysis she did not want to live, so she planned to commit suicide. Then she tuned in the "Hour of Power" and through the happy faces and joyful music she received hope. That was enough to change her from suicidal thoughts. She became a possibility thinker. Why? Because she found comfort. She committed her life to Jesus Christ and dared to believe she could earn her own way in life and not be dependent on others. That's exactly what she did. She became a life insurance salesperson. In gratitude to God, she dared to believe she could save enough dollars to buy a star in the Crystal Cathedral. She shared with me last week and said, "You know, Dr. Schuller, I'm just a little pebble." I said to her, "Penny, if there were no pebbles, there would be no beaches. The pebbles make up the beaches of the world!"

# Job's Representative

A while ago I received a letter from a gentleman. He identified himself as Dallas J. Anderson and enclosed his resume, which was very impressive. It included undergraduate work in art at Saint Olaf College in Minnesota, and nine years of graduate work in sculpture at the Royal Danish Academy of Fine Arts. He enclosed a portfolio with photographs of a plaster model of a sculpture he called *Job*. He was planning to reproduce it in bronze. It looked magnificent—like a work of Michelangelo. He said he would like to donate the bronze statue to the gardens of the Crystal Cathedral.

I was thrilled, to say the least, but I wrote him and said, "Thank you, Dallas, but for me the work should be done in marble, not in bronze. It should be carved so that the form will glisten and ripple. I feel that marble sculpting has a humanity that bronze does not. Furthermore, the whole subject is faith versus healing, poverty versus the possibility of prosperity. Such loss and torment would be stated much more strongly if it were in white against a dark base." I asked him, "Can you possibly reproduce this job in marble without losing its emotion?"

He answered, "It's odd that you should request this because last year I was in Vermont, and I purchased this exquisite chunk of white Vermont marble, seven feet high. My answer is, 'Yes! I would love to do it!'"

So for the next year and a half, Dallas Anderson quietly carved away. Finally on Thanksgiving morning 1983, the statue was unveiled. At its base are four verses from the Book of Job. On one side, carved in dark granite, is the text, "The Lord gave, the Lord has taken away. Blessed be the name of the Lord" (*see* Job 1:21). On the other side,

"Though he slay me yet will I trust him" (*see* Job 13:15). On another, "I know my Redeemer lives" (*see* Job 19:25). And on the fourth side, "When he has tried me I shall come forth as gold" (*see* Job 23:10).

Who needs to be tried? We all do. The truth is that every day is a trial. If you're in business, you know what I'm talking about. You are tried in the marketplace every day and the customer either likes your product or he doesn't. You come forth either as gold or as tin, depending upon the quality of product and service you offer.

# The Courage to Try

I ran into a young man in an airport in Texas. He happened to be carrying a copy of my book *Tough Times Never Last, But Tough People Do*. He recognized me. He came up to me and said, "Can I have your autograph?"

I was glad to give it.

He said, "Dr. Schuller, this book has really been helping me, because I'm in absolute bankruptcy. I started my own business, but I've lost everything I ever had."

He had a tear in his eye, but continued. "You know, my business was going pretty well. I expanded, with a new plant and more equipment. I was making quite a bit of money. Suddenly the other people who owed me money didn't pay. The little businesses went down the tubes. Then, a couple of big businesses went down the tubes. I looked at my Accounts Receivable and suddenly everything that I had expected to take in had evaporated. My Accounts Receivable were worth nothing. When that happened, I went under, too! That's where I am today. But I saw this book and it's helping."

I said, "Well, first of all, sir, let me correct you. You haven't lost everything you had."

He said, "Oh, but I have."

I said, "No, I don't think so. You haven't lost everything you had. You had something before you had a business. You had a dream. And you had the nerve to try. You haven't lost that."

He said, "I think I have."

I said, "Oh, no! Nobody ever loses courage! Courage isn't something you lose, because courage is always an option."

Courage is a choice. And it's always there for you to choose. You can choose to start over. And remember—every competitor is a winner! Nobody who competes can ever be a total loser, because the total loser is the guy who didn't dare to try. Every competitor is a winner, because he has courage.

Never, never, never, believe that God wants you to be a failure. There may be a round when you get knocked down. There may be a season that is not good. You may go through a really tough period. But just because you've lost the battle doesn't mean you will lose the war.

# EXTRAORDINARY LOVE

# Every Blessing Is a Burden

I remember when Gretchen, my youngest daughter, asked me to buy her a puppy for Christmas. "Honey," I said, "we've already got two dogs." We have a little acreage, so there is room for the dogs to run. Besides, they are trained for security purposes. After several days of begging, I finally consented. In a weak moment, I said yes. Well, when Carol, my older daughter, found out I was going to buy Gretchen a puppy, she started in on me. "Daddy, I asked you for a puppy three years ago and you said no. I asked you the next year and you still said no. And now you are letting Gretchen have one? That's not fair!" So in another weak moment I said, "Okay, Carol, you can have one, too."

Every blessing is a burden! I now have two puppies! I have lost my kitchen because it's the only room in the house that doesn't have carpeting. (And it's the only room suitable for training puppies.) But the puppies are beautiful and the children love them. (So do I, unfortunately.) I can't help but love the little darlings. A couple of little blessings—but they are a burden!

# "God Loves You and So Do I"

Every Sunday I ask members of my congregation to turn around and shake hands with somebody near them and say, "God loves you and so do I!" And just about every week I see a few people with gloomy expressions who reluctantly turn to the persons next to them, shake hands, and say, "God loves you and so do I." And do you know what? When they turn back around and face me, a light comes on! They are smiling and their faces are actually bright!

The most tragic blind spot in any personal philosophy of life is the concept that "if I'm greedy I'll get ahead." Nothing could be further from the truth. "Whatever a man sows, that shall he also reap" (*see* Galatians 6:7).

# Still Singing

I recently conducted a funeral service for the man who has been at my side longer than any other person, except for my wife. I graduated from seminary in June of 1950. My first assignment was at a little church of thirty-three members in Chicago, Illinois. The church was divided. It was split because of some contradictions. The people didn't know how to resolve them. They never learned that the lion could lie down with the lamb.

I went to that little church. The ruling elder, the vice-president of the church, was Bain Fisher. He met me at the depot. That was the beginning of a dear friendship. Together we worked to save that church. And I must say, we were successful.

Five years later, the Reformed Church in America, the oldest denomination in the United States of America, invited me to come to California and start a new church. Before I accepted, I wanted to go out there and look over the place. But the denomination didn't have the money to send me. When Bain Fisher, who worked for the Santa Fe Railroad, found out about it, he said, "I don't want to lose you, but you ought to check it out." And he gave me a round-trip train ticket.

Fifteen years ago, Bain joined me in California. What a faithful, loyal servant he has been to our church.

He was my friend for thirty-three years. Then he got lung cancer some months ago. Then they found cancer in the brain. Soon after, we got the call that he passed away quietly. I asked his wife, Charlotte, "Was he conscious at the end?"

She said, "Not quite to the end. He fell asleep about four hours before he passed away, but up until then he was still singing."

I said, "Singing? What was he singing?"

She said, "Oh, his favorite songs. He sang, 'Jesus loves me! this I know,' and "O how I love Jesus, O how I love Jesus, O how I love Jesus because He first loved me!' "

# The Magnificent Madonna

I have a friend in Chicago named Don Paset. He owns the largest art and antique store, the Donrose Galleries, on the North Shore. When I visited the art gallery recently, I wandered through its garden. There was a life-size, very stylized, modern bronze statue of the Madonna. There is no face. You supply the features with your imagination. Yet there is no doubt that it's the Madonna.

I was really struck by how beautiful she was. I asked Don how much he wanted for her. He said, "She's not for sale. It's a very, very, important piece by an important contemporary sculptor." I continued to study her beauty. Where the womb would be, there is a hollow in the bronze. In the hollow is a large number six. It, of course, represents the unborn infant. The top of the six represents the head, and the rest of the body of the six represents the body of the unborn child.

As I looked at the statue a young woman near me asked, "Dr. Schuller, why is the baby shaped like a six?"

I said, "I don't know. I didn't talk to the sculptor, but I have my own interpretation that I read into it: On the sixth day, God created Adam and Eve. All of His hopes and dreams were pinned on Adam and Eve. They blew it. So He sent Jesus. When Jesus was born it was as if God went back to the sixth day to try again. He's pinning His last hopes for the human race on Jesus—'The new Adam,' as the Scriptures tell us. 'The second Adam.' God's trying once more."

# God Patches Up the Holes

Recently I was in Sioux Falls, South Dakota, where a young couple came up to greet me following a speaking engagement. They held a little baby. They told me how the "Hour of Power" helped them through a terribly difficult time. The young man said, "Three years ago my wife was killed in a tragic car accident." Then the young woman said, "And just thirty days later, my husband was driving at night and was killed in an accident." In unison they said, "God introduced us to each other." As they looked lovingly at each other they said, "Now we're married and it's beautiful! Thank you for 'Hour of Power.' It gives us hope." And then the husband made this classic statement: "God patches up the holes!"

# Different Music

I remember the story of the two old Dutchmen, sitting on a park bench. The night had come and the moon started to shine. Not far from the bench where they sat, a river flowed, and from the river came a chorus of crickets. Pete, the first old gentleman, listened to the crickets and said, "Crickets sure do sing." John, sitting next to him, agreed, saying, "Yep, they sure know how to sing." Just then he heard the voices of the choir coming from a nearby church and remarked, "Beautiful music, isn't it?" Pete said, "Yeah, and to think they do it just by rubbing their legs together."

Each heard different music—one was listening to the crickets and one was listening to the choir. What you hear depends on where you're coming from and where you're going! When you come to our church, I want you to hear one thing: the note of real love—the love of Jesus Christ.

# The Unknown Singer

Here's a story that I love. It's a true story. It happened in the Paris opera house. A famous singer was planning to sing that night. The house was packed. The curtain was raised. But the singer did not enter the stage. Instead, the house manager stepped to the microphone and made the following announcement: "I am afraid that due to illness the man you've come to hear will not be performing tonight. Someone will be standing in for him." The manager mentioned the stand-in's name, but no one heard it over the groan of disappointment. It was a difficult situation. The unknown singer sang with everything he had. When he finished there was nothing but a stony silence. Suddenly, from one of the high balconies, a little boy stood up and cried, "Daddy, I think you are wonderful!" Then the crowd broke into thunderous applause.

Where do I find my inner security? How do I find my self-esteem? Not through my position. Actually that is a very threatening and vulnerable spot to be in. I don't find self-esteem through performance, because I'm never satisfied with it. Instead, I find it through a Person, a special Person named Jesus Christ. Like that little boy, Jesus says to me, *Schuller, I think you're wonderful.*

# Reason to Live

I was asked to visit a young man, twenty-one years of age, who was suicidal. He was living in an institution in Southern California where young men and young women are kept when they are severely mentally handicapped, when there's no hope of recovery.

I went to see him. He said, "Dr. Schuller, I cannot live. I cannot read. I cannot write. My life is totally useless. If I could believe in God, I could live. But I can't believe in God."

I said, "Why not?"

He replied, "Why would God make a useless person like me? I am of no value to anyone."

I was praying for the right answer for this young man, and just then, a nurse walked into our room. I recognized her because she is a member of our church. I remembered talking to her only a few months before when her husband died. She didn't have any income so she was forced to go out and find a job. She had been totally dependent upon her now-deceased husband. Then, suddenly, she had to go back to work at the age of forty-eight. She tried to use her nursing experience, but the hospitals didn't want her. Finally, she took the only nursing job she could find. It was a job at this institution where nobody wanted to work.

Now, here she was. She came bouncing into the room. "Hello, Dr. Schuller! How are you?"

"I'm fine. How are you?"

"Wonderful! I really enjoy this work."

I said, "You do?"

"Oh, yes. I meet the nicest people." Then she came up to the twenty-one-year-old boy whom I was visiting. She tweaked him on the cheek and said, "Johnny, how are you today?"

When he looked up at her, she put her arm around him and said, "Did you know that I really do love you, Johnny?" She looked at me and said, "I don't think he believes that I really do love him. But I do. He's such a sweet guy."

After she left the room, I turned to Johnny and said, "Johnny, your life is not totally useless. You help create a job opportunity for this widow and you help her to forget her own problems. She loves you. Can't you see it?"

He said, "Yeah, I guess so. Do you really think she loves me, Dr. Schuller?"

I said, "Of course, she does!"

Still unconvinced, he said, "Do you really think she loves me, Dr. Schuller?"

I said, "Johnny, I know she does!" I must have said it that time in such a way that he started to cry. I hugged him and he hugged me.

Here was Johnny with an enormous need. And here was a widow with a tremendous need. Two needs collide and a spark ignites. Now that's a principle of life.

# Turn Your Problems Into Partners

One of the most inspiring women in our congregation was Sara Rasmussen. I told her story in my book *Move Ahead With Possibility Thinking*. Sara and Norm were about to have their fifth child. They already had four sons, and so they prayed for a girl. At the baby shower the word was, "Think Pink." All the gifts were wrapped in pink paper; all the ribbons were pink. The baby was born and it was a girl. They named her Leah. However, a few months later they found out Leah had Down's syndrome. Nevertheless, they loved her!

They decided not to try to conquer their problem, but to redeem it. They loved little Leah and as she became a junior high school student, she needed peer companionship. So they went to various California adoption agencies and brought mongoloid children nobody else wanted into their home. Soon they had two, three, four, five mongoloid children join their family.

Finally, they moved up to a big old house with lots of empty land where, the last I heard, Sara and her husband and Leah had about twenty-six of these children! They turned their problem into a partner. They're more than conquerors through Christ who loves us.

# Beautiful Sammy Brook

Many know the story of Peggy Brook. She already had two little boys when Sammy was born. He was such a beautiful baby. But after a few months, he seemed to have problems with his eyes. She said, "I was so happy when finally I got an apointment with an ophthalmologist." He held up darling little Sammy and looked into one eye. He said the pupil response seemed to be good. Then he looked in the other eye. He said that the voluntary muscle response seemed to be good. But when he looked the third time, his response was silence. Finally he pulled out a chart and said, "The optic nerve is very dull."

Then, without looking at Peggy, he said, "You know, the retina is made up of many little, tiny nerves. They branch into the larger nerves until they converge at the center in the optic nerve. The optic nerve sends all signals to the brain, where they are deciphered. In Sammy's case," he said as he drew some lines to illustrate how we see, "I can't find the little nerves. And the optic nerve is almost nonexistent."

Peggy said, "Will he be able to read?" The doctor answered, "Well, he might be able to see forms. He might be able to tell the difference between light and shadow. At best that will be all he'll be able to see."

Peggy walked out of there holding her little Sammy, her beautiful little baby. And then suddenly, the word came to her: *blind*. Her Sammy was blind! All her hopes turned to ashes. Peggy and her husband wept that night and the next night, and they prayed and held hands and claimed the Bible promises for healing. They asked Jesus, but they got no hope. He never assured them that there would be a healing.

Peggy went through all the emotions: guilt, fear, and anger toward God. But then she remembered what a minister said: "Be positive, thank God anyway." Peggy said, "I began to praise God for Sammy, and Jesus touched me. He didn't touch Sammy. He touched me. In a vision, like a dream, I saw God at the moment of Sammy's conception. I saw Him in heaven holding a beautiful, blond, blue-eyed baby boy. He was looking around the world for a home for this very special baby. He saw a rich man's house, but passed it by. He saw a poor man's house, but He said, *Not there*. Then He saw a home where an unmarried woman did not want a child. He passed her by. And then He saw our little home with the Bible and the cross on the wall. He said, *This is the kind of home that deserves a special gift like Sammy*. And He gave Sammy to me."

Peggy said, "At that moment, all of my negative emotions disappeared. I had nothing but praise to give to God for my beautiful little Sammy—blind, but bright and beautiful!"

# The Language of Silence

As you may know, I travel a lot. I was on a plane recently. I overheard the stewardess say, "I've been out of this for a year. I'm just back on the job today."

When she pushed her cart past my seat, I said, "I'm curious. I heard you say that you've been gone for a year. I hope it's been a happy holiday."

Her eyes immediately filled with tears and she said, "No, not really. I lost a little boy."

"Oh, my, I'm sorry." I reached out to her and we gave each other a hug. I asked, "What helped you?"

She said, "So many people meant well, but what they said didn't help me. They said, 'God wanted your little baby, so He took it.' That didn't help—it made me angry at God. Others said, 'Your little baby is now a bud in the bouquet of heaven.' That didn't help me, either. These things help some people, I'm sure. But they didn't help me."

I asked again, "What helped you?"

She said, "A couple came, I really didn't know them. They were Christians. They had lost a little boy, and I knew about their loss. It was tragic, like mine. But when they came, they didn't say anything. They just reached out and hugged me and we cried. That did it."

The silence healed. The stillness helped. For silence has a language all its own.

# A Sixty/Forty Proposition

When I was in college, one of the professors said to us, his students, "The secret of a successful marriage is this: Marriage is not a 50/50 proposition. A 50/50 proposition is one where nobody is giving anything.

"Rather, the secret of a happy marriage is 60/40. The husband gives in sixty percent of the time and expects his wife to give in forty percent of the time. The wife gives in sixty percent of the time and expects her husband to give in forty percent of the time. In a 60/40 proposition, you don't clash in the middle and say, 'Now, it's your turn.' Instead, you intersect and overlap, because you're each giving sixty percent."

"Give and it will be given to you." It's the secret in business; it's the secret in interpersonal relationships. And it's the secret of powerful, mountain-moving, miracle-working religion.

# Poco's Accident

My daughter Carol was coming home at about ten o'clock one night. We live out in the country, so it is not uncommon to see a dead opossum in the street. As she approached the house, she saw what appeared to be a dead opossum in the reflected headlights. She pulled the car to a stop in the road, got out, realized immediately it was not an opossum. It was our pet dog Poco. Our little Lhasa apso had gotten out, run into the street, and was injured. Carol was shocked when she saw him lying there in the street, apparently dead. But then she heard a whimper and on one foot hopped over to him. Through tears she said, "Poco!" He responded with a painful whimper. Carol tried to lift the weight of the injured dog but she lost her balance and fell. She got back up, but with only one foot she couldn't carry the weight. Just then a car came by and the driver saw this young girl with only one leg trying to lift an injured dog. The driver stopped, jumped out of the car, and said, "May I help you?"

Weeping, Carol said, "Yes, this is my dog. He's been hurt and I know what it's like to get hurt when you've been hit by a car at night. Please help me."

The driver picked up little Poco, who was whimpering, and put him on the front seat. Carol hopped in beside him. *When you care, you really carry.* The good news is that Poco had only a broken jaw and recovered nicely.

# You'll Have to Give It Away

Many years ago, my son and I built a little mountain cabin on a remote piece of property up in the mountains in California. It took us a couple of years. We saved our coins and we fixed it up nice and pretty. Finally there was a time when we had it just right. We had a radio in there and a little television set as well. We also had a little place where we could play records and tapes. Our fishing poles were in there and my son had his skis in there. It was well equipped. And then we went up there one weekend to have a nice little rest and we found the door ajar. Then we found a window broken. And we found that all of our property had been stolen. And about that time I got a call from the police department. I was asked to come in and identify the stolen equipment. They thought they'd gotten it all. They asked if I would sign a complaint. They gave me a piece of paper. So I signed, whatever it was. I really don't remember what I signed. Later on I received word that they had caught a couple of men who had ripped us off. I was told they'd been sent to jail. That was it.

I must tell you—I had some bad feelings toward those invisible thieves. Awful feelings. I think it's basically the invasion of your privacy. End of the story? Not quite.

Two, or was it three, years later, I was back in the mountains with my little daughter. We were going through one of the dime stores, buying some balloons for a party. I thought I saw some sinister eyes probing me, from a customer who seemed to be walking up and down the other aisle. And I almost got the feeling that he was following me or staring at me. I went to the cash register and then this character came right up to me. He had on grubby-looking clothes, long hair, and was unshaven. He came real close, with his hands in his pockets, and asked, "Are you Dr. Schuller?" I said, "Yes."

His eyes spoke, he had a smile, tears were in his eyes, his lips trembled. He said, "Will you forgive me?" I said, "Forgive you for what?" He said, "I broke into your home two years ago. I stole your recorder. I stole your television. I stole the skis and the fishing poles." Tears were rolling down his cheeks.

He said, "I went to jail, but that's when it happened." I said, "What?" He said, "I started watching you on television. One of the things I stole from you was a book with your name on it. And somebody's kid was with me. He said, 'You know what? I think this is the Robert Schuller who's on television.' And I said, 'Do you think we ripped him off?' He said, 'Could be.' " Then he said, "I saw you on television and when you asked people to accept Jesus Christ, I did." He continued, "I'm now a Christian. I go to a Bible study here in the mountains, every Wednesday night. Me and a bunch of other kids are born again." He said, "I'm so sorry I did it." And I could tell what he wanted, so I opened my arms and he embraced me. Do you know what? When you really take Christ in your life, you have a connection to the Source of Love that will never let you go. You'll experience salvation and forgiveness of sins. And, you'll never be able to keep it. You'll have to give it away.

# Plant a Powerful Seed

I was in Minneapolis recently. I had to speak to about six thousand Methodists. In the forum that followed, one of the ministers asked me this question: "Dr. Schuller, what are you and your congregation doing to fight racism? And what are you doing to fight the social injustices? I never hear you preach any sermons against these sins." I answered him with this story: I was born on an Iowa farm. Every spring my brother and I had to go and pick cockleburs. Cockleburs are ugly, horrible weeds, and every year we had to pull them out, pile them up, and burn them. One spring my father plowed the ground and planted alfalfa. Alfalfa sends roots down twelve feet into the ground. It grew so thick that the cockleburs did not grow—they were choked out.

The positive solution to loneliness, boredom, lust, promiscuity, racism, social injustice, or any sin you can imagine, is not to be against them, but to plant something else so powerful that it consumes the problem. Love is that satisfying! It lifts you beyond temptations. Once you've enjoyed good music, you won't be interested in any other kind. If you are happily married and have a beautiful love in Christ, pornography isn't tempting. Once you've grown alfalfa, cockleburs don't stand a chance. Love is the greatest because it's the answer to every sin you can imagine. Love is the greatest because it's available for all. Love is the greatest because it's the positive solution to every problem.

# INDEX OF NAMES

Truitt, George  48

Valente, Charlotte  121
Van Buren, Abby  126

Walsh, Homer  89
Wayne, John  78
Weaver, Eula  144
Wilcox, Ella  Wheeler  203
Wilson, Patty  43
Wolcott, William  246
Woolworth, Frank  82
Wright, Hazel  263, 264

Ziglar, Zig  201, 202

# INDEX OF TITLES

# INDEX OF TOPICS

## ABOUT THE AUTHOR
## ROBERT H. SCHULLER

Known throughout the world for his "Hour of Power" television program, many inspirational books, and a syndicated newspaper column, Dr. Robert H. Schuller has touched the lives of millions and has been presenting life-changing truths in story form for over thirty years. He is the dynamic pastor and founder of the Crystal Cathedral in Garden Grove, California.

## ABOUT THE EDITOR
## ROBERT A. SCHULLER

Robert A. Schuller, son of Robert H. Schuller, is a graduate of Hope College and Fuller Theological Seminary. He has been ordained into the Reformed Church of America and presently serves as senior pastor at Rancho Capistrano Community Church in San Juan Capistrano, California.